Testable JavaScript

Mark Ethan Trostler

O'REILLY®

Beijing · Cambridge · Farnham · Köln · Sebastopol · Tokyo

Testable JavaScript

by Mark Ethan Trostler

Printed in the United States of America.

Published by O'Reilly Media, Inc., 1005 Gravenstein Highway North, Sebastopol, CA 95472.

O'Reilly books may be purchased for educational, business, or sales promotional use. Online editions are also available for most titles (*http://my.safaribooksonline.com*). For more information, contact our corporate/institutional sales department: 800-998-9938 or *corporate@oreilly.com*.

Editors: Simon St. Laurent and Meghan Blanchette	**Proofreader:** Rachel Head
Production Editor: Christopher Hearse	**Indexer:** Lucie Haskins
Copyeditor: Audrey Doyle	**Cover Designer:** Randy Comer
	Interior Designer: David Futato
	Illustrator: Rebecca Demarest

January 2013:   First Edition

Revision History for the First Edition:

2013-01-14   First release

See *http://oreilly.com/catalog/errata.csp?isbn=9781449323394* for release details.

ISBN: 978-1-449-32339-4

[LSI]

For Inslee, Walter, and Michelle—Trostlers Trostlers Trostlers Woo!

Table of Contents

Preface

You have to test your code, so why not make the process as easy and painless as possible? Client-side JavaScript is especially difficult to test properly, as we have very little control over the environment within which our code runs. Multiple operating systems, multiple versions of operating systems, multiple browsers, and multiple versions of browsers, not to mention plug-ins, extensions, different languages, zoom levels, and who knows what else, all conspire to hinder the performance of our applications. These permutations slow down, break, crash, and eat our applications for lunch. It's a jungle out there! Server-side JavaScript gives us significantly more control, as by and large, we control the execution environment. However, Rhino and Node.js applications do not have the full gamut of mature tools, the testing procedures, and the ecosystem that other languages do. Further, the asynchronous nature of Node.js complicates testing. It is interesting that a language so intertwined with asynchronous execution has essentially zero built-in support for that mode of execution.

Regardless, testing—especially JavaScript testing—is complicated. Our best shot at taming this complexity is to take full control of what we actually do control: the code. Code exists across a continuum, from someone else's to yours on one axis and from legacy to nonlegacy on the other.

What is legacy code? I'm a fan of Michael Feathers's definition in his excellent book, *Working Effectively with Legacy Code* (Prentice Hall): legacy code is code without tests. This code either will not survive or will never be touched by anyone. When the time comes to touch legacy code, it gets rewritten. Take a look at your current project; any code that does not have tests will likely be rewritten. Probably not by the author of the code, but by whoever is now tasked with dealing with it—either enhancing or bug-fixing it. Unless tests are written, this is dead code that will have to be rewritten. The code may be spectacular, but the only way it will survive is if it never causes bugs *and* if no one ever requests enhancements or new features for it. Even then, how happy are you to ship production code with no tests? Even if the code "worked" before, are you content to keep rolling the dice? Is your company, which owns the code, content to keep rolling the dice? Typically the piper must be paid, and this code will just get rewritten. It's too bad the company had to pay to have this possibly spectacular code written twice, but such is the case with legacy code.

As you can see in the matrix shown in Figure P-1, it is very easy for any legacy code you've written to fall into someone else's hands and be rewritten. That path is typically less painful than bringing someone else's legacy code up to speed with tests. It is very easy to move from side to side in this matrix, as code changes hands constantly, moving into and out of your purview with great agility. Moving "down" is the hardest path for code to take; writing tests for existing code is a job no one wants to do, and most people will go to impressively great lengths to avoid it—typically resulting in a complete rewrite.

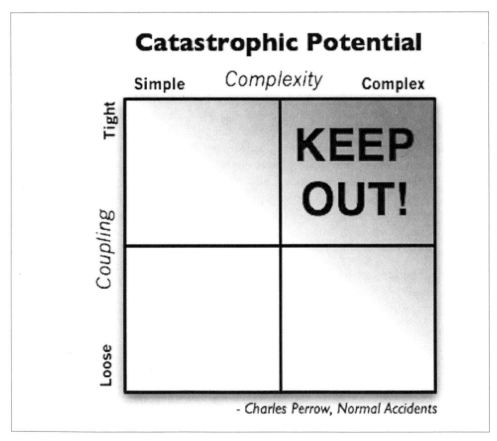

Figure P-1. Current versus legacy code

Unfortunately, moving up in this matrix happens with some regularity. Code that starts out with tests can lapse into legacy code if it falls into the wrong hands. Vigilance is required to keep tests up to date as more enhancements and features are bolted on, but this is a *much* simpler process than writing tests for code without any (or with very few) tests.

The Goal of This Book

This book aims to keep your JavaScript code in the lower-right quadrant of Figure P-1 by taking a holistic approach to development. It's not just about "writing tests" or "testing first," but rather understanding how the choices you make while coding, good and bad, will affect you (your code and your employment) down the road.

Starting with the good habits of structuring your code syntactically and semantically for testability, writing the right tests at the right times, running them regularly, and monitoring their results will keep you in that lower-right sweet spot in the matrix.

This book attempts to bridge the gap between sane development practices and Java-Script. JavaScript is a weird little language. Starting with its senseless name, JavaScript was originally used by nonprogrammers to add some interactivity to web pages. Even if "real" programmers used the language in its early days, the dynamics between the language, the DOM, and the browser environment took some getting used to.

As more and more professional programmers started working with the language, best practices began to be understood and codified. Tools for working with JavaScript, debuggers, test harnesses, IDE support, and more began to emerge. The language itself was modified using lessons learned from several years out in the wild. JavaScript was starting to grow, and grow up. But a lot of weirdness remains, and more powerful tools are still around the corner.

With the advent of server-side JavaScript via Node.js, PhantomJS and other applications can now be written entirely in JavaScript. Not too long ago, that was not only impossible, but also thought to be insane. No one is laughing now!

This book attempts to pull together lessons learned from decades of study and experience with testing and quality assurance (QA), and to apply those lessons to JavaScript. Almost all the examples and code snippets in this book are written in JavaScript (some Perl has snuck in there!).

Who This Book Is For

This book's primary target audience is people who encounter JavaScript professionally. Beginning, intermediate, or guru-level developers are all welcome, as this book has something for everyone.

JavaScript may not be the only language you use, but you write or test significantly sized chunks of it. Someone is paying you (hopefully good!) money to wrangle JavaScript to run either in the browser or, lucky you, on the server. If you are dealing with JavaScript every day with an application of any size, this book is right up your alley.

This book is also for you if you are on a QA or tools team that must test JavaScript—Chapter 3 through Chapter 7 are right in your wheelhouse. This books aims to make testing as easy as possible, and then automate all of it. Hopefully, this book will make people's lives easier. That's just how I roll.

If you write only a little JavaScript, this book still has lots of good information for you —especially the chapters on complexity (Chapter 2), event-based architectures (Chapter 3), and debugging (Chapter 7). The remaining chapters still have good information within, mind you! But they probably do not directly address your pain points. A lot of pain has led to my writing this book—I've learned from previous mistakes and hard work, and so should you! Learning good habits from the start will make you much more productive and happy.

Who This Book Is Not For

Sadly, this book is not for everyone. If you already are interested in learning JavaScript, you should learn the basics of the language elsewhere and then come back to this book. If you write clean, bug-free, fully documented and commented code with an automated build continuously running all of your unit and integration tests with full code coverage reports and automatically deploy into staging environments, well, there might not be a lot for you here. Maybe take a quick look at Chapter 7 in case you ever have to do any debugging, or check out Chapter 6 for kicks.

If you do not use JavaScript often, you can probably put this book down right now.

Who I Am

I am a relatively recent convert to JavaScript, coming to it after a very long and enjoyable time with Perl. Oh sure, I have used the language for 10+ years, but I never really took it very seriously. Making things "blink" and performing other seemingly useless UI tricks were all it appeared to be good for.

Douglas Crockford really opened my eyes to the depth and sophistication of the language with his excellent "Crockford on JavaScript" talks, available on YouTube on the YUI Library channel (*http://bit.ly/XUdcax*). If you need to be further convinced, or if some of your friends are giving you grief about JavaScript, watching these videos will effect a change in mindset.

I spent two and a half years as a frontend developer on Yahoo! Mail, which was rewritten from scratch during my tenure. I am confident that our team experienced every possible problem, issue, trouble, disaster, and triumph in utilizing client-side JavaScript during the rewrite. Most of the content of this book was drawn directly from that experience.

I am currently a Software Engineer in Test at Google, putting all of those hard-earned lessons to good use, and I hope you can too.

What You Will Learn from This Book

There are two things to learn from this book: the right way and the wrong way! There is, of course, a continuum between "right" and "wrong." After you have finished reading this book, I would like you to be coding or looking at someone else's code and know *why* you feel good or feel bad about it. If you can already tell what is wrong with code, good for you. When I look at code for the first time, either what I wrote or what someone else wrote, I get a good or bad feeling pretty quickly: either I understand the code almost immediately (a good feeling), or my eyes glaze over (a bad feeling). It is nice to be able to articulate to the author issues with his code; hopefully Chapter 2 will give you not only a more concrete sense of good versus bad, but also a shared vocabulary to communicate back to the author.

Writing unit tests for client-side JavaScript can be daunting. That means too many people don't do it. This is not OK, for a variety of reasons spelled out in this book (and in many others!). But rather than wagging a finger, this book provides you with the tools and code to get you started. Getting started is the hardest part, and this book will get you on your way to writing unit tests for client-side JavaScript.

Clearly, just writing tests is not enough. You also have to run them. Ideally, you can run them easily at any time in your development environment, and also as part of an automated build process. What about code coverage for those tests? What about integration tests, performance tests, and load tests? What about code coverage for all of *those* tests? How about a continuous build environment that takes care of all of that for you? Finally, how can you structure your code such that all of this testing and automation is easier rather than harder? How about running tests on both client- and server-side JavaScript?

These topics and more (debugging, anyone?) are all covered within this book, so get ready for a wild ride through the world of JavaScript development. The overriding theme is writing and maintaining "testable" code.

Content

This book will tackle testable code in several steps. First we will investigate complexity. Then we will look at an architecture choice that attempts to limit complexity and coupling. With that as our foundation, we will move on to testing, both at the functional level and at the application level. We will gain a thorough understanding of code coverage and debugging, and then finish it all off with a healthy dose of automation. By the end of the book, you will have a fuller grasp of the "what" and the "how" of testable JavaScript.

Chapter 1, Testable JavaScript

The overrriding theme of this book is writing and maintaining "testable" code. But what is testable code? Why should we strive to write it? And how do we do so? We will begin by exploring all of these questions, and taking a look at some popular development methodologies and how they relate to testable code. Ultimately, whatever practice you may choose to follow, the key to writing testable code lies in keeping it small, clear, uncomplicated, and loosely coupled."

Chapter 2, Complexity

Complexity is the root of many problems, not just testability. These problems include understandability and maintainability, both of which are key metrics for quality code. Some systems and applications are inherently complex; in fact, most applications are complex, but there are right ways and wrong ways to handle and express that complexity. Obviously, breaking down the more complex pieces into smaller, simpler chunks is a big first step. Reducing coupling and fan-out are other ways to manage complexity. We will investigate all of these methods, and more, in our quest for testable JavaScript.

Chapter 3, Event-Based Architectures

After our discussion on complexity, we will dive deeper into event-based architecture. This application-level architecture can greatly reduce complexity and coupling while providing easy ways to break down your application into smaller, more self-sufficient pieces. Regardless of whether your application is server-side, client-side, or (most likely) both, an event-based architecture solves many of the problems enumerated in Chapter 2. Even if it is not suitable as the overall architecture for every application, there certainly is a place within the overall structure to leverage event-based architecture concepts and practices.

Chapter 4, Unit Tests

There is a lot of controversy about unit testing. How important is it? Unit tests do not find every bug. Like all other tools, unit tests are a piece of the testability puzzle. Describing code as "testable" does not imply that tests are available for that code; rather, it implies that writing tests for that code would be straightforward. Unit tests are special in that they typically are the only kind of test developers write. They are also invasive, requiring that you isolate the code under test and execute it separately from the application. This makes unit testing potentially difficult, as being able to run code at the level of a single method, in isolation, can be very difficult. A large part of *Testable JavaScript* ensures that your code can be executed in isolation, thereby making unit tests much simpler to write. While unit tests do not find every bug (or even most bugs), the ones they do find are worth the effort involved in running them. It is also important that your test code adheres to the same high standards and principles as the code you are testing.

Chapter 5, Code Coverage

Code Coverage typically goes hand in hand with unit testing. Code coverage can be a good measure of unit-test efficacy; however, we will see that this is not always the case. Yet code coverage is not just for unit testing anymore! All kinds of testing can benefit from code coverage measurements, including integration, manual, and performance testing. We will investigate the good and the bad of code coverage metrics and how to generate, view, and make sense of them.

Chapter 6, Integration, Performance, and Load Testing

Of course, there is much more to testing than just unit testing. Integration, manual, performance, functional, and other types of testing all play an important role in finding and ferreting out bugs. Regardless of who does the testing—the developers, the QA team, or even your unwitting users—these other kinds of tests will get done whether you like it or not. The ability to easily test the application as a whole is also vitally important. Modularizing functionality allows the test code to be more clearly linked to the implemented functionality, which helps developers fix bugs faster. Using code coverage during these tests can quickly show executed code during black-box testing. Plenty of great JavaScript-based tools are available for developers to leverage for integration and performance testing, and we will take a closer look at some of those tools to give you an idea of what can be accomplished.

Chapter 7, Debugging

The code we write is not perfect, no matter how perfect it seems when we first write it. Our code will have bugs. Lots of bugs. Stuff you thought about and stuff you did not even conceive of will bedevil your code. Your tests, someone else's tests, or a user using your application will find the bugs. Bugs found by tests are by far the easiest to fix, which is another great reason to maximize your tests. Bugs found by users running production code are far more difficult to track down. The upshot is that you will have to debug not only your code but also someone else's. I'll share some tips and tricks for debugging both Node.js and browser code. Get a good debugging environment set up, because you will be doing a lot of it.

Chapter 8, Automation

Finally, doing things manually over and over again is not only not sustainable but also not very fun. Writing software is one of the most manual processes in the world, but testing and maintaining software does not have to be. Running tests, generating code coverage reports, performing static analysis, minifying and compressing code, and deploying and rolling back code to and from production and other environments should all be part of an automated process. Automation ensures that whatever happens, success or failure, it will happen quickly and, more importantly, in a way that can be repeated. You will fail. Tests will fail, a production launch will fail, and things will go wrong that will have absolutely nothing to do with your code. That is life. It is critical that you can recover from those failures (along with the failures you have caused) as quickly and seamlessly as possible.

If You Like (or Don't Like) This Book

If you like—or don't like—this book, by all means, please let people know. Amazon reviews are one popular way to share your happiness (or lack of happiness), or you can leave reviews at the book's website (*http://oreil.ly/Testable-JavaScript*).

That website also provides a link to errata, giving you a way to let us know about typos, errors, and other problems with the book. These errata will be visible on the page immediately, and we'll confirm them after checking them out. O'Reilly can also fix errata in future printings of the book and on Safari, making for a better reader experience pretty quickly.

Recap

Writing testable code will make your life, and the lives of all who follow you, much, much easier. From fewer bugs to more easily fixed ones, from easier testing to simpler debugging, testable JavaScript is your gateway to sanity.

This book attempts to show you the path toward that sanity. After reading the entire book you will have a very good understanding of what writing and maintaining testable JavaScript actually entails. But that is only the beginning. You must fit these practices and patterns into your daily life as a developer. You must resist the temptation to be "lazy" and not write tests, when you are instead just kicking the can down the road for either yourself or someone else to clean up your mess. Testable JavaScript is code that will last. If you are currently writing legacy code, do yourself and your employer a favor and start writing current code. I hope you will find that not only is that effort not difficult, but it can also be extremely rewarding, and maybe even fun!

How to Contact Us

We have tested and verified the information in this book to the best of our ability, but you may find that features have changed (or even that we have made a few mistakes!). Please let us know about any errors you find, as well as your suggestions for future editions, by writing to:

O'Reilly Media, Inc.
1005 Gravenstein Highway North
Sebastopol, CA 95472

800-998-9938 (in the U.S. or Canada)
707-829-0515 (international/local)
707-829-0104 (fax)

We have a web page for this book, where we list errata, examples, and any additional information. You can access this page at *http://oreil.ly/Testable-JavaScript*.

To comment or ask technical questions about this book, send email to *bookques tions@oreilly.com*.

For more information about our books, courses, conferences, and news, see our website at *http://www.oreilly.com*.

Find us on Facebook: *http://facebook.com/oreilly*

Follow us on Twitter: *http://twitter.com/oreillymedia*

Watch us on YouTube: *http://www.youtube.com/oreillymedia*

Conventions Used in This Book

The following typographical conventions are used in this book:

Italic
    Indicates new terms, URLs, email addresses, filenames, and file extensions.

`Constant width`
    Used for program listings, as well as within paragraphs to refer to program elements such as variable or function names, databases, data types, environment variables, statements, and keywords.

`Constant width bold`
    Shows commands or other text that should be typed literally by the user.

`Constant width italic`
    Shows text that should be replaced with user-supplied values or by values determined by context.

 This icon signifies a tip, suggestion, or general note.

 This icon indicates a warning or caution.

Using Code Examples

This book is here to help you get your job done. In general, if this book includes code examples, you may use the code in your programs and documentation. You do not need to contact us for permission unless you're reproducing a significant portion of the code. For example, writing a program that uses several chunks of code from this book does not require permission. Selling or distributing a CD-ROM of examples from O'Reilly books does require permission. Answering a question by citing this book and quoting example code does not require permission. Incorporating a significant amount of example code from this book into your product's documentation does require permission.

We appreciate, but do not require, attribution. An attribution usually includes the title, author, publisher, and ISBN. For example: "*Testable JavaScript* by Mark Ethan Trostler (O'Reilly). Copyright 2013 ZZO Associates, 978-1-449-32339-4."

If you feel your use of code examples falls outside fair use or the permission given above, feel free to contact us at *permissions@oreilly.com*.

Safari® Books Online

 Safari Books Online (*www.safaribooksonline.com*) is an on-demand digital library that delivers expert content in both book and video form from the world's leading authors in technology and business.

Technology professionals, software developers, web designers, and business and creative professionals use Safari Books Online as their primary resource for research, problem solving, learning, and certification training.

Safari Books Online offers a range of product mixes and pricing programs for organizations, government agencies, and individuals. Subscribers have access to thousands of books, training videos, and prepublication manuscripts in one fully searchable database from publishers like O'Reilly Media, Prentice Hall Professional, Addison-Wesley Professional, Microsoft Press, Sams, Que, Peachpit Press, Focal Press, Cisco Press, John Wiley & Sons, Syngress, Morgan Kaufmann, IBM Redbooks, Packt, Adobe Press, FT Press, Apress, Manning, New Riders, McGraw-Hill, Jones & Bartlett, Course Technology, and dozens more. For more information about Safari Books Online, please visit us online.

Thanks!

A Big Thank You to everyone who helped me cobble together this book, starting with my former employer, Yahoo!, which green-lighted the time I needed to spend writing during "business hours"; thanks Julia and Randy! Also a Big Shout-Out to the amazing frontend team working on Yahoo! Mail, especially those based in Rancho Bernardo—I'm looking at you, Brian, Jeff, Hung, Dan, Mily, Steve, and Scott. Thanks to my manager here at Google, Matt Evans, and the rest of our team for letting me continue to pursue my goal of developing sane software.

A special thank you to everyone who contributes to open source technology. It is amazing that there continue to be fewer reasons to use commercial software, which is quite ironic for someone in the commercial software business. It is clear that money is not the be-all and end-all motivator, and it warms the cockles of my heart that passion trumps money every time. Hey employers, the intersection of your employees' passion and your product is how quality work actually gets done!

Thanks to Doug Crockford and his excellent series of talks that inspired me to take JavaScript seriously.

Big props to Shelley Powers and Davis Frank for reviewing the book and providing lots of great feedback that improved the book greatly. Of course, the buck stops with me, so if anything is not up to snuff it is all on me. JavaScript is changing rapidly and the language and tools are constantly evolving, but I hope the concepts presented in this book (if not all of the tools) will remain relevant for a long time. Poor Audrey Doyle had the unfortunate task of copyediting this manuscript, and she knocked it out of the park! I now have proof that at least one person read the book cover to cover—thanks Audrey!

Finally, much love to my family—Walter, Inslee, and especially Michelle, who has had to live with the gestation process of this book for too long. Now, on to the next one?

## CHAPTER 1

Testable JavaScript

Your ideas are unique; your code is not. Almost every industry has been completely revolutionized by machines; yet strangely, the computer science industry has not. Programmers are essentially doing the exact same things we have been doing for 40 years or so. We write code by hand, and that code gets compiled or interpreted and then executed. We look at the output and determine whether we need to go around again. This cycle of development has remained unchanged since the dawn of computer science. Our machines are orders of magnitude faster, RAM and secondary storage sizes are unimaginably large, and software has grown increasingly complex to take advantage of these developments. Yet we still write code by hand, one keystroke at a time. We still litter our code with "print" statements to figure out what is going on while it runs. Our development tools have indeed grown increasingly powerful, but with every hot new language, tooling starts all over again. The bottom line is that writing software remains an almost entirely manual process in a world of incredible automation, and most of that automation is due to the fruits of our software-writing labors. The very act of writing software one character at a time is the height of hypocrisy.

While the bulk of any code you write has been written before, either in the language you are currently using or in another one, every application is unique, even if yours is doing exactly the same thing as your competitor's. Unique or not, to succeed the application must also work. It does not have to be beautiful. It does not have to be the absolute fastest, nor does it have to be the most feature-rich. But it does have to work.

Applications are, at their core, just message-passing systems with some input and output. The amount of complexity built on top of that standard idiom continues to increase. With the advent of JavaScript, we must apply the lessons learned not only from other languages, but also from JavaScript itself to make our code testable. As JavaScript applications grow in size, on both the client and the server, we must be extremely careful to apply the best practices and lessons learned by our forefathers and tweak them to fit well with JavaScript.

Figure 1-1 shows the microprocessor cost per transistor cycle over the course of three decades.[1] This ridiculous graph of cost per cycle of CPUs, following Moore's law, keeps trending inexorably downward. Hardware refresh rate is indeed progressing far beyond anything seen in the software side of the world.

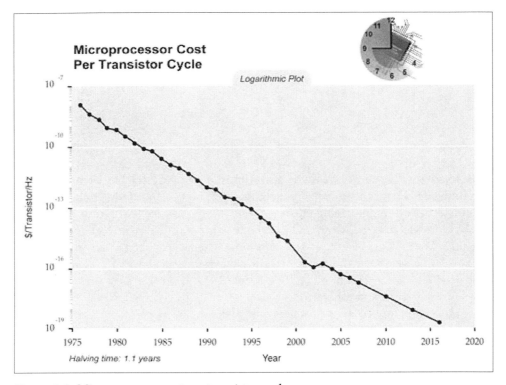

Figure 1-1. Microprocessor cost per transistor cycle

Enormous benefits have been achieved by programming machines to stamp out objects faster and smaller than ever before. In order to reach the incredible scale of global production, these rows of machines, assembled into factories, rely on standardization. Yet software engineers still sit in front of their individual computers, pecking away on their keyboards one character at a time.

Prior Art

While writing software is still an extremely manual process, there have been *a lot* of attempts to codify and standardize what developers should do to create a more repeat-

---

1. By Wgsimon [own work: CC-BY-SA-3.0 (*http://bit.ly/XUdmi9*)].

able process for writing "good" code. These processes, of course, hope to steer the wayward developer into writing "clean" and "bug-free" code. However, as with most things in life, "you gotta wanna"—and the results of employing any of the processes or methodologies covered in the following sections depend directly on the willingness of the developers to "buy in" to the system. The meat of this book is not about how or which methodology to use or choose, but what to do and think about when actually programming. Let's run through some of the current thinking.

Agile Development

This is a big one that is a placeholder for a lot of practices. The Agile approach is mainly a response to the "waterfall" model of software application development that occurs using a serialized process of discrete stages. For example, first the specification is written, then coders code, then testers test, then the application is deployed, and then we go back to updating the specification for new features. Each step in the process happens serially and in isolation. So, while the specification is written, the coders and testers wait. While the coders code, the testers wait, while the testers test, everyone waits, and so on.

Agile development tries to be more flexible and allow each stage to occur in parallel. Software that works is the top priority. Instead of waiting around for large chunks of time for the previous step to be perfect before handoff, each team iterates over shorter cycles, so things are always happening. Big chunks of work get broken down into smaller chunks that can be more easily estimated. Agile seeks to break down the walls between each group in the development cycle so that they work together and therefore reduce the time between deliverables. Collaboration with customers helps to define the final deliverable.

Note that the use of Agile methods does not necessarily mean your application is completed faster or with higher quality. Agile's biggest strength is the way it deals with changes. In the waterfall model, any change would require running through the entire process all over again. Agile's shorter cycles allow changes to be more easily incorporated into the final product. You might be using Agile already if you hear the words *fail fast*, *release often*, *backlog*, *standup*, or any phrase with the word *continuous*. Most modern development utilizes Agile to some extent. Figure 1-2 shows the canonical chart of the Agile development process.

There is a lot going on in Figure 1-2, but the basic idea is that quick iteration and constant interaction will accelerate the delivery of quality software.

Agile itself does not mandate how software is written; rather, it recommends several methodologies that fit well with the Agile philosophy. For example, "user stories" are plain sentences by "users" about what features they need from the application. These stories are ideally fed back into the product as feature requests for the application. A user is anyone who uses your application or API, from someone sitting at home to a developer in another group who can contribute to help define the feature set of the final application. Pair programming is another development methodology often associated with Agile. In its purest form, pair programming is two programmers sitting at the same desk, staring at the same monitor, with one keyboard and mouse, writing software together. While one programmer is typing, the other is actively debugging and thinking about the code. Two minds are typically better than one, so issues are found and resolved more quickly than if the two programmers were working in isolation.

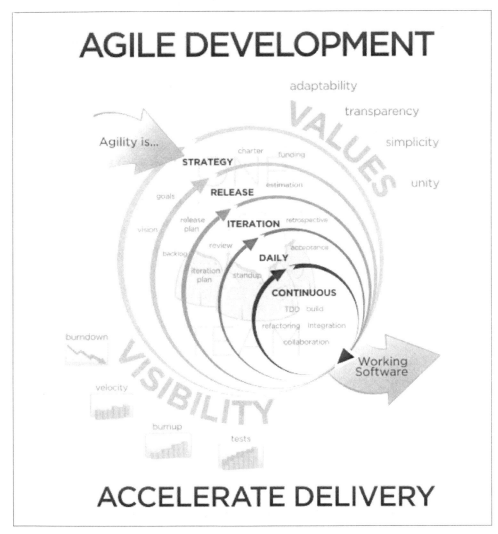

Figure 1-2. The Agile development process (courtesy of Dbenson and VersionOne, Inc.)

Test-Driven Development

Test-driven development (TDD) is a recommended practice of Agile software development. TDD wants you to write your tests first, before you write any code. These tests provide the expectations to which your code must conform. After you write tests that fail (as there initially is no code to make the tests work), you then start writing code that makes your tests pass. As your tests stay one step ahead of your development, you will never have any code that is not covered by a test. That is the theory, at least. In reality, what tends to happen is developers start to go down this path and initial tests are written, but the code soon overtakes the tests. Hey, at least you got some tests out of the bargain!

TDD clearly works best when you are starting a new project or module. It is also most successful if only unit tests are required. Writing full integration tests before any code exists is daunting! TDD also provides a great reason/excuse to rewrite existing legacy code. If a developer's choice is "write a bunch of tests for already existing code" or "write your own new code starting with tests," most likely the developer will choose the latter option. Of course, developers do not always have a choice; just do not expect happy faces and high fives from them if writing tests for an already existing codebase is the path chosen to move forward.

Regardless, TDD is not a bad thing; in fact, it can be a very good thing. TDD is great at beginnings, whether an entire application or a single module—everyone is excited to write new code, and if the "cost" of writing that new code is writing tests first, so be it. And as there is no code at the beginning, the "cost" of writing tests is minimal.

An interesting study in 2005 on Canadian undergraduates found that TDD made programmers more productive because they wrote more tests. While that is debatable, what is more interesting is that the researchers "also observed that the minimum quality increased linearly with the number of programmer tests, independent of the development strategy employed."[2] It is good to know that the number of tests is proportional to higher code quality. The conclusion one could draw is that any methodology that gets developers to write more tests before, during, or after coding is a very good thing.

Behavior-Driven Development

Behavior-driven development (BDD) builds on TDD to provide developers and non-developers a common language to describe correct application and module behavior. The common language is just your everyday language. For example, instead of writing a test called `testEmptyCart`, you would provide a description that defines the behavior

---

2. Erdogmus, Hakan, Marco Torchiano, and Maurizio Morisio. January 2005. "On the Effectiveness of the Test-First Approach to Programming." *Proceedings of the IEEE Transactions on Software Engineering* 31(3): pp 226-237; NRC 47445.

of the module under test, such as "the shopping cart should not allow you to check out if it is empty." Using a common language to define tests or expectations allows anyone to more easily understand what is being tested, as well as helping to define what the tests and expectations should be.

BDD utilizes Agile user stories to define tests against the code. The user stories can then be directly translated into tests. The user stories typically must follow a specific template of the form: As a [someone] I want to [something] so that [result].

Each blank is filled in appropriately, as in a Yahoo! Mail user I want to attach a picture to my email so that my recipients can see it. This user story can then be translated into a set of feature requirements and tests for the Yahoo! Mail product.

BDD is great for formalized feedback from people not on your team (technical or not), to help you understand how your system should operate. The user stories can usually be directly translated into tests—and anything that promotes focused testing (and more of it) is a very good thing!

The Best Approach?

This book is intended to neither advocate nor explicate any development methodology, and by that measure I think it succeeds admirably. Waterfall, spiral, Agile, and other methodologies are all well and good, but none necessarily leads to testable code, let alone testable JavaScript. Similarly, TDD, BDD, and other forms of development also do not necessarily lead to testable JavaScript. What does lead to testable JavaScript? A commitment to writing clear, loosely coupled, and well-commented code that you know will be maintained by someone else will lead to testable JavaScript. Writing, reading, and maintaining testable JavaScript does not require test-driven, behavior-driven, or any other "-driven" development practices. However, following any practice that emphasizes tests along with code is a good thing. The most important thing to internalize is that the code you write does not exist in a vacuum. Any code you write professionally will be looked at, compiled, debugged, and finally used by not only yourself, but hopefully someone else too. In the end, you are writing code for other people to maintain, study, and use.

Code Is for People

This has been beaten into our heads a lot lately, and I am not going to let up on that trend! The code we write is not for computers, it is for people. Writing software is a hands-on business. Computers just want the bits; JavaScript, C++, Java, Perl, Lisp, or whatever else all gets compiled down to the CPU's extremely limited instruction set. The CPU does not know if it is running a "compiled" or "interpreted" language. The

CPU does not care about comments or semicolons or whitespace. The CPU is blissfully unaware of the structure, syntax, or semantics of any of the myriad computer programming languages people use. A JavaScript program looks just like a C++ program, which looks exactly like a Perl program to the CPU.

At the lowest level, the success or failure of our programs is intertwined with the machine language code that the CPU executes; but we rarely, if ever, see that. We see only the original code. The CPU does not care what you are trying to do, but people do.

Software starts with *intent*. What are you trying to do? What is this piece of code trying to accomplish? Why are you writing it? These are important questions that either you or your coworkers must ask every day. You transform that initial intent (the "whats" and the "whys") into actual code: the "hows." This book is mostly concerned with the "hows." Figuring out what you are trying to do and why you are trying to do it are the necessary first steps toward getting to the "how" part of your job, but the rubber really hits the road when you are actually *dealing* with the "hows." Books on programming languages help with the lowest-level "how"; then software-pattern books go one layer higher. This book hopes to clearly explain the top layer of the "how" totem pole: "how" to write testable code and "how" to test it.

But before we can get to the "how," it is important to understand the "what" and the "why" of software development.

Why do we want to write testable code? What is testable code?

Why

"Writing software is the hardest thing people do," says Douglas Crockford (*http://bit.ly/ XUdoGJ*), which means it is extremely important that software be as human-friendly as possible. Testable code is easier to test, which means it is easier to maintain, which means it is easier for people (yourself included) to understand it, which makes it easier to maintain, which in turn makes it easier to test.

We have gone in a circle, but it is a virtuous circle. There is no Platonic ideal of perfect code; testability, maintainability, and understandability are interlocked, and there are lots of opinions about what these things are and how to get there with software. However, finding and fixing bugs is much simpler with testable, maintainable, and understandable code. And you as a programmer will spend at least half of your time finding and fixing bugs, either in your code or in someone else's, so be nice to yourself and try to make that time as pleasant as possible.

Why testable

Testing code, using any kind of testing, is a required activity. Either you test it or someone else does, even if it is the end user simply using your application. Nothing is perfect the first time, or any subsequent time thereafter. Even one of the simplest JavaScript programs:

```
x = x + 1;
```

can have problems. What if x is a string? What if x is infinity? What if x is an object? As our programs get more complicated, we can only hope to test the most common paths for sanity. Exhaustive testing is impossible. Writing code that is easy to test, or "testable," at least gives testers a fighting chance to accomplish the most basic and hopefully ever-more advanced testing.

Why maintainable

Programmers do not always write code from scratch. Sometimes we are tasked with debugging and maintaining someone else's code. That someone else may be long gone, just as you are long gone from the code you wrote at your previous company. While you are maintaining someone else's code, someone else is maintaining yours. Besides making the world a better place, code that is testable is also more "maintainable." Usually you do not have a full picture of what your changes will affect, and having tests, made possible by testable code, can help you figure out the extent and ramifications of your seemingly little changes. When you know how the code works—specifically, what will happen when you make changes to it—you have maintainable code. This is code you are not afraid of. This is code that you can more easily share with members of your team. This is code that does not need to be rewritten solely to understand it. As an application increases in size, the number of people with full knowledge of the code dwindles rapidly. Even these people can be surprised that a seemingly innocuous change has affected functionality elsewhere.

Why understandable

The third feature of quality software, which is intertwined with the other two, is the ability to look at code and understand it. How long does it take when staring at a piece of code to understand what it does? Clearly, being able to test it (and have tests for it) goes a long way toward helping you understand what the code is doing. But can you look at a method or function and understand not only the author's intent but also the "how"? If you cannot understand either code you wrote six months ago or code someone else wrote, you have a serious problem. Looking at a piece of code and understanding it is not only satisfying, but also necessary to properly fulfill your job requirements. Conversely, if you have written code that you no longer understand, you have failed. Code is for people to understand, maintain, and test. You write code for other people, which means your peers must be able to relatively quickly understand your code. If code is not understood, it can be neither tested nor maintained. In those circumstances, code typically gets completely rewritten. You may be throwing out crap or you may be throwing out awesome code that is 99% bug-free, but how could anyone ever know that? If it is not testable, maintainable, and understandable, it is trash.

What

So "what" exactly is "testable" code? What does "maintainable" code look like? What kind of code is "understandable" code? Let us dig a bit deeper into those questions. We will see numerous examples of "what" all of this looks like throughout this book.

What is testable

Testable code is code that is easy to test. Bet you didn't see that coming! But what makes code easy to test? In general, the features that make code easy to test are the same ones that make it easy to maintain, and more understandable: there's less of it, and it's less complex code, fully commented, and loosely coupled. These features and more make code "testable." By exploiting testability features and using tools focused on testing, you make your code more and more testable.

What is maintainable

Maintainable code is code that can be handed over to other team members and peers with a minimum of handholding and transition. Code that is testable with good tests and is understandable is more maintainable than complex, uncommented code without tests. Maintainable code can live a full product life cycle: it does not need to be rewritten, either partially or fully, when passed off from person to person. Code that you can fix and change, without having to fully understand everything the code does but with the confidence that your changes have not broken something else, is maintainable code.

What is understandable

How long will it take when looking at a piece of code—either a function or an even smaller piece—for you to understand it? Does the original author need to explain it to you step by step? Or can you "get" it yourself in a reasonable amount of time? Simple, small, and commented code tends to be more understandable. Being able to test your assumptions about the code by running it in isolation also helps greatly in terms of understanding. It is vitally important that code is understandable; otherwise, it will be thrown away and rewritten.

How

Understanding the "why" and the "what" leads us to the "how." This book is primarily concerned with how you can write, test, and maintain testable, maintainable, and understandable code. Clearly, testing and maintaining code that is already testable, maintainable, and understandable will make your job easier. Starting with this solid foundation will make you much more productive, and productive people are happy people, and happy people are productive people! It's one of those virtuous circles again. I like virtuous circles.

How testable

Writing testable code is easier when you start with a blank slate (isn't everything easier when you start with a blank slate?). Some development methodologies, such as TDD and BDD, can lead to testable code, but not necessarily. This is because having tests for code does not automatically make that code testable. However, when you think about testing from the start, your code typically will end up more testable than code written from scratch without regard to testing. I do not demand that you use TDD or BDD when writing code; however, I think it is a great idea to start with testing in mind, and I believe that testing constantly is necessary to writing testable code. Writing tests or the UI first is not a requirement for testable code, but writing unit tests first (TDD) or integration tests first (BDD) speaks to a fundamental notion of testable code: the sooner the code can be executed and tested, the better. I would like to squeeze a third approach in between TDD and BDD: test-while-driven development (TWDD). The tests and the code are in a chicken-and-egg situation: either one can come first, as long as the other comes immediately afterward—meaning, do not write a lot of tests and no code, and do not write a lot of code and no tests. Instead, write a little code and then quickly write a little test. Or perhaps write a little test and then write a little code.

Again, this does not necessarily lead to testable code. You can still write crap with a lot of tests. While you are writing little bits of code and little tests, remember the bigger picture: write small, isolatable chunks of code with minimal dependencies and minimal complexity. That mindset is the essence of this book.

How maintainable

You can achieve maintainable code in much the same way you achieve testable code: by writing small bits of simple, isolatable code—small because the fewer the lines of code, the fewer the bugs; simple because simple code is easier to maintain; and isolatable so that changes made to the code will affect as few other pieces of the code as possible. We will investigate several methods for keeping your code small and isolated throughout this book.

How understandable

Not surprisingly, writing understandable code follows the same principles. Simple code is more quickly understood. Having tests along with the code gives further insight into the intent and inner workings of the code. Comments greatly aid in understandability.

Writing code is similar to composing chapters in a novel: several small chapters are easier to understand than a few large ones. Being verbose in both comments (inserting comment blocks before methods) and code (choosing meaningful variable names, following best practices, following a consistent coding style, etc.) enhances understandability. Your peers tasked with maintaining your code are not morons. Give them some signposts to aid in their understanding, and your code will not have to be thrown away and rewritten.

Beyond Application Code

Your job does not end with writing small chunks of testable code. You also get to test it! Writing testable code makes testing it, and finding bugs within it, much easier. No developer wants to attempt to debug a giant mound of code, especially if said developer did not write it.

Testing

Unit tests are a developer's first line of defense. Not only do unit tests force you, the developer, to understand your code, but they also help you to document and debug your code. Beyond unit testing, integration testing helps to ensure that everything is working together as planned—especially client-side JavaScript, which runs on many different browsers on an increasing number of platforms (desktops, tablets, and phones). Finally, performance testing and load testing help to ensure that your application is performing to specification. Each step up the testing ladder exercises your code at different levels of abstraction. Each test type finds bugs in different usage scenarios. Fully testing code requires tests at all levels of abstraction. And still you will have bugs in production; there is no magic bullet.

Debugging

Regardless of the number of tests you conduct, debugging is a fact of life for software developers. Fortunately, JavaScript has some very nice tools that are constantly improving to help. Leveraging these tools will help make your debugging life easier, which is nice, as you will probably spend much more time debugging your code than writing it.

Whether you are debugging locally or remotely, many powerful tools are available for step-by-step debugging and resource management.

Recap

Testable JavaScript does not automatically flow from Agile, waterfall, TDD, BDD, or whatever other software development philosophy you might follow. Testable JavaScript is a commitment to small, loosely coupled, bite-sized chunks of simple code. How you arrive at that code is up to you. This book will hopefully provide insight into achieving this state of coded bliss.

Writing testable code will make your life, and the lives of all who follow you, much easier. From fewer bugs to more easily fixed ones, from easier testing to simpler debugging, testable JavaScript is your gateway to sanity.

Most importantly, do not forget that you are writing code for people, not for the compiler. People, yourself included, will have to maintain your code going forward, so make everyone's life easier, including your own, and write testable JavaScript.

## CHAPTER 2

Complexity

Complex: bad. Simple: good. We touched on this already, and it's still true. We can measure complexity with some accuracy via static analysis. Measures such as JSLint, cyclomatic complexity, lines of code, and fan-in and fan-out are important. However, nothing measures complexity as accurately as showing your code to a coworker or colleague.

Code can be complex for a number of reasons, from the serious "this is a hairy algorithm" to the mundane "a JavaScript newbie wrote it and it's nasty," and everything in between. Analyzing the complexity of static code is a great starting point toward creating testable JavaScript.

Maintainable JavaScript is clear, consistent, and standards-based. Testable JavaScript is loosely coupled, short, and isolatable. The magic happens when your code is both maintainable and testable. Since you will spend about 50% of your time testing and debugging your code, which is significantly more time than you will spend coding it (*http://bit.ly/XUdoXl*), you might as well make code maintenance as easy on yourself and others as possible.

Complexity is the bane of every software project. While some complexity is unavoidable, in many cases complexity can be avoided. Being able to recognize which parts of your application are complex, and understanding why, will allow you to reduce its overall complexity. As always, recognizing the problem is the first step toward fixing it.

It is also important to note that the algorithms your code relies on may be complex as well. In fact, typically these complex algorithms are what make your code unique and useful. If your core algorithms were not complex, someone probably would have already created your application. However, unavoidable (in fact, beneficial) algorithm complexity is no excuse for writing complicated code. Although the details, and perhaps the code, surrounding your algorithm may be complex, of course there is a lot more to your application than some core algorithms.

Code Size

As code size grows, code complexity increases and the number of people who understand the entire system shrinks. As the number of modules increases, integration testing
becomes increasingly difficult and the number of module interaction permutations
grows. It is not surprising, therefore, that the number-one indicator of bugs/bug po-
tential is code size. The more code you have, the greater the chance it will have bugs in
it (*http://bit.ly/XUdmPf*). The total amount of code necessary for your project may not
change, but the number of statements in a method can. The amount of code in each file
is also changeable. Large methods are difficult to test and maintain, so make more small
ones. In an ideal world, functions have no side effects and their return value(s) (if any)
are completely dependent on their parameters. Code rarely gets to live in that world,
but it is something to keep in mind while writing code, along with "how am I going to
test this thing?"

One method that can keep functions minimally sized is command query separation.
Commands are functions that *do* something; queries are functions that *return* something. In this world, commands are setters and queries are getters. Commands are tested
using *mocks* and queries are tested using *stubs* (more on this in Chapter 4). Keeping
these worlds separate, along with enhancing testability, can provide great scalability
returns by ensuring that reads are separated from writes. Here is an example of command
query separation using Node.js:

```
function configure(values) {
    var fs = require('fs')
        , config = { docRoot: '/somewhere' }
        , key
        , stat
    ;

    for (key in values) {
        config[key] = values[key];
    }

    try {
        stat = fs.statSync(config.docRoot);
        if (!stat.isDirectory()) {
            throw new Error('Is not valid');
        }
    } catch(e) {
        console.log("** " + config.docRoot +
            " does not exist or is not a directory!! **");
        return;
    }

    // ... check other values ...
    return config;
}
```

Let's take a quick look at some test code for this function. In Chapter 4 we will discuss the syntax of these tests in greater detail, so for now we'll just look at the flow:

```
describe("configure tests", function() {
    it("undef if docRoot does not exist", function() {
        expect(configure({ docRoot: '/xxx' })).toBeUndefined();
    });

    it("not undef if docRoot does exist", function() {
        expect(configure({ docRoot: '/tmp' })).not.toBeUndefined();
    });

    it("adds values to config hash", function() {
        var config = configure({ docRoot: '/tmp', zany: 'crazy' });
        expect(config).not.toBeUndefined();
        expect(config.zany).toEqual('crazy');
        expect(config.docRoot).toEqual('/tmp');
    });

    it("verifies value1 good...", function() {
    });

    it("verifies value1 bad...", function() {
    });

    // ... many more validation tests with multiple expects...
});
```

This function is doing too much. After setting default configuration values, it goes on to check the validity of those values; in fact, the function under test goes on to check five more values. The method is large and each check is completely independent of the previous checks. Further, all of the validation logic for each value is wrapped up in this single function and it is impossible to validate a value in isolation. Testing this beast requires many tests for each possible value for each configuration value. Similarly, this function requires many unit tests, with all of the validation tests wrapped up inside the unit tests for the basic working of the function itself. Of course, over time more and more configuration values will be added, so this is only going to get increasingly ugly. Also, swallowing the thrown error in the `try/catch` block renders the `try/catch` block useless. Finally, the return value is confusing: either it is undefined if any value did not validate, or it is the entire valid hash. And let's not forget the side effects of the `console.log` statements—but we will get to that later.

Breaking this function into several pieces is the solution. Here is one approach:

```
function configure(values) {
    var config = { docRoot: '/somewhere' }
        , key
    ;

    for (key in values) {
```

```
        config[key] = values[key];
    }

    return config;
}

function validateDocRoot(config) {
    var fs = require('fs')
      , stat
    ;

    stat = fs.statSync(config.docRoot);
    if (!stat.isDirectory()) {
        throw new Error('Is not valid');
    }
}

function validateSomethingElse(config) { ... }
```

Here, we split up the setting of the values (query, a return value) with a set of validation functions (commands, no return; possible errors thrown). Breaking this function into two smaller functions makes our unit tests more focused and more flexible.

We can now write separate, isolatable unit tests for each validation function instead of having them all within the larger "configure" unit tests:

```
describe("validate value1", function() {
    it("accepts the correct value", function() {
        // some expects
    });

    it("rejects the incorrect value", function() {
        // some expects
    });
});
```

This is a great step toward testability, as the validation functions can now be tested in isolation without being wrapped up and hidden within the more general "configure" tests. However, separating setters from the validation now makes it possible to avoid validation entirely. While it may be desirable to do this, usually it is not. Here is where command query separation can break down—we do not want the side effect of setting the value without validating it simultaneously. Although separate validation functions are a good thing for testing, we need to ensure that they are called.

The next iteration might look like this:

```
function configure(values) {
    var config = { docRoot: '/somewhere' };
    for (var key in values) {
        config[key] = values[key];
    }
```

```
    validateDocRoot(config);
    validateSomethingElse(config);
    ...

    return config;
}
```

This new configuration function will either return a valid `config` object or throw an error. All of the validation functions can be tested separately from the `configure` function itself.

The last bit of niceness would be to link each key in the `config` object to its validator function and keep the entire hash in one central location:

```
var fields {
    docRoot: { validator: validateDocRoot, default: '/somewhere' }
    , somethingElse: { validator: validateSomethingElse }
};

function configure(values) {
    for (var key in fields) {
        if (typeof values[key] !== 'undefined') {
            fields[key].validator(values[key]);
            config[key] = values[key];
        } else {
            config[key] = fields[key].default;
        }
    }

    return config;
}
```

This is a great compromise. The validator functions are available separately for easier testing, they will all get called when new values are set, and all data regarding the keys is stored in one central location.

As an aside, there still is a problem. What is to stop someone from trying the following?

```
config.docRoot = '/does/not/exist';
```

Our validator function will not run, and now all bets are off. For objects, there is a great solution: use the new ECMAScript 5 `Object` methods. They allow object property creation with built-in validators, getters, setters, and more, and all are very testable:

```
var obj = { realRoot : '/somewhere' };
Object.defineProperty(obj, 'docRoot',
    {
        enumerable: true
        , set: function(value) {
            validateDocRoot(value); this.realRoot = value; }
    }
);
```

Now the following:

```
config.docRoot = '/does/not/exist';
```

will run the set function, which calls the validate function, which will throw an exception if that path does not exist, so there is no escaping the validation.

But this is weird. This assignment statement might now throw an exception and will need to be wrapped in a try/catch block. Even if you get rid of the throw, what do you now set config.docRoot to if validation fails? Regardless of what you set it to, the outcome will be unexpected. And unexpected outcomes spell trouble. Plus, the weirdness of the internal and external names of docRoot versus realRoot is confusing.

A better solution is to use private properties with public getters and setters. This keeps the properties private but everything else public, including the validator, for testability:

```
var Obj = (function() {
    return function() {
        var docRoot = '/somewhere';
        this.validateDocRoot = function(val) {
            // validation logic - throw Error if not OK
        };
        this.setDocRoot = function(val) {
            this.validateDocRoot(val);
            docRoot = val;
        };
        this.getDocRoot = function() {
            return docRoot;
        };
    };
}());
```

Now access to the docRoot property is only possible through our API, which forces validation on writes. Use it like so:

```
var myObject = new Obj();
try {
    myObject.setDocRoot('/somewhere/else');
} catch(e) {
    // something wrong with my new doc root
    // old value of docRoot still there
}
// all is OK
console.log(myObject.getDocRoot());
```

The setter is now wrapped in a try/catch block, which is more expected than wrapping an assignment in a try/catch block, so it looks sane.

But there is one more issue we can address—what about this?

```
var myObject = new Obj();
myObject.docRoot = '/somewhere/wrong';

// and then later...
var dR = myObject.docRoot;
```

Gah! Of course, none of the methods in the API will know about or use this spurious docRoot field created erroneously by the user. Fortunately, there is a very easy fix:

```
var Obj = (function() {
    return function() {
        var docRoot = '/somewhere';
        this.validateDocRoot = function(val) {
            // validation logic - throw Exception if not OK
        };
        this.setDocRoot = function(val) {
            this.validateDocRoot(val);
            docRoot = val;
        };
        this.getDocRoot = function() {
            return docRoot;
        };
        Object.preventExtensions(this)
    };
}());
```

Using `Object.preventExensions` will throw a `TypeError` if anyone tries to add a property to the object. The result: no more spurious properties. This is very handy for all of your objects, especially if you access properties directly. The interpreter will now catch any mistyped/added property names by throwing a `TypeError`.

This code also nicely encapsulates command query separation with a setter/getter/validator, all separate and each testable in isolation. The validation functions could be made private, but to what end? It is best to keep them public, not only so that they can be tested more easily, but also because production code might want to verify whether a value is a legitimate docRoot value or not without having to explicitly set it on the object.

Here is the very clean test code—short, sweet, isolatable, and semantic:

```
describe("validate docRoot", function() {
    var config = new Obj();

    it("throw if docRoot does not exist", function() {
        expect(config.validateDocRoot.bind(config, '/xxx')).toThrow();
    });

    it("not throw if docRoot does exist", function() {
        expect(config.validateDocRoot.bind(config, '/tmp')).not.toThrow();
    });
});
```

Command query separation is not the only game in town and is not always feasible, but it is often a good starting point. Code size can be managed in a number of different ways, although breaking up code along command query lines plays to one of JavaScript's great strengths: eventing. We will see how to use this to our advantage later in this chapter.

JSLint

While JSLint does not measure complexity directly, it does force you to know what your code is doing. This decreases complexity and ensures that you do not use any overly complicated or error-prone constructs. Simply put, it is a measure of code sanity. With inspiration from the original "lint" for C, JSLint analyzes code for bad style, syntax, and semantics. It detects the bad parts[1] of your code.

Refactoring bad code and replacing it with good code is the essence of testable JavaScript. Here is an example:

```
function sum(a, b) {
    return
        a+b;
}
```

That example was simple enough. Let's run it through JSLint:

```
Error:
    Problem at line 2 character 5: Missing 'use strict' statement.
return
    Problem at line 2 character 11: Expected ';' and instead saw 'a'.
return
    Problem at line 3 character 8: Unreachable 'a' after 'return'.
a+b;
    Problem at line 3 character 8: Expected 'a' at column 5,
not column 8.
a+b;
    Problem at line 3 character 9: Missing space between 'a' and '+'.
a+b;
    Problem at line 3 character 10: Missing space between '+' and 'b'.
a+b;
    Problem at line 3 character 10: Expected an assignment or
function call and instead saw an expression.
a+b;
```

---

1. Douglas Crockford defines and explains these bad parts in JavaScript: The Good Parts (O'Reilly).

Wow! Four lines of mostly nothing code generated seven JSLint errors! What is wrong? Besides a missing use strict statement, the biggest problem is the carriage return character after the return. Due to semicolon insertion, JavaScript will return unde fined from this function. JSLint has caught this error, and is complaining about other whitespace issues in this function.

Not only is whitespace relevant for readability, but in this case it also causes an error that is very hard to track down. Use whitespace sanely, as JSLint requires; you cannot test what you cannot read and understand. Code readability is the fundamental step toward testable code. Programs are written for other programmers to maintain, enhance, and test. It is critically important that your code is readable. JSLint provides a good measure of readability (and sanity).

Here is the corrected code:

```
function sum(a, b) {
    return a + b;
}
```

Let's look at one more seemingly innocuous snippet:

```
for (var i = 0; i < a.length; i++)
    a[i] = i*i;
```

This time JSLint cannot even parse the entire chunk, and only gets this far:

```
Error:
    Problem at line 1 character 6: Move 'var' declarations to the top
of the function.
    for (var i = 0; i < a.length; i++)
        Problem at line 1 character 6: Stopping. (33% scanned).
```

The first issue is the var declaration in the for loop. JavaScript variables are all either global- or function-scoped. Declaring a variable in a for loop does *not* declare that variable for only the for loop. The variable is available inside the function that contains the for loop. By using this construct, you have just created a variable named i that is available anywhere throughout the enclosing function. This is what JSLint is telling us about moving the declaration to the top of the function. By writing the code this way, you are confusing yourself and, even worse, the next programmer who maintains this code.

While this is not mission-critical, you should get out of the habit of declaring variables anywhere other than at the beginning of a function. JavaScript variables are function-scoped, so be proud that you understand this key differentiator between JavaScript and other common languages! Move the declaration to the top of the enclosing function, where it makes sense.

OK, after we've moved the declaration up, JSLint now says the following:

```
Error:
    Problem at line 2 character 28: Unexpected '++'.
for (i = 0; i < a.length; i++)
    Problem at line 3 character 5: Expected exactly one space between
 ')' and 'a'.
a[i] = i*i;
    Problem at line 3 character 5: Expected '{' and instead saw 'a'.
a[i] = i*i;
    Problem at line 3 character 13: Missing space between 'i' and '*'.
a[i] = i*i;
    Problem at line 3 character 14: Missing space between '*' and 'i'.
a[i] = i*i;
```

JSLint is displeased with ++. The prefix and postfix ++ and - - operators can be confusing. This may be their least problematic form of usage and represents a very common programming idiom, so perhaps JSLint is being a bit harsh here, but these operators are a holdover from C/C++ pointer arithmetic and are unnecessary in JavaScript, so be wary of them. In cases when these operators can cause confusion, be explicit about their use; otherwise, you are probably OK. The Big Picture is that you must ensure that your code is readable and understandable by others, so as usual, do not get too cute or optimize prematurely.

JSLint also wants braces around all loops, so put braces around all your loops. Not only will the one line in your loop probably expand to more than one line in the future and trip someone up in the process, but also some static analysis tools (e.g., minifiers, code coverage generators, other static analysis tools, etc.) can get confused without braces around loops. Do everyone (including yourself) a favor, include them. The extra two bytes of "cost" this will incur are far outweighed by the readability of the resultant code.

Here is the JSLint-approved version of the preceding code:

```
for (i = 0; i < a.length; i = i + 1) {
    a[i] = i * i;
}
```

What is especially troubling about the original code is that there are no bugs in it! It will compile and run just fine, and will do what it was intended to do. But programs are written for other programmers, and the latent confusion and poor readability of the original code will become a liability as the codebase grows and the code is maintained by people other than the original author (or is maintained by the original author six months after he wrote it, when the intent is no longer fresh in his mind).

Rather than going through all of JSLint's settings and exhortations, I'll direct you to the JSLint website (*http://bit.ly/XUdnmb*), where you can read about JSLint and its capabilities. Another good source of information is Crockford's *JavaScript: The Good Parts*, which provides details on "good" versus "bad" JavaScript syntactic constructs. JSLint and Crockford's book are great first steps toward testable JavaScript. JSLint can be a bit prescriptive for some; if you have a good reason to feel very strongly against what JSLint proposes and can articulate those feelings clearly to members of your group, check out JSHint (*http://bit.ly/XUdpKV*), a fork of JSLint that is more flexible and forgiving than JSLint. JSLint can also read configuration settings in comments at the top of your Java-Script files, so feel free to tweak those. I recommend using a standard set of JSLint configuration options throughout your application.

As a quick aside, there is a larger problem here that JSLint cannot resolve: use of a for loop is not idiomatic JavaScript. Using the tools provided by the language clears up just about all the issues JSLint had with the original loop:

```
a.forEach(function (val, index) {
    a[index] = index * index;
});
```

Use of the forEach method ensures that the array value and index are scoped properly to just the function callback. Equally important is the fact that this construct shows future maintainers of your code that you know what you are doing and are comfortable with idiomatic JavaScript.

Although this immediately fixes all the issues we had with the original code, at the time of this writing the forEach method unfortunately is not available natively in all browsers —but not to worry! Adding it is simple; do not try to write it yourself, but rather utilize Mozilla's standards-based implementation (*http://mzl.la/XUdq1m*). The definition of the algorithm is here (*http://bit.ly/XUdqhN*). It is important to note that the callback function receives three arguments: the value, the current index, and the object itself, not just the array element. While you can write a barebones version of forEach in fewer lines, do not be tempted to do this; use the standards-based version. You can easily add this snippet of code to the top of your JavaScript to ensure that forEach is available in every context. Not surprisingly, IE 8 and earlier do not have native forEach support. If you are sure your code will not run in those environments or if you are writing server-side JavaScript, you are good to go.

Unfortunately, adding this snippet of code will increase the size of the code that must be downloaded and parsed. However, after minification it compresses down to 467 bytes and will only be fully executed once on IE 8 and earlier.

This seems to be a good compromise, as the standard forEach method has a function-scoped index variable, so no attempted variable declaration in the initializer is even possible. Plus, we don't have to deal with the ++ post-conditional, and the braces are right there for you. Using the "good" features of JavaScript and programming idiomatically always leads to cleaner and more testable code.

In Chapter 8 we will integrate JSUnit into our build to keep a close eye on our code.

Cyclomatic Complexity

Cyclomatic complexity is a measure of the number of independent paths through your code. Put another way, it is the minimum number of unit tests you will need to write to exercise all of your code. Let's look at an example:

```
function sum(a, b) {
    if (typeof(a) !== typeof(b)) {
        throw new Error("Cannot sum different types!");
    } else {
        return a + b;
    }
}
```

This method has a cyclomatic complexity of 2. This means you will need to write two unit tests to test each branch and get 100% code coverage.

 In the preceding code, I used the !== operator even though typeof is guaranteed to return a string. While not strictly necessary, in this case using !== and === is a good habit, and you should use them everywhere. The JSLint website and Crockford's *JavaScript: The Good Parts* provide more details. Using strict equality will help you to more quickly uncover bugs in your code.

Generating the cyclomatic complexity of your code is simple using a command-line tool such as jsmeter (*http://bit.ly/XUdqOI*). However, determining what is optimal in terms of cyclomatic complexity is not so simple. For instance, in his paper "A Complexity Measure" (*http://bit.ly/XUdrlS*), Thomas J. McCabe postulated that no method should have a cyclomatic complexity value greater than 10. Meanwhile, a study that you can read about (*http://bit.ly/XUdu11*) states that cyclomatic complexity and bug probability will not correlate until cyclomatic complexity reaches a value of 25 or more. So why try to keep the cyclomatic complexity value less than 10? Ten is not a magic number, but rather a reasonable one, so while the correlation between code and bugs may not begin until cyclomatic complexity reaches 25, for general sanity and maintainability purposes keeping this number lower is a good idea. To be clear, code with a cyclomatic complexity value of 25 is *very* complex. Regardless of the number of bugs in that code currently, editing a method with that much complexity is almost assured to *cause* a bug. Table 2-1 shows how Aivosto.com (*http://bit.ly/XUdrSY*) measures "bad fix" probabilities as cyclomatic complexity increases (*http://bit.ly/XUduxY*).

Table 2-1. Cyclomatic complexity and bad fix probability

Cyclomatic complexity	Bad fix probability
1–10	5%
20–30	20%
> 50	40%
Approaching 100	60%

An interesting tidbit is apparent from this table: when fixing relatively simple code there is a 5% chance you will introduce a new bug. That is significant! The "bad fix" probability increases fourfold as cyclomatic complexity gets above 20. I have never seen a function with cyclomatic complexity reaching 50, let alone 100. If you see cyclomatic complexity approaching either of those numbers, you should scream and run for the hills.

Also, the number of unit tests necessary to test such a beast is prohibitive. As McCabe notes in the aforementioned paper, functions with complexities greater than 16 were also the least reliable.

Reading someone else's code is the most reliable indicator of code quality and correctness (more on that later). The reader must keep track of what all the branches are doing while going over the code. Now, many scientists have conducted studies on short-term memory; the most famous of these postulates that humans have a working memory of "7 plus or minus 2" items (a.k.a. Miller's Law),[2] although more recent research suggests the number is lower. However, for a professional programmer reading code, that cyclomatic complexity value can be higher for shorter periods of time, but it doesn't have to be. Exactly what battle are you fighting to keep your code more complex? Keep it simple!

Large cyclomatic complexity values are usually due to a lot of `if/then/else` statements (or `switch` statements, but you are not using those as they are not one of the "good parts," right?). The simplest refactoring fix, then, is to break the method into smaller methods or to use a lookup table. Here is an example of the former:

```
function doSomething(a) {
    if (a === 'x') {
        doX();
    } else if (a === 'y') {
        doY();
    } else {
        doZ();
    }
}
```

This can be refactored using a lookup table:

---

2. Miller, G.A. 1956. "The Magical Number Seven, Plus or Minus Two: Some Limits on Our Capacity for Processing Information." *Psychological Review* 63(2): pp. 81–97.

```
function doSomething(a) {
    var lookup = { x: doX, y: doY }, def = doZ;
    lookup[a] ? lookup[a]() : def();
}
```

Note that by refactoring the conditional into a lookup table we have *not* decreased the number of unit tests that are necessary. For methods with a high cyclomatic complexity value, decomposing them into multiple smaller methods is preferable. Instead of a lot of unit tests for a single function, now you will have a lot of unit tests for a lot of smaller functions, which is significantly more maintainable.

Adding cyclomatic complexity checks as a precommit hook or a step in your build process is easy. Just be sure that you actually look at the output and act on it accordingly! For a preexisting project, break down the most complex methods and objects first, *but not before writing unit tests*! Certainly, the number-one rule of refactoring is "do no harm," and you cannot be sure you are obeying this rule unless you have tests to verify the "before" and "after" versions of your code.

jscheckstyle (*http://bit.ly/XUdsq5*) is a very handy tool for computing the cyclomatic complexity of each of your functions and methods. In Chapter 8 we will integrate jscheckstyle with the Jenkins tool to flag code that may be overly complex and ripe for refactoring, but let's sneak a quick peek at it now.

The following code will install the jscheckstyle package:

```
% sudo npm install jscheckstyle -g
```

Now let's run it against any JavaScript source file:

```
findresult-lm:~ trostler$ jscheckstyle firefox.js
The "sys" module is now called "util". It should have a similar
interface.
jscheckstyle results - firefox.js
```

Line	Function	Length	Args	Complex...
8	doSeleniumStuff	20	0	1
26	anonymous	1	0	1
31	startCapture	17	1	1
39	anonymous	6	1	1
40	anonymous	4	1	1
44	anonymous	3	1	1
49	doWS	40	2	2

```
| 62    | ws.onerror   | 4 | 1 | 1 |
| 67    | ws.onopen    | 4 | 1 | 1 |
| 72    | ws.onmessage | 6 | 1 | 2 |
| 79    | ws.onclose   | 9 | 1 | 1 |
```

This outputs a list of all the functions present in the file, the number of lines in each function, the number of arguments for each function, and the cyclomatic complexity of each function. Note that the number of lines includes any blank lines and comments, so this measure is more relative than the other values, which are absolute.

Also note that in this output the bulk of these functions are contained within other functions—in fact, there are only three top-level functions in this file. The anonymous function on line 26 is within the doSeleniumStuff function. There are three anony mous functions within the startCapture function, and the doWS function contains the four ws.* functions. This tool unfortunately does not clearly capture the hierarchy of functions within a file, so beware of it.

jscheckstyle can also output JSON and HTML using the —json and —html command-line options.

A utility such as jscheckstyle provides you with an at-a-glance view of your underlying source code. While there are no absolutes when it comes to coding practice and style, cyclomatic complexity has been proven to be a valid measure of code complexity, and you would do well to understand its implications.

Reuse

The best way to reduce code size is to decrease the amount of code you write. The theory is that using third-party (either external or internal) code that is production-ready and maintained by someone else takes a good chunk of responsibility away from you. Almost everyone uses third-party code, open source or not, in their programs. Jeffrey Poulin, while at Loral Federal Systems, estimated that up to 85% of code in a program is not application-specific; only 15% of the code in a program makes it unique. In his 1995 paper "Domain Analysis and Engineering: How Domain-Specific Frameworks Increase Software Reuse" (*http://bit.ly/XUdv54*), he says the following:

> A typical application will consist of up to 20% general-purpose domain-independent software and up to another 65% of domain-dependent reusable software built specifically for that application domain. The remainder of the application will consist of custom software written exclusively for the application and having relatively little utility elsewhere.

He illustrates the three classes of software—application-specific, domain-specific, and domain-independent—as shown in Figure 2-1.

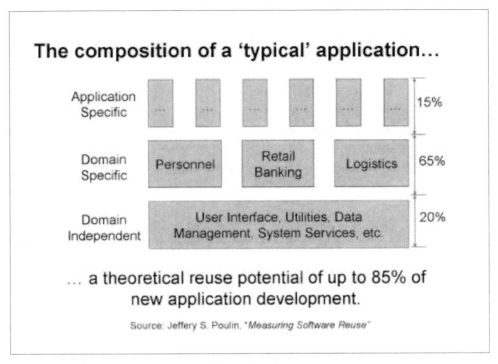

Figure 2-1. The composition of a typical application

For JavaScript, the domain-independent code is the client-side framework such as YUI, or Node.js on the server side. The domain-specific software consists of other third-party modules you use in your application. You write the application-specific code.

Client-side JavaScript runs on many platforms (OS + browser combinations), and it would be insane for any web application to attempt to account for this. Using a good JavaScript framework is an absolute must in almost every circumstance. Frameworks such as YUI, Closure, and jQuery handle the bulk of the generic boilerplate code that makes application-specific code runnable across many platforms. Framework-provided façades give your code a consistent interface across browsers. Frameworks provide utilities, plug-ins, and add-ons that greatly reduce the size of your code. On the server side, Node.js uses the Node Package Manager tool (a.k.a. npm) to utilize modules uploaded to the npm registry (*http://bit.ly/XUdvlF*) in order to handle a large number of generic tasks.

Using event handling, a very basic and extremely important part of writing JavaScript, as an example, one can quickly see the dangers of not reusing code. While events are key to client-side JavaScript due to browser UIs, Node.js also makes extensive use of events and event callbacks. Yet there is nothing in the JavaScript language specification itself for handling events. These decisions were left up to the browser manufacturers, who were (and are) actively competing against one another. Not surprisingly, this led to fragmentation, until the World Wide Web Consortium (W3C) stepped in and attempted to standardize client-side JavaScript events. Having to handle event registration and handler discrepancies in each browser is painful and very error-prone. Using a JavaScript framework solves these browser incompatibility problems for free. There are varying levels of support for the ECMAScript5 standard across browsers (especially Internet Explorer before version 9), so your favorite new language feature may not be present in a significant percentage of run-time environments. Do not get stuck supporting only one particular browser when you can support almost any modern browser, again for free, using a third-party framework.

Node.js also has a growing number of third-party modules that you can use via npm. A quick look at the npm registry (*http://bit.ly/XUdsX3*) shows the large number of modules available. Of course, the quality of the modules varies, but if nothing else, you can see how others have solved a problem similar to (if not the same as) yours to get you started.

Beyond basic JavaScript frameworks, there are a very large number of components available for use. It is your duty to use available prior art before attempting to roll your own code. Concentrate on the 15% that makes your application unique, and "offshore" the grunt work to well-established third-party libraries.

Equally important as reusing other people's code is reusing your own code. In the "Fan-In" (page 38) section we will discuss how you can discover code of yours that is not being reused properly (we will continue that discussion in Chapter 8, when we cover the dupfind tool). The general rule of thumb is that if you find that you are writing a chunk of code twice, it is time to pull the code into its own function. Whatever "extra" time you spend making the code sharable will pay dividends in the future. If the same chunk of code is required in two places, it will only be a matter of time before it is required in three places, and so on. Be vigilant about duplicated code. Do not let it slide "this one time." As always, an ounce of prevention is worth a pound of cure, especially when debugging software.

Fan-Out

Fan-out is a measure of the number of modules or objects your function directly or indirectly depends on. Fan-out (and fan-in) were first studied in 1981 by Sallie Henry and Dennis Kafura, who wrote about them in "Software Structure Metrics Based on Information Flow," published in *IEEE Transactions on Software Engineering*. They postulated that 50% to 75% of the cost of software is due to maintenance, and they wanted to measure, as early as the design phase as possible, the complexity of software to be written. Building on previous work that demonstrated that greater complexity led to lower-quality software, they figured that if complexity could be measured and controlled while (or even before) the software was being built, everyone would win. They were familiar with McCabe's work on measuring cyclomatic complexity and its relationship to software quality (published in 1976 and referenced earlier in this chapter) and other lexical analysis techniques, but they were convinced that they could get a better complexity measurement by measuring the underlying structure of the code instead of just counting tokens.

So, using information theory and analyzing flows between functions and modules, they cooked up a formula for a complexity measurement:

```
(fan_in * fan_out)²
```

They then calculated this value (and some variants) using the Unix OS and found a 98% correlation between it and "software changes" (i.e., bug fixes). To wit: the more complex a function or module measured by their formula, the more likely there were to be bugs in that function or module.

So, what the heck are fan-in and fan-out? Here is their definition of fan-out:

> The fan-out of procedure A is the number of local flows from procedure A plus the number of data structures which procedure A updates.

In this definition, a local flow for A is counted as (using other methods B and C):

1 if A calls B
2 if B calls A and A returns a value to B, which B subsequently utilizes
3 if C calls both A and B, passing an output value from A to B

So, adding all of those flows for function A, plus the number of global structures (external to A) that A updates, produces the fan-out for function A. Fan-in is defined similarly, as we will see shortly.

Calculating this value and the corresponding value for fan-in for all of your functions, multiplying those two numbers together, and squaring the result will give you another number that measures the complexity of a function.

Using this measure, Henry and Kafura note three problems inherent in highly complex code. First, high fan-in and fan-out numbers may indicate a function that is trying to do too much and should be broken up. Second, high fan-in and fan-out numbers can identify "stress points" in the system; maintaining these functions will be difficult as they touch many other parts of the system. And third, they cite *inadequate refinement*, which means the function needs to be refactored, because it is too big and is trying to do too much, or there is a missing layer of abstraction that is causing this function to have high fan-in and fan-out.

Building on function complexity measures, Henry and Kafura note that one can generate module complexity values, and from there one can measure the coupling between the modules themselves. Applying the lessons from the function level, one can determine which modules have high complexity and should be refactored or perhaps demonstrate that another layer of abstraction is necessary. They also found that typically the vast majority of a module's complexity is due to a small number of functions (three!), regardless of the module's size. So beware of the one "mongo" function that does way too much, while most of the other functions do very little!

Henry and Kafura also looked at function length (using lines of code) and found that only 28% of functions containing fewer than 20 lines of code had an error, whereas 78% of functions with more than 20 lines of code had errors. Keep it short and small, people!

Intuitively, it makes sense that functions with large fan-out are more problematic. Java-Script makes it very easy to declare and use global variables, but standards-based Java-Script tells us to not use the global space and instead to namespace everything locally. This helps to reduce fan-out by taking away part of the fan-out definition ("the number of data structures A updates"), but we still must account for our functions' local flows.

You can inspect this easily by seeing how many foreign objects your function requires. The following example uses YUI's asynchronous require mechanism to pull in the my Module chunk of JavaScript code. A detailed discussion of this is available here (*http:// bit.ly/XUdvCj*); the main point to understand here is that we are telling YUI about a dependency of our code, which YUI will fetch for us. It will then execute our callback when the dependency has been loaded:

```
YUI.use('myModule', function(Y) {
    var myModule = function() {
        this.a = new Y.A();
        this.b = new Y.B();
        this.c = new Y.C();
    };
    Y.MyModule = myModule;
}, { requires: [ 'a', 'b', 'c' ] });
```

The fan-out for the myModule constructor is 3 (in this case, the objects are not even being used; they are just being created and stored for future methods, but they are still required here, so they count against the constructor's fan-out). And this is without the constructor being instantiated and used yet. Three is not a bad number, but again that number will grow when an outside object instantiates myModule and uses any return value from any local myModule method it calls. Fan-out is a measure of what you need to keep track of in your head as you edit this method. It is a count of the external methods and objects this method manipulates.

Regardless of whether we are counting local flows, Miller's Law argues that trying to remember and track more than seven things is increasingly difficult. Later reanalysis has brought that number down to four.[3] The point is that there is no specific number that is a danger indicator, but when fan-out is greater than 7 (or even 4) it is time to look at what is going on and possibly refactor. Excessive fan-out belies other issues, namely tight coupling, which we will also investigate in this chapter.

High fan-out can be problematic for even more reasons: the code is more complex, making it harder to understand and therefore test; each direct dependent must be mocked or stubbed out during testing, creating testing complexity; and fan-out is indicative of tight coupling, which makes functions and modules overly brittle.

A strategy to tame fan-out without eventing involves creating an object that encapsulates some of the fanned-out modules, leaving the original function with the single dependency on that new module. This obviously makes more sense as the fan-out of the original function increases, especially if the newly factored-out module can be reused by other functions as well.

Consider the following code, which has a fan-out of at least 8:

```
YUI.use('myModule', function(Y) {
    var myModule = function() {
        this.a = new Y.A();
        this.b = new Y.B();
        this.c = new Y.C();
        this.d = new Y.D();
        this.e = new Y.E();
        this.f = new Y.F();
        this.g = new Y.G();
        this.h = new Y.H();
    };
    Y.MyModule = myModule;
}, { requires: [ 'a', 'b', 'c', 'd', 'e', 'f', 'g', 'h' ] });
```

Testing this thing is going to be problematic; it needs to be refactored. The idea is to pull out a subset of related modules into another module:

```
YUI.use('mySubModule', function(Y) {
    var mySubModule = function() {
        this.a = new Y.A();
        this.b = new Y.B();
        this.c = new Y.C();
        this.d = new Y.D();
    };
    mySubModule.prototype.getA = function() { return this.a; };
    mySubModule.prototype.getB = function() { return this.b; };
    mySubModule.prototype.getC = function() { return this.c; };
    mySubModule.prototype.getD = function() { return this.d; };
    Y.MySubModule = mySubModule;
```

3. Cowan, Nelson. 2001. "The Magical Number 4 in Short-Term Memory: A Reconsideration of Mental Storage Capacity." *Behavioral and Brain Sciences* 24(1): pp. 87–114; discussion, pp. 114–185.

```
    }, { requires: [ 'a', 'b', 'c', 'd'] });

YUI.use('myModule', function(Y) {
    var myModule = function() {
        var sub = new Y.MySubModule();
        this.a = sub.getA();
        this.b = sub.getB();
        this.c = sub.getC();
        this.d = sub.getD();
        this.e = new Y.E();
        this.f = new Y.F();
        this.g = new Y.G();
        this.h = new Y.H();
    };
    Y.MyModule = myModule;
}, { requires: [ 'mySubModule', 'e', 'f', 'g', 'h' ] });
```

Here we have created a level of indirection between MyModule and modules a, b, c, and d and reduced the fan-out by three, but has this helped? Strangely, it has, a little. Even this brain-dead refactoring has made our testing burden for MyModule lighter. The total number of tests did increase a little because now MySubModule must also be tested, but the point is not to decrease the total amount of overall testing, but instead to make it easier to test each module or function.

Clearly, this unsophisticated refactoring of MyModule to reduce its fan-out is not ideal. The modules or objects that are refactored should in some way be related, and the submodule they are refactored to should provide a more intelligent interface to the underlying objects than just returning them whole cloth. Using the façade pattern is really what is expected, wherein the factored-out submodules are presented to the original module with a simpler and more unified interface. Again, the total number of tests will increase, but each piece will be easier to test in isolation. Here is a quick example:

```
function makeChickenDinner(ingredients) {
    var chicken = new ChickenBreast()
        , oven  = new ConventionalOven()
        , mixer = new Mixer()
        , dish  = mixer.mix(chicken, ingredients)

    return oven.bake(dish, new FDegrees(350), new Timer("50 minutes"));
}

var dinner = makeChickenDinner(ingredients);
```

This function *fans out* like crazy. It creates five external objects and calls two methods on two different objects. This function is *tightly coupled* to five objects. Testing it is difficult, as you will need to stub in all the objects and the queries being made to them. Mocking the mixer's mix method and the oven's bake method will be difficult, as both return values as well. Let's see what a unit test for this function might look like:

```
describe("test make dinner", function() {

    // Mocks
    Food = function(obj) {};
    Food.prototype.attr = {};
    MixedFood = function(args) {
        var obj = Object.create(Food.prototype);
        obj.attr.isMixed = true; return obj;
    };
    CookedFood = function(dish) {
        var obj = Object.create(Food.prototype);
        obj.attr.isCooked = true; return obj;
    };
    FDegrees = function(temp) { this.temp = temp };
    Meal = function(dish) { this.dish = dish };
    Timer = function(timeSpec) { this.timeSpec = timeSpec; };
    ChickenBreast = function() {
        var obj = Object.create(Food.prototype);
        obj.attr.isChicken = true; return obj;
    };
    ConventionalOven = function() {
        this.bake = function(dish, degrees, timer) {
            return new CookedFood(dish, degrees, timer);
        };
    };
    Mixer = function() {
        this.mix = function(chicken, ingredients) {
            return new MixedFood(chicken, ingredients);
        };
    };
    Ingredients = function(ings) { this.ings = ings; };
    // end Mocks

    it("cooked dinner", function() {
        this.addMatchers({
            toBeYummy: function(expected) {
                return this.actual.attr.isCooked
                    && this.actual.attr.isMixed;
            }
        });

        var ingredients = new Ingredients('parsley', 'salt')
            , dinner = makeChickenDinner(ingredients)
            ;
        expect(dinner).toBeYummy();
    });
});
```

Wow, that is a lot of code! And what are we actually testing here? We had to mock out all referenced objects and their referenced objects, plus create a new `Ingredients` object to execute the `makeChickenDinner` method, which then instantiates and utilizes our mocked-up object hierarchies. Mocking and replacing all of those other objects is a lot of work to just unit-test a single method. The whole thing is problematic. Let's refactor it and make it testable.

This function requires five objects—`ChickenBreast`, `ConventionalOven`, `Mixer`, `FDegrees`, and `Timer`—and five is near the upper limit of fan-out that is comfortable. Not only is the fan-out high, but also the coupling is very tight for all of those objects. Coupling and fan-out usually go hand in hand, but not always. We can reduce coupling via injection or eventing, and we can reduce fan-out by using façades that encompass multiple objects. We will investigate coupling more fully later in this chapter.

The first façade that we can create involves the oven. Creating an oven, setting its temperature, and setting its timer are ripe for abstraction. Then we inject the façade to reduce the coupling, which leaves us with this:

```
function Cooker(oven) {
    this.oven = oven;
}
Cooker.prototype.bake = function(dish, deg, timer) {
    return this.oven.bake(dish, deg, timer);
};
Cooker.prototype.degrees_f = function(deg) {
    return new FDegrees(deg);
};
Cooker.prototype.timer = function(time) {
    return new Timer(time);
};

function makeChickenDinner(ingredients, cooker) {
    var chicken = new ChickenBreast()
        , mixer = new Mixer()
        , dish  = mixer.mix(chicken, ingredients)

    return cooker.bake(dish
      , cooker.degrees_f(350)
      , cooker.timer("50 minutes")
    );
}

var cooker = new Cooker(new ConventionalOven())
    , dinner = makeChickenDinner(ingredients, cooker);
```

`makeChickenDinner` now has two tightly coupled dependencies, `ChickenBreast` and `Mixer`, and an injected façade to handle the cooking chores. The façade does not expose the entire API of the oven, degrees, or timer, just enough to get the job done. We have really just spread the dependencies around more evenly, making each function easier to test and less tightly coupled, with less fan-out.

Here is the new test code for our refactored method:

```
describe("test make dinner refactored", function() {

    // Mocks
    Food = function() {};
    Food.prototype.attr = {};
    MixedFood = function(args) {
        var obj = Object.create(Food.prototype);
        obj.attr.isMixed = true;
        return obj;
    };
    CookedFood = function(dish) {
        var obj = Object.create(Food.prototype);
        obj.attr.isCooked = true;
        return obj;
    };
    ChickenBreast = function() {
        var obj = Object.create(Food.prototype);
        obj.attr.isChicken = true;
        return obj;
    };
    Meal = function(dish) { this.dish = dish };
    Mixer = function() {
        this.mix = function(chicken, ingredients) {
            return new MixedFood(chicken, ingredients);
        };
    };
    Ingredients = function(ings) { this.ings = ings; };
    // end Mocks

    it("cooked dinner", function() {
            this.addMatchers({
                toBeYummy: function(expected) {
                return this.actual.attr.isCooked
                    && this.actual.attr.isMixed;
            }
        });

        var ingredients = new Ingredients('parsley', 'salt')
            , MockedCooker = function() {};

        // Local (to this test) mocked Cooker object that can actually
        //    do testing!
        MockedCooker.prototype = {
            bake: function(food, deg, timer) {
                expect(food.attr.isMixed).toBeTruthy();
                food.attr.isCooked = true;
                return food
                }
            , degrees_f: function(temp) { expect(temp).toEqual(350); }
            , timer: function(time) {
                expect(time).toEqual('50 minutes');
            }
```

```
    };

    var cooker = new MockedCooker()
      , dinner = makeChickenDinner(ingredients, cooker)
      ;

    expect(dinner).toBeYummy();
  });
});
```

This new test code got rid of several generically mocked-out objects and replaced them with a local mock that is specific to this test and can actually do some real testing using **expects** within the mock itself.

This is now much easier to test as the Cooker object does very little. We can go further and inject FDegrees and Timer instead of being tightly coupled to them. And of course, we can also inject or create another façade for Chicken and maybe Mixer—you get the idea. Here's the ultimate injected method:

```
function makeChickenDinner(ingredients, cooker, chicken, mixer) {
    var dish = mixer.mix(chicken, ingredients);
    return cooker.bake(dish
      , cooker.degrees_f(350)
      , cooker.timer('50 minutes')
    );
}
```

Here are the dependencies we injected (we will discuss dependency injection fully in just a bit) and the corresponding code to test them:

```
describe("test make dinner injected", function() {
    it("cooked dinner", function() {
        this.addMatchers({
            toBeYummy: function(expected) {
                return this.actual.attr.isCooked
                    && this.actual.attr.isMixed;
            }
        });

        var ingredients = ['parsley', 'salt']
          , chicken = {}
          , mixer = {
              mix: function(chick, ings) {
                  expect(ingredients).toBe(ings);
                  expect(chicken).toBe(chick);
                  return { attr: { isMixed: true } };
              }
          }
          , MockedCooker = function() {}
          ;

        MockedCooker.prototype = {
```

```
            bake: function(food, deg, timer) {
                expect(food.attr.isMixed).toBeTruthy();
                food.attr.isCooked = true;
                return food
                }
            , degrees_f: function(temp) { expect(temp).toEqual(350); }
            , timer: function(time) {
                expect(time).toEqual('50 minutes');
            }
        };

        var cooker = new MockedCooker()
            , dinner = makeChickenDinner(ingredients, cooker
                        , chicken, mixer)
        ;

        expect(dinner).toBeYummy();
    });
});
```

All of the generic mocks are gone and the test code has full control over the mocks passed in, allowing much more extensive testing and flexibility.

When injecting and creating façades, it can become a game to see how far back you can pull object instantiation. As you head down that road, you run directly into the ultimate decoupling of event-based architectures (the subject of the next chapter).

Some may argue that abstracting functionality away behind façades makes code more complex, but that is not true. What we have done here is created smaller, bite-sized pieces of code that are significantly more testable and maintainable than the original example.

Fan-In

Most of what we discussed about fan-out also applies to fan-in, but not everything. It turns out that a large fan-in can be a very good thing. Think about common elements of an application: logging, utility routines, authentication and authorization checks, and so on. It is good for those functions to be called by all the other modules in the application. You do *not* want to have multiple logging functions being called by various pieces of code—they should all be calling the same logging function. That is code reuse, and it is a very good thing.

Fan-in can be a good measure of the reuse of common functions in code, and the more the merrier. In fact, if a common function has very low fan-in, you should ensure that there is no duplicated code somewhere else, which hinders code reuse.

In some cases, though, high fan-in is a bad thing. Uncommon and nonutility functions should have low fan-in. High(er) levels of code abstraction should also have low fan-in (ideally, a fan-in of 0 or 1). These high-level pieces of code are not meant to be used by lots of other pieces of code; typically they are meant to be used by just one other piece, usually to get them started once and that is it.

Here is the "official" fan-in definition:

> The fan-in of procedure A is the number of local flows into procedure A plus the number of data structures from which procedure A retrieves information.

You get the idea: watch out for a piece of code that has large fan-in and large fan-out, as this is not desirable due to the high complexity and high amount of coupling that result.

Fan-in helps you identify code reuse (or not). Code reuse is good; scattered logging and debugging functions across your code are bad. Learn to centralize shared functions (and modules) and use them!

Coupling

While fan-out counts the number of dependent modules and objects required for a module or function, coupling is concerned with how those modules are put together. Submodules may reduce the absolute fan-out count, but they do not reduce the amount of coupling between the original module and the original dependent. The original module still requires the dependent; it is just being delivered via indirection instead of explicitly.

Some metrics try to capture coupling in a single number. These metrics are based on the six levels of coupling defined by Norman Fenton and Shari Lawrence Pfleeger in *Software Metrics: A Rigorous & Practical Approach, 2nd Edition* (Course Technology) way back in 1996. Each level is given a score—the higher the score, the tighter the coupling. We will discuss the six levels (from tightest to loosest) in the following subsections.

Content Coupling

Content coupling, the tightest form of coupling, involves actually calling methods or functions on the external object or directly changing its state by editing a property of the external object. Any one of the following examples is a type of content coupling with the external object O:

```
O.property = 'blah'; // Changing O's state directly

// Changing O's internals
```

```
O.method = function() { /* something else */ };

// Changing all Os!
O.prototype.method = function() { /* switcheroo */ };
```

All of these statements content-couple this object to O. This kind of coupling scores a 5.

Common Coupling

Slightly lower on the coupling spectrum is common coupling. Your object is commonly coupled to another object if both objects share a global variable:

```
var Global = 'global';
Function A() { Global = 'A'; };
Function B() { Global = 'B'; };
```

Here objects A and B are commonly coupled. This scores a 4.

Control Coupling

Next up is control coupling, a slightly looser form of coupling than common coupling. This type of coupling controls how the external object acts based on a flag or parameter setting. For example, creating a singleton abstract factory at the beginning of your code and passing in an env flag telling it how to act is a form of control coupling:

```
var absFactory = new AbstractFactory({ env: 'TEST' });
```

This scores a big fat 3.

Stamp Coupling

Stamp coupling is passing a record to an external object that only uses part of the record, like so:

```
// This object is stamp coupled to O
O.makeBread( { type: wheat, size: 99, name: 'foo' } );

// Elsewhere within the definition of O:
O.prototype.makeBread = function(args) {
    return new Bread(args.type, args.size);
}
```

Here we pass a record to the makeBread function, but that function only uses two of the three properties within the record. This is stamp coupling. Stamp coupling scores a 2.

Data Coupling

The loosest coupling of them all is data coupling. This type of coupling occurs when objects pass messages to one another, with no transfer of control to the external object. We will investigate this much further in Chapter 3. Data coupling scores a measly 1.

No Coupling

The last form of coupling (and my personal favorite), with absolutely zero coupling whatsoever between two objects, is the famed "no coupling." No coupling scores a perfect 0.

Instantiation

While not formally a part of the coupling jargon, the act of instantiating a nonsingleton global object is also a very tight form of coupling, closer to content coupling than common coupling. Using `new` or `Object.create` creates a one-way, tightly coupled relationship between the objects. What the creator does with that object determines whether the relationship goes both ways.

Instantiating an object makes your code responsible for that object's life cycle. Specifically, it has just been created by your code, and your code must now also be responsible for destroying it. While it may fall out of scope when the enclosing function ends or closes, any resources and dependencies the object requires can still be using memory— or even be executing. Instantiating an object foists responsibilities on the creator of which you must be aware. Certainly, the fewer objects your code instantiates, the clearer your conscience will be. Minimizing object instantiations minimizes code complexity; this is a nice target to aim for. If you find that you are creating a lot of objects, it is time to step back and rethink your architecture.

Coupling Metrics

The point of naming and scoring each type of coupling, besides giving us all a common frame of reference, is to generate metrics based on coupling found in functions, objects, and modules. An early metric calculates the coupling between two modules or objects by simply adding up the number of interconnections between the modules or objects and throwing in the maximum coupling score.[4] Other metrics try to measure the coupling inherent in a single module.[5] A matrix has also been created between all modules in an application to view the overall coupling between each of them.[6]

The point here is that a number or set of numbers can be derived to determine how tightly or loosely coupled a system or set of modules is. This implies that someone

---

4. Fenton, Norman, and Austin Melton. 1990. "Deriving Structurally Based Software Measures." *Journal of Systems and Software* 12(3): pp. 177–187.

5. Dhama, Harpal. 1995. "Quantitative Models of Cohesion and Coupling in Software." *Journal of Systems and Software* 29(1): pp. 65–74.

6. Alghamdi, Jarallah. 2007. "Measuring Software Coupling." Proceedings of the 6th WSEAS International Conference on Software Engineering, Parallel and Distributed Systems, Corfu Island, Greece, February 16–19, 2007. Available online (*http://bit.ly/XUdtKo*).

"above" the system is trying to determine its state. For our purposes, *we* are the programmers looking at this stuff every day. Once we know what to look for, we can find it and refactor if necessary. Again, code inspections and code reviews are an excellent way to find code coupling, instead of relying on a tool to root out coupling metrics.

Coupling in the Real World

Let's look at some examples of coupling in JavaScript. The best way to understand loose coupling is to take a look at tight coupling:

```
function setTable() {
    var cloth = new TableCloth()
        , dishes = new Dishes();
    this.placeTableCloth(cloth);
    this.placeDishes(dishes);
}
```

This helper method, presumably belonging to a `Table` class, is trying to set the table nicely. However, this method is *tightly coupled* to both the `TableCloth` and `Dishes` objects. Creating new objects within methods creates a tight coupling.

This method is not isolatable due to the tight coupling—when I'm ready to test it I also need the `TableCloth` and `Dishes` objects. Unit tests really want to test the `setTable` method in isolation from external dependencies, but this code makes that difficult.

As we saw in the cooking example earlier, globally mocking out the `TableCloth` and `Dishes` objects is painful. This makes testing more difficult, although it is certainly possible given JavaScript's dynamic nature. Mocks and/or stubs can be dynamically injected to handle this, as we will see later. However, maintenance-wise this situation is less than ideal.

We can borrow some ideas from our statically typed language friends and use injection to loosen the coupling, like so:

```
function setTable(cloth, dishes) {
    this.placeTableCloth(cloth);
    this.placeDishes(dishes);
}
```

Now testing becomes much simpler, as our test code can just pass in mocks or stubs directly to the method. Our method is now much easier to isolate, and therefore much easier to test.

However, in some instances this approach will just push the problem farther up the stack. Something, somewhere is going to have to instantiate the objects we need. Won't those methods now be tightly coupled?

In general, we want to instantiate objects as high as possible in the call stack. Here is how this method would be called in an application:

```
function dinnerParty(guests) {
    var table = new Table()
        , invitations = new Invitations()
        , food = new Ingredients()
        , chef = new Chef()
        , staff = new Staff()
        , cloth = new FancyTableClothWithFringes()
        , dishes = new ChinaWithBlueBorders()
        , dinner;

    invitations.invite(guests);
    table.setTable(cloth, dishes);
    dinner = chef.cook(ingredients);
    staff.serve(dinner);
}
```

This issue here, of course, is what if we wanted to have a more casual dinner party and use a paper tablecloth and paper plates?

Ideally, all our main objects would be created up front at the top of our application, but this is not always possible. So, we can borrow another pattern from our statically typed brethren: factories.

Factories allow us to instantiate objects lower in the call stack but still remain loosely coupled. Instead of an explicit dependency on an actual object, we now only have a dependency on a `Factory`. The `Factory` has dependencies on the objects it creates; however, for testing we introduce a `Factory` that creates mocked or stubbed objects, not the real ones. This leads us to the end of this line of thinking: abstract factories.

Let's start with just a regular `Factory`:

```
var TableClothFactory = {
    getTableCloth: function(color) {
        return Object.create(TableCloth,
            { color: { value: color }});
    }
};
```

I have parameterized the tablecloth's color in our `Factory`—the parameter list to get a new instance mirrors the constructor's parameter list. Using this `Factory` is straight-forward:

```
var tc = TableClothFactory.getTableCloth('purple');
```

For testing, we do not want an actual `TableCloth` object. We are trying to test our code in isolation. We really just want a mock or a stub instead:

```
var TableClothTestFactory = {
    getTableCloth: function(color) {
        return Y.Mock(); // Or whatever you want
    };
```

Here I'm using YUI's excellent mocking framework. We will investigate this deeper in Chapter 4. The code looks almost exactly the same to get a mocked version of a Table Cloth object:

```
var tc = TableClothTestFactory.getTableCloth('purple');
```

If only there were *some way* to reconcile these two factories so that our code always does the right thing... Of course, there is: all we need to do is create a factory to generate the appropriate TableCloth factory, and then we'll really have something!

```
var AbstractTableClothFactory = {
    getFactory: function(kind) {
        if (kind !== 'TEST') {
            return TableClothFactory;
        } else {
            return TableClothTestFactory;
        }
    }
};
```

All we did here was parameterize a Factory so that it returns an actual Factory that in turn returns the kind of TableCloth object requested. This monster is called an abstract factory. For testing, we just want a mocked object; otherwise, we want the real deal. Here is how we use it in a test:

```
var tcFactory = AbstractTableClothFactory.getFactory('TEST')
  , tc = tcFactory.getTableCloth('purple');
        // We just got a Mock'ed object!
```

Now we have a way to instantiate objects without being tightly coupled to them. We have moved from very tight content coupling to much looser control coupling (that's two less on the coupling scale; woo!). Testing now becomes much simpler, as we can create versions of factories that return mocked versions of objects instead of the "real" ones, which enables us to test *just* our code, without having to worry about all of our code's dependencies.

Testing Coupled Code

It is interesting to note the type and amount of testing required to test the various levels of coupled code. Not too surprisingly, the more tightly coupled the code is, the more resources are required to test it. Let's go through the levels.

Content-coupled code is difficult to test because unit testing wants to test code in isolation, but by definition content-coupled code is tightly coupled with at least one other object external to it. You need the entire set of unit-testing tricks here to try to test this code; typically you must use both mocked objects and stubs to replicate the environment within which this code expects to run. Due to the tight coupling, integration testing is also necessary to ensure that the objects work together correctly.

Commonly coupled code is easier to unit-test as the shared global variable can be easily mocked or stubbed out and examined to ensure that the object under test is reading, writing, and responding to that variable correctly.

Control-coupled code requires mocking out the controlled external object and verifying it is controlled correctly, which is easy enough to accomplish using a mock object.

Stamp-coupled code is easily unit-tested by mocking out the external object and verifying the passed parameter was correct.

Data-coupled code and noncoupled code are very easily tested through unit testing. Very little or nothing needs to be mocked or stubbed out, and the method can be tested directly.

Minimize coupling, and your testing will be easier.

Dependency Injection

We touched on injection only briefly earlier, so let's take a closer look at it now. Dependencies make code complex. They make building more difficult, testing more difficult, and debugging more difficult; pretty much everything you would like to be simpler, dependencies make harder. Managing your code's dependencies becomes an increasingly larger time sink as your application grows.

Injection and mocking are loosely related. Injection deals with constructing and injecting objects into your code, and mocking is replacing objects or method calls with canned dummy versions for testing. You could (and should!) use an injector to insert mocked versions of objects into your code for testing. But you should not use a mocking framework in production code!

Factoring out dependencies or manually injecting them into constructors or method calls helps to reduce code complexity, but it also adds some overhead: if an object's dependencies are to be injected, another object is now responsible for correctly constructing that object. Haven't we just pushed the problem back another layer? Yes, we have! The buck must stop somewhere, and that place is typically at the beginning of your application or test. Maps of object construction are dynamically defined up front, and this allows any object to be easily swapped out for another. Whether for testing or for upgrading an object, this is a very nice property to have.

A dependency injector can construct and inject fully formed objects into our code for us. Of course, an injector must be told how to actually construct these objects, and later, when you actually want an instance of that object, the injector will hand you one. There is no "magic" (well, perhaps a little); the injector can only construct objects you specify. Injectors get fancy by providing lots of different ways to describe exactly how your objects are constructed, but do not get lost in the weeds: you tell the injector how to construct an object (or have the injector pass control to your code to construct an object).

There is one more bit that injectors handle along with object construction: scope. Scope informs the injector whether to create a new instance or reuse an existing one. You tell the injector what scope each object should have, and when your code asks for an object of that type the injector will do the right thing (either create a new instance or reuse an existing one).

In Java this is all accomplished by subclasses and interfaces—the dependent needs an instance of an interface or superclass, and the injector supplies a concrete instantiation of an implementing class or specific subclass. These types can be (mostly) checked at compile time, and injectors can guard against passing in null objects. While JavaScript does have the `instanceof` operator, it has neither type checking nor the notion of implementing an interface type. So, can we use dependency injection in JavaScript? Of course!

We know that instantiating dependent objects in constructors (or elsewhere within an object) tightly couples the dependency, which makes testing more difficult—so let the injector do it.

Let's take a brief look at knit (*http://bit.ly/XUdwGa*), a Google Guice-like (*http://bit.ly/XUdwWL*) injector for JavaScript. We know this code is "bad":

```
var SpaceShuttle = function() {
    this.mainEngine = new SpaceShuttleMainEngine();
    this.boosterEngine1 = new SpaceShuttleSolidRocketBooster();
    this.boosterEngine2 = new SpaceShuttleSolidRocketBooster();
    this.arm = new ShuttleRemoteManipulatorSystem();
};
```

With all of those objects being instantiated within the constructor, how can we test a `SpaceShuttle` without its real engines and arm? The first step is to make this constructor injectable:

```
var SpaceShuttle = function(mainEngine, b1, b2, arm) {
    this.mainEngine = mainEngine;
    this.boosterEngine1 = b1;
    this.boosterEngine2 = b2;
    this.arm = arm;
};
```

Now we can use `knit` to define how we want our objects constructed:

```
knit = require('knit');
knit.config(function (bind) {
    bind('MainEngine').to(SpaceShuttleMainEngine).is("construtor");
    bind('BoosterEngine1').to(SpaceShuttleSolidRocketBooster)
      .is("constructor");
    bind('BoosterEngine2').to(SpaceShuttleSolidRocketBooster)
      .is("constructor");
    bind('Arm').to(ShuttleRemoteManipulatorSystem).is("constructor");
```

```
        bind('ShuttleDiscovery').to(SpaceShuttle).is("constructor");
        bind('ShuttleEndeavor').to(SpaceShuttle).is("constructor");
        bind('Pad').to(new LaunchPad()).is("singleton");
    });
```

Here, the `SpaceShuttleMainEngine`, `SpaceShuttleSolidRocketBooster`, and `Shut tleRemoteManipulatorSystem` objects are defined elsewhere, like so:

```
    var SpaceShuttleMainEngine = function() {
        ...
    };
```

Now whenever a `MainEngine` is requested, `knit` will fill it in:

```
    var SpaceShuttle = function(MainEngine
        , BoosterEngine1
        , BoosterEngine2
        , Arm) {
        this.mainEngine = MainEngine;
        ...
    }
```

So the entire `SpaceShuttle` object with all of its dependencies is available within the `knit.inject` method:

```
    knit.inject(function(ShuttleDiscovery, ShuttleEndeavor, Pad) {
        ShuttleDiscovery.blastOff(Pad);
        ShuttleEndeavor.blastOff(Pad);
    });
```

`knit` has recursively figured out all of `SpaceShuttle`'s dependencies and constructed `SpaceShuttle` objects for us. Specifying `Pad` as a singleton ensures that any request for a `Pad` object will always return that one instantiation.

Suppose as time passes, Mexico creates an even more awesome `ShuttleRemoteManipu latorSystem` than Canada's. Switching to use that arm instead is trivial:

```
    bind('Arm').to(MexicanShuttleRemoteManipulatorSystem).is("constructor");
```

Now all objects that require an `Arm` will get Mexico's version instead of Canada's without changing any other code.

Besides swapping out objects easily for newer or different versions, an injector framework can also inject mock or test objects into your application by changing the bindings.

Testing a `SpaceShuttle` blastoff without actually blasting it off is a nice option that an injector allows easily by simply changing the bindings.

The AngularJS framework (*http://bit.ly/XUdxdb*) also makes heavy use of dependency injection via regular expressions. Besides easing testing, controllers and other pieces of functionality can specify which objects they need to do their work (by function parameter lists) and the correct objects will be injected.

Dependency injection really shines the larger an application grows, and since all non-trivial applications will grow, utilizing dependency injection from the beginning gives your code a great head start.

Comments

Testable JavaScript has a comment block before every function or method that will be unit-tested. How else could you (or anyone else) possibly know what and how to test? While maintaining code, seeing comment blocks before functions (especially public functions) keeps the maintainer informed. You may think that having tests is more important and perhaps replaces the need for correct comments, but I disagree. Writing effective comments and keeping them up to date is an integral part of a developer's job. Reading code is a more straightforward way to understand it, as opposed to relying on (or reading) the tests for it. While comments for methods are the most important, any comments referencing hard-to-understand code from programmer to programmer are invaluable. It is important that your comments explain both why and how the method exists and what exactly it does. Further, by taking advantage of structured comments, you can easily transform all of your hard work into readable HTML for all to browse.

Comments and tests should not be an either-or proposition. You are a professional programmer, so you can write tests and maintain comment blocks for, at minimum, all public methods. You should only use comments within methods to explain something that is not clear from the surrounding context. If you comment within a function, it is extremely important that you keep those comments up to date! It is far more preferable to have no comments in your code than to have incorrect comments.

YUIDoc

YUIDoc (*http://bit.ly/XUdzC0*) is a Node.js package available via npm. Installation is easy:

```
% npm -g install yuidocjs
```

The yuidoc executable is now available to transform all of your beloved comments into pretty HTML. In this section, I will discuss version 0.3.28, the latest version available at the time of this writing.

YUIDoc comments follow the Javadoc convention of starting with /** and ending with */. In fact, you can run YUIDoc on any language whose block comment tokens are /* and */.

YUIDoc provides seven primary tags. Each comment block must contain one and only one of these primary tags; the exhaustive list of tags is available here (*http://bit.ly/XUdA8Q*).

Ideally, you should be able to write unit tests using *only* the function or method YUIDoc.

Generating YUIDoc from the `yuidoc` command-line tool is simple. YUIDoc, however, wants to work with directories, so unlike with JSDoc (discussed next), you are not able to generate one JavaScript file's worth of documentation. But unless you are debugging the YUIDoc in your code, that is rarely done anyway.

A typical command line looks like this:

```
% yuidoc -o yuidoc -c src/yuidoc.json src
```

where `yuidoc` is the name of the output directory where all the HTML will go and `src` is the root of your JavaScript files to recurse over to generate the documentation. The *yuidoc.doc* configuration file can just be an empty JSON object for our purposes:

```
% cat src/yuidoc.json
{}
```

Here is a JavaScript file with YUIDoc notation:

```
/**
 * Provides some mathematical functions
 *
 * @class Math
**/

/**
 * This function accepts two operands, 'a' and 'b' and returns
 * their sum (or concatenation if they are strings)
 *
 * @method sum
 * @param {Number or String} a first operand
 * @param {Number or String} b second operand
 * @return {Number or String} The 'summed' value
 */
exports.sum = function(a, b) { return a + b };

/**
 * This function accepts two operands, 'a' and 'b' and returns
 * their product
 *
 * @method product
 * @param {Number} a first operand
 * @param {Number} b second operand
 * @return {Number} The product
 */
exports.mult = function(a, b) { return a * b };
```

Running this JavaScript through YUIDoc generates a page similar to Figure 2-2.

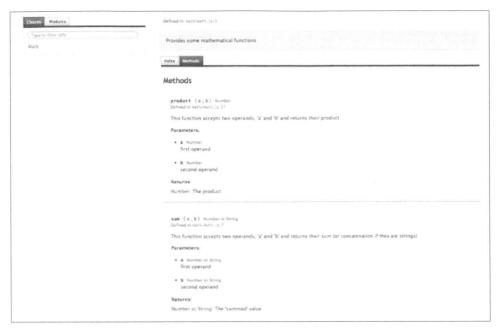

Figure 2-2. Generated HTML from YUIDoc directives

This looks just like the API documentation for YUI3 (*http://bit.ly/XUdy0M*). I think YUIDoc generates nicer templates (with searching!) and its tag library is more JavaScript-friendly than that of JSDoc. Of course, feel free to play with both and decide which one works best for your project.

JSDoc

Similar to YUIDoc is JSDoc (*http://bit.ly/XUdy0U*). It utilizes a similar but larger set of tags (*http://bit.ly/XUdAWm*).

Google's Closure Compiler (*http://bit.ly/XUdyxU*) leverages JSDoc tags when minifying, optimizing, and compiling your code, which is nice as you can kill two birds with one stone.

JSDoc is a little goofy to get set up. It is a Java program that relies on the locations of its JAR file and a set of template files. After downloading and unzipping the package, it is easiest to set two environment variables, `JSDOCDIR` and `JSDOCTEMPLATEDIR`. `JSDOCDIR` is set to be the directory where *jsrun.jar* exists, which is in the *jsdoc-toolkit* directory after the bundle has been unzipped. For starters—and maybe forever, unless you want to create your own HTML templates for JSDoc to use—`JSDOCTEMPLATEDIR` should point to *$JSDOCDIR/templates/jsdoc* to use the default templates provided by JSDoc.

Once you have set those two environment variables, you can use the *jsrun.sh* shell script provided by the distribution, located in *$JSDOCDIR*. So, your command line to JSDoc a file looks like this:

```
% /bin/sh $JSDOCDIR/jsrun.sh -d=<output dir> <JavaScript file>
```

This will generate a set of HTML files and place them into *<output dir>*. In this JSDoc-friendly JavaScript file, note the subtle differences between the JSDoc tags and the YUI-Doc tags shown earlier:

```
/**
 * This function accepts two operands, 'a' and 'b' and returns
 * their sum (or concatenation if they are strings)
 *
 * @name sum
 * @function
 * @param {Number or String} a first operand
 * @param {Number or String} b second operand
 * @returns {Number or String} The 'summed' value
 */
exports.sum = function(a, b) { return a + b };

/**
 * This function accepts two operands, 'a' and 'b' and returns
 * their product
 *
 * @name product
 * @function
 * @param {Number} a first operand
 * @param {Number} b second operand
 * @returns {Number} The product
 */
exports.mult = function(a, b) { return a * b };
```

When run through JSDoc, like so:

```
/bin/sh $JSDOCDIR/jsrun.sh -d=jsdoc mySum.js
```

the code will output several HTML files into the *jsdoc* directory. The most interesting of the HTML looks like Figure 2-3.

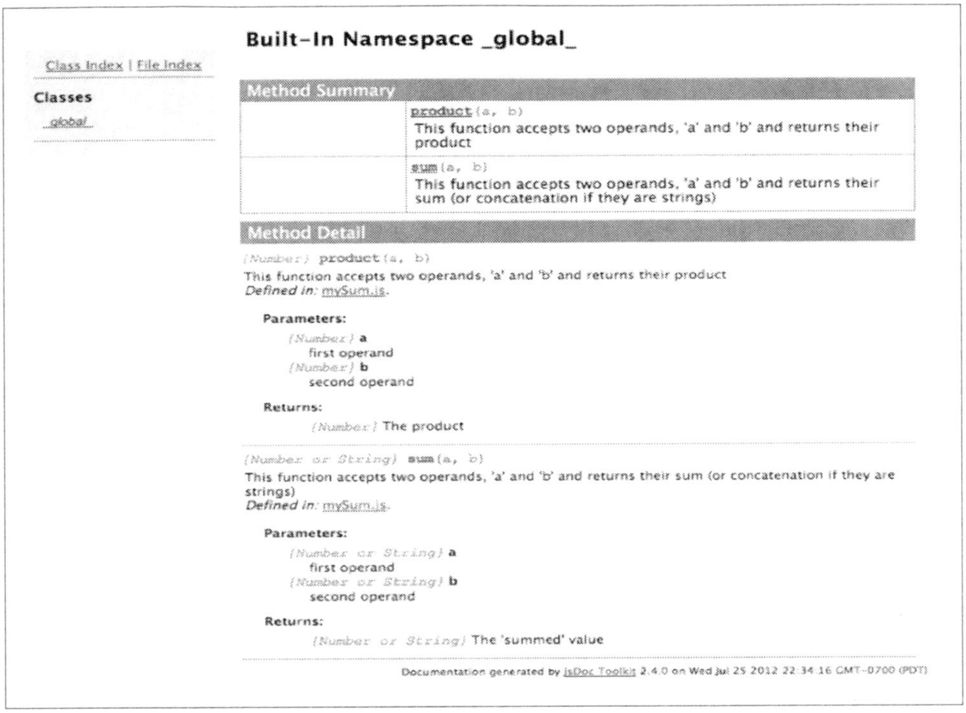

Figure 2-3. HTML generated by jsdoc directives

It's very cute, but the tags are the HTML output and are not as zesty as in YUIDoc. Your mileage will vary.

Docco/Rocco

According to the product website, "Docco is a quick-and-dirty, hundred-line-long, literate-programming-style documentation generator"—quite a mouthful indeed. Docco (*http://bit.ly/XUdyOv*) is the parent of a family of programs that all do the same thing: pull out Markdown-styled comments from your source code and HTML-ize the comments in the left column matched with the syntax-highlighted code in the right column. This is best understood with an example; for instance, the Docco website is generated by Docco.

Rocco is a Docco clone written in Ruby that, strangely enough, does a smarter job of formatting JavaScript code than Docco (which is written in CoffeeScript). The Rocco (*http://bit.ly/XUdBK7*) website is (surprisingly) generated by Rocco.

The biggest hurdle to using Rocco is installing Ruby to run it if Ruby is not already available. The next dependency is Pygments, a syntax highlighting utility written in

Python. Rocco will attempt to use the Pygments web service if it is not installed locally, but it is doubtful that you'll want your code shipped across the wire to be syntax-highlighted using the Pygments web service. Pygments depends on Python, so once Python is installed Pygments can be installed like so:

```
% sudo easy_install Pygments
```

Rocco also needs a Markdown parser; take rdiscount for a spin:

```
% sudo gem install rdiscount
```

Finally, install Rocco:

```
% sudo gem install rocco
```

Now simply run Rocco on your code:

```
% rocco myJavascript.js
```

By default, a file of the same name but with an *.html* extension will be created in the current directory (you can change this with the -o option to specify another directory where the HTML file should be saved).

All comments are stripped from the source and placed on the left side of the resultant web page, lined up with the code it relates to on the right side of the generated HTML.

So, this basic JavaScript:

```
/**
 * This function accepts two operands, 'a' and 'b' and returns their
 * sum (or concatenation if they are strings)
 */
exports.sum = function(a, b) { return a + b };

/**
 * This function accepts two operands, 'a' and 'b' and
 * returns their product
 */
exports.mult = function(a, b) { return a * b };
```

generates the HTML page shown in Figure 2-4.

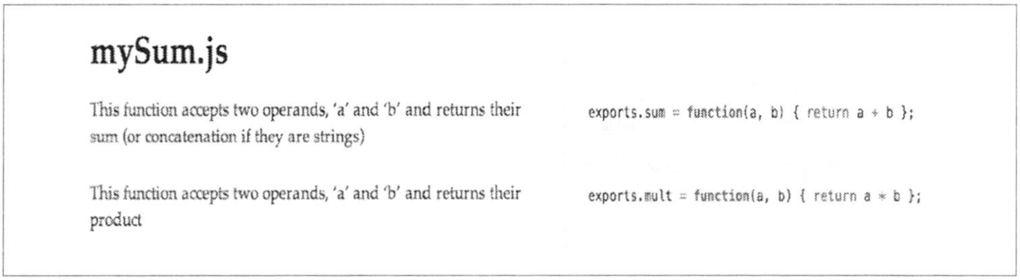

Figure 2-4. Generated HTML from Rocco directives

Pretty snazzy! Beyond YUIDoc or JSDoc, Rocco and friends provide a different view of your code.

The Human Test

In the end, the most relevant test of complexity is your coworker. Show her your code. What is her reaction? Can she understand it? Follow it? Comprehend what it does and why? This informal code review process is a great gateway to a more formal review. Formalized software inspections (*http://bit.ly/XUdC0y*), studied by Fagan, have been shown to find 60% to 90% of all program defects. That is an incredible percentage. The Fagan inspection process is a very formalized, repeatable, data-collecting code review process that I will not discuss in detail here; however, it's worth mentioning that no other method even comes close to finding such a large percentage of bugs. When you are really ready to get serious about finding bugs, Fagan inspections are as serious as it gets.

Back in not-quite-so-serious-ville, informal code reviews or walkthroughs are also excellent tools to gauge complexity, maintainability, and testability. In six months you probably will not be looking at the same chunk of code you are looking at now, but someone else will be. Even if you are, you will likely not remember what you did and why you did it.

This is where well-commented code comes to the fore. Up until now we have discussed what makes code complex and how to reduce that complexity. But there is no such thing as zero complexity. Writing software is hard. Writing good software is even harder. Douglas Crockford believes that writing software is the most complicated thing humans do (*http://bit.ly/XUdCh0*). You can help to simplify your code by commenting it heavily.

An Enerjy study (*http://bit.ly/XUdmPf*) found that two of the three leading metrics for "fault-prone" code are based on comments, namely comment blocks at the beginning of functions. Missing and incorrect comment blocks before functions are the leading indicators of fault-prone code.

Comments (correct comments!) require a full understanding of the code. More comments require more understanding. How difficult is it to have a full understanding of a given function? When you're writing a function for the first time is clearly the time when you're most likely to have a full understanding of what the function is doing. That is the time to comment the code. Try commenting the function even before you start writing it, as you would write a test before writing a function using test-driven development (TDD). Going forward, any changes also should be commented. Even if you never see this code again, someone else will—and there will likely be bugs in your code that she will have to fix.

Comments also make code more testable. They are signposts of what and how to test. Comments force you to understand your code. They act as a mini self-review of your code. This is especially important when it is unclear what the range of expected return values for a function may be, and what those values may mean. Commented function blocks before function definitions must make clear exactly what the function expects in its parameter list and what is returned, as well as what the return values mean. Ideally, such a function has no side effects, but if it does they must be explicitly stated in the comment block. This demonstrates that you realize this function has side effects, and what exactly those side effects are.

Interestingly, `if` statements without braces are also a leading indicator of fault-proneness in source code, so remember to always use braces!

Complexity really boils down to the difficulty someone else will have reading your code. Twenty minutes is the *upper* bound of typical adult concentration. If it takes a coworker more than 20 minutes to understand, in general, the gist of your code—not the entire application, but just a method or object abstracted from the whole—something is wrong. The onus is on *you* to make your code understandable. Some complexity is unavoidable; rarely is a lot of complexity unavoidable.

Code size works the same way. Your code size will grow over time. Minimizing code size and maximizing understandability does not mean limiting the amount of code in your application. It does mean limiting the amount of code in each function, module, and file. You can still have lots of functions, modules, and files; that's OK. As long as their individual sizes are reasonable and they are understandable, complexity is kept at a minimum.

Therefore, it is imperative that you understand the code you are writing. You can demonstrate your understanding by providing comments, especially when you know you are breaking a "rule." If you cannot explain in comments why you are doing what you are doing, certainly no one else will understand it either. When someone else begins to maintain your code, bad bugs may crop up, and it's likely that it will be scrapped and rewritten by the new maintainer. What a waste! Write it right the first time!

Recap

Code complexity comes in many shapes and sizes. Most complexity can be measured; however, the most important measurements cannot. Static code analysis will make large strides in cleaning up your code and make it more testable. Using well-understood patterns from static languages and standards-based JavaScript will help keep your code testable, and therefore maintainable.

Dependencies play a large role in code complexity. They must be constructed, destroyed, understood, and maintained. Instantiating dependencies is a dangerous business. If the process can be offloaded to an injector, all the better.

Writing good documentation in code comments is also crucial for making complex code more approachable. Generating YUIDoc, JSDoc, or Rocco-style documentation automatically with each build will greatly ease code complexity. Of course, writing comments initially is barely half the battle. Keeping the comments up to date is equally if not more important.

However, there is no substitute for Fagan inspections and code reviews in terms of finding bugs and ensuring that your code is not overly complex.

There are no magic bullets reducing the complexity of your code. The first step is to understand and realize where the complexity lies. There are many industry-standard books about modeling and refactoring code and the various patterns that can be used to factor and refactor your code—however, there are two "bibles" in the field: *Refactoring: Improving the Design of Existing Code*, by Martin Fowler (Addison-Wesley), and *Code Complete: A Practical Handbook of Software Construction*, by Steve McConnell (Microsoft Press). All of the dirty details are available in these two books, and therefore, both are very highly recommended. It is rarely possible to completely eliminate complexity, but it can be minimized, and in cases where it cannot, there must be robust and correct comments explaining in clear terms exactly what is going on. Of course, having tests for that code is also especially important.

## CHAPTER 3

Event-Based Architectures

Using factories of various abstractions, façades, and other patterns is not the only way to decouple dependencies and isolate code. A more JavaScript-oriented approach involves the use of events. The functional nature of JavaScript makes it an ideal language for event-based programming.

The Benefits of Event-Based Programming

At their core, all applications revolve around message passing. Tight coupling can occur because the code needs to have a reference to another object so that it can send the object a message and perhaps receive a reply. These objects are global, passed in, or injected via a function parameter, or they are instantiated locally. Our use of factories in the preceding chapter enabled us to pry away the local instantiation requirement; however, we still need the object to be available locally in order to pass messages to it, which means we still must deal with global or injected dependencies. Global dependencies are dangerous: any part of the system can touch them, making bugs very difficult to track down; we can accidentally change them if we have a variable by the same or a similar name declared locally; and they cause data encapsulation to break since they are available everywhere, making debugging very difficult. JavaScript makes declaration and use of global variables very easy, and the environment typically provides several global variables (e.g., the `window` object in the `global` scope), as well as global functions and objects (e.g., the `YUI` object, or `$` from jQuery). This means we must be careful to not just dump variables into the global scope, as there already are a lot of them there.

If we want to neither instantiate objects locally nor put them in the global namespace, we are left with injection. Injection is not a panacea, though, as we now must have setter functions and/or update constructors to handle injection, and more importantly, we now must deal with the care and feeding of either factories or a dependency injection framework. This is boilerplate code that must be maintained and managed and is code that is not specific to our application.

To recap, the problem with dependencies arises because we need to interact with other pieces of code that may be internal or external to our application. We may need to pass parameters to this other code. We may expect a result from this other code. This code may take a long time to run or return. We may want to wait for this code to finish and return before continuing, or keep plowing ahead while it churns away. Typically, this is all accomplished by holding direct references to other objects. We have these references; we shake them up by calling methods or setting properties, and then get the results.

But event-based programming provides an alternative way to pass messages to objects. By itself, the use of events is not much different from calling a method with a level of indirection through an event-handling framework. You still need to have a local reference to the object to throw an event to it, or to listen for events coming from it.

Interestingly, the JavaScript language has no formal support for events and callbacks; historically, the language has only provided functions as first-class objects. This allowed JavaScript to ditch the interface-based model of Java event listeners wherein everything must be an object, leading to some very clunky syntax. The event model provided by the DOM in browsers brought event-based JavaScript programming to the core, followed by the Node.js approach of asynchronous programming utilizing callbacks extensively.

Event-based programming all boils down to two primary pieces: the call and the return. It transforms the call into a parameterized thrown event and the return into a parameterized callback. The magic occurs when the requirement for a local reference to make these calls and returns is abstracted away, allowing us to interact with other code without having to have a local reference to it.

The Event Hub

The idea behind events is simple: methods register with an event hub, advertising themselves as capable of handling certain events. Methods utilize the hub as the single central location to which to throw event requests and from which to await responses. Methods can both register for and throw events. Methods receive asynchronous responses via callbacks. Your application's classes or methods require only one reference to the event hub. All communication is brokered through the event hub. Code running in a browser or on a server has equal access to the hub.

A typical web application is tightly coupled to the web server itself, as shown in Figure 3-1.

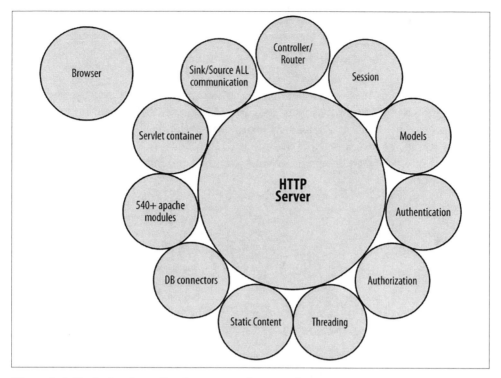

Figure 3-1. Typical web application centered on a web server

As you can see in the figure, browsers and clients are off on their own, connecting to an HTTP server laden with services and modules. All extra services are tightly coupled to the HTTP server itself and provide all the other required services. Furthermore, all communication between clients and modules is brokered through the HTTP server, which is unfortunate, as HTTP servers are really best for just serving static content (their original intent). Event-based programming aims to replace the HTTP server with an event hub as the center of the universe.

As the following code shows, all we need to do is add a reference to the hub to join the system. This works great for multiple clients and backends all joining the same party:

```
eventHub.fire(
    'LOG'
    , {
        severity: 'DEBUG'
        , message: "I'm doing something"
    }
);
```

Meanwhile, somewhere (anywhere) else—on the server, perhaps—the following code listens for and acts on the LOG event:

```
eventHub.listen('LOG', logIt);
function logIt(what) {
    // do something interesting
    console.log(what.severity + ': ' + what.message);
}
```

The event hub joins these two otherwise disconnected pieces of code. Disregard what is happening behind the scenes; messages are being passed between event hub clients regardless of their location. Figure 3-2 illustrates the relationship between the hub and all of its connected modules. Note that the HTTP server is no longer the center of the universe, but is relegated to being a service-providing module similar to all other connected modules.

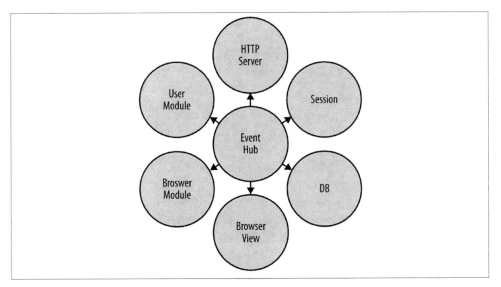

Figure 3-2. Clients (browsers and server-side clients) all connected to the same event hub

But now are we commonly coupled? As we discussed in Chapter 2, common coupling is the second tightest form of coupling, wherein objects share a common global variable. Regardless of whether the EventHub object is global or is passed into each object as a parameter, this is not common coupling. While all objects use the common EventHub, they do not alter it or share information through it by changing its state. This is an important distinction and an interesting case for an EventHub versus other kinds of global objects. Although all communication between objects is brokered through an EventHub object, there is no shared state in the EventHub object.

Using the Event Hub

So, the game is to have pieces join the hub and start firing, listening for, and responding to events. Instead of making method calls (which requires a local instantiation of an object, coupling, fan-out, and local mocking and stubbing), throw an event and (possibly) wait for the response (if you need one).

A hub can run wherever you like on the server side. Clients can connect to it and fire and subscribe to events.

Typically, browser-based clients fire events and server-based clients consume them, but of course any client can fire and consume events.

This architecture plays to JavaScript's functional strengths and encourages small bits of tightly focused code with minimal dependencies. Using events instead of method calls greatly increases testability and maintainability by encouraging developers to write smaller chunks of code with minimal dependencies. Anything external to a module is provided as a service instead of being wrapped within a dependency. The only function calls should be to the hub or to methods local to the object or module.

Let's take a look at some canonical login logic. Here is the standard Ajax-based login using the YUI framework:

```
YUI().add('login', function(Y) {
    Y.one('#submitButton').on('click', logIn);
    function logIn(e) {
        var username = Y.one('#username').get('value')
            , password = Y.one('#password').get('value')
            , cfg = {
                data: JSON.stringify(
                    {username: username, password: password })
                , method: 'POST'
                , on: {
                    complete: function(tid, resp, args) {
                        if (resp.status === 200) {
                            var response = JSON.parse(resp.responseText);
                            if (response.loginOk) {
                                userLoggedIn(username);
                            } else {
                                failedLogin(username);
                            }
                        } else {
                            networkError(resp);
                        }
                    }
                }
            }
            , request = Y.io('/login', cfg)
            ;
    }
}, '1.0', { requires: [ 'node', 'io-base' ] });
```

At 27 lines of code, that login isn't too bad. Here is the equivalent using event-based programming (using the YUI Event Hub module):

```
YUI().add('login', function(Y) {
    Y.one('#submitButton').on('click', logIn);
    function logIn(e) {
        var username = Y.one('#username').get('value')
          , password = Y.one('#password').get('value')
        ;
        eventHub.fire('logIn'
          , { username: username, password: password }
          , function(err, resp) {
            if (!err) {
                if (resp.loginOk) {
                    userLoggedIn(username);
                } else {
                    failedLogin(username);
                }
            } else {
                networkError(err);
            }
        });
    }

}, '1.0', { requires: [ 'node', 'EventHub' ] });
```

This code is only 18 lines long, representing a whopping 33% code savings. But in addition to fewer lines of code, testing is simplified. To illustrate this, let's conduct a unit test of the standard Ajax version and compare it to a unit test of the event-hub-based version. (We will discuss unit tests in detail in Chapter 4, so don't get too bogged down in the syntax if you are not familiar with YUI Test (*http://bit.ly/XUdCxH*). We'll start with the Ajax version, beginning with the setup:

```
YUI().use('test', 'console', 'node-event-simulate'
  , 'login', function(Y) {

    // Factory for mocking Y.io
    var getFakeIO = function(args) {
        return function(url, config) {
            Y.Assert.areEqual(url, args.url);
            Y.Assert.areEqual(config.data, args.data);
            Y.Assert.areEqual(config.method, args.method);
            Y.Assert.isFunction(config.on.complete);
            config.on.complete(1, args.responseArg);
        };
    }
      , realIO = Y.io;
```

This is standard boilerplate YUI code that loads the external modules our tests depend on, including our `login` module, which we will be testing. The code also includes the factory for creating a mocked `Y.io` instance, which is YUI's veneer over `XMLHttpRe quest`. This object will ensure that the correct values are passed to it. Finally, we keep a reference to the real `Y.io` instance so that it can be restored for other tests.

Here is the test itself:

```
var testCase = new Y.Test.Case({
    name: "test ajax login"
    , tearDown: function() {
        Y.io = realIO;
    }
    , testLogin : function () {
        var username = 'mark'
            , password = 'rox'
        ;

        Y.io = getFakeIO({
            url: '/login'
            , data: JSON.stringify({
                username: username
                , password: password
            })
            , method: 'POST'
            , responseArg: {
                status: 200
                , responseText: JSON.stringify({ loginOk: true })
            }
        });

        userLoggedIn = function(user) {
            Y.Assert.areEqual(user, username); };
        failedLogin  = function() {
            Y.Assert.fail('login should have succeeded!'); };
        networkError = function() {
            Y.Assert.fail('login should have succeeded!'); };

        Y.one('#username').set('value', username);
        Y.one('#password').set('value', password);
        Y.one('#submitButton').simulate('click');
    }
});
```

The preceding code is testing a successful login attempt. We set up our fake `Y.io` object and mock the possible resultant functions our login module calls to ensure that the correct one is used. Then we set up the HTML elements with known values so that clicking Submit will start the whole thing off. One thing to note is the `teardown` function that restores Y.io to its original value. The mocking of Y.io is a bit clunky (although not horribly so), as Ajax only deals with strings and we need to keep track of the HTTP status from the server. For completeness, here is the rest of the test module, which is all boilerplate:

```
var suite = new Y.Test.Suite('login');
suite.add(testCase);

Y.Test.Runner.add(suite);

//Initialize the console
new Y.Console({
    newestOnTop: false
}).render('#log');

Y.Test.Runner.run();
});
```

Let's now look at a unit test for the event-based code. Here is the beginning portion:

```
YUI().use('test', 'console', 'node-event-simulate'
    , 'login', function(Y) {

    // Factory for mocking EH
    var getFakeEH = function(args) {
        return {
            fire: function(event, eventArgs, cb) {
                Y.Assert.areEqual(event, args.event);
                Y.Assert.areEqual(JSON.stringify(eventArgs),
                                   JSON.stringify(args.data));
                Y.Assert.isFunction(cb);
                cb(args.err, args.responseArg);
            }
        };
    };
});
```

Here we see the same boilerplate at the top and a similar factor for mocking out the event handler itself. Although this code is slightly cleaner, some unfortunate ugliness crops up when comparing the two objects for equality, as YUI does not provide a standard object comparator method.

Here is the actual test:

```
var testCase = new Y.Test.Case({
    name: "test eh login"
    , testLogin : function () {
        var username = 'mark'
            , password = 'rox'
        ;

        eventHub = getFakeEH({
```

```
        event: 'logIn'
        , data: {
            username: username
            , password: password
        }
        , responseArg: { loginOk: true }
    });

    userLoggedIn = function(user) {
        Y.Assert.areEqual(user, username); };
    failedLogin  = function() {
        Y.Assert.fail('login should have succeeded!'); };
    networkError = function() {
        Y.Assert.fail('login should have succeeded!'); };

    Y.one('#username').set('value', username);
    Y.one('#password').set('value', password);
    Y.one('#submitButton').simulate('click');
    }
});
```

This is very similar to the previous code. We get a mocked version of the event hub, prime the HTML elements, and click the Submit button to start it off. The exact same post-test boilerplate code present from the previous Ajax test is also necessary here to complete the example (refer back to that code if you want to see it again!).

This example illustrates that the base code and the test code are smaller for the event-based example, while providing more semantic usage and more functionality. For example, the event-based code handles cross-domain (secure or not) communication without any changes. There is no need for JSONP, Flash, hidden iframes, or other tricks, which add complexity to both the code and the tests. Serialization and deserialization are handled transparently. Errors passed as objects, not as HTTP status codes, are buried within the response object. Endpoints are abstracted away from URLs to arbitrary strings. And finally (and perhaps most importantly), this kind of event-based architecture completely frees us from the tyranny of instantiating and maintaining tightly coupled pointers to external objects.

The test code for Ajax requests really grows when using more of the features of XMLHttpRequest and Y.io, such as the success and failure callbacks, which also need to be mocked. There are more complex usages that require more testing complexity.

Responses to Thrown Events

There are three possible responses to a thrown event: no response, a generic response, or a specific response. Using events for message passing is simplest when no reply is necessary. In a typical event system, sending events is easy but getting replies is problematic. You could set up a listener for a specific event directly tied to the event that was just fired. This approach is similar to giving each event a unique ID; you could then listen for a specifically named event containing the request ID to get the response. But that sure is ugly, which is why eventing has typically been relegated to "one-way" communication, with logging, UI actions, and notifications (typically signifying that something is now "ready") being the most common event use cases. However, two-way asynchronous communication is possible using callbacks, which handle generic and specific responses. Let's look at some examples.

Obviously, if *no response* is necessary, we can simply throw the event and move on:

```
eventHub.fire('LOG', { level: 'debug', message: 'This is cool' });
```

If a specific response to the thrown event is not necessary and a more *generic response* is sufficient, the remote listener can throw the generic event in response. For example, if a new user registers a generic USER_REGISTERED event, a generic response may be the only "reply" that is necessary:

```
// somewhere on server
eventHub.on('REGISTER_USER', function(obj) {
    // stick obj.name into user DB
    eventHub.fire('USER_REGISTERED', { name: obj.name });
});

// somewhere global
eventHub.on('USER_REGISTERED', function(user) {
    console.log(user.name + ' registered!');
});

// somewhere specific
eventHub.fire('REGISTER_USER', { name: 'mark' });
```

In this example, the REGISTER_USER event handler is sitting on a server writing to a database. After registering the user by adding him to the database, the handler throws another event, the USER_REGISTERED event. Another listener listens for this event. That other listener then handles the application's logic after the user has been registered—by updating the UI, for example. Of course, there can be multiple listeners for each event, so perhaps one USER_REGISTERED event can update an admin panel, another can update the specific user's UI, and yet another can send an email to an administrator with the new user's information.

Finally, in some cases a *specific response* sent directly back to the event thrower is required. This is exactly the same as making a method call, but asynchronously. If a direct reply is necessary, an event hub provides callbacks to the event emitter. The callback is passed as a parameter by the event emitter to the hub. For example:

```
// Somewhere on the server
eventHub.on('ADD_TO_CART'
    , function(userId, itemId, callback) {
        d.cart.push(itemId);
        callback(null, { items: userId.cart.length });
});
```

```
// Meanwhile, somewhere else (in the browser, probably)
function addItemToCart(userId, itemId) {
    eventHub.fire('ADD_TO_CART'
      , { user_id: userId, item_id: itemId }
      , function(err, result) {
        if (!err) {
                console.log('Cart now has: ' + result.cart.items + ' items');
        }
    });
}
```

Here, we fire a generic `ADD_TO_CART` event with some information and we wait for the callback. The supplied callback to the event hub is called with data provided by the listener.

Event-Based Architectures and MVC Approaches

How do event-based architectures compare with Model-View-Controller (MVC) approaches? They are actually quite similar. In fact, event-based architectures help to enforce the separation of concerns and modularity that MVC advocates.

But there are a few differences between the two, with the biggest difference being that in event-based architectures models are turned inside out, eliminated, or pulled apart, depending on how you like to think about these things. For example, using MVC, a `Model` class is instantiated for each database row; this class provides the data and the methods that operate on that data. In an event-based architecture, models are simple hashes storing only data; this data is passed using events for listeners (you can call them models, I suppose) to operate on. This separation of data and functionality can provide greater testability, memory savings, greater modularity, and higher scalability, all with the benefits of putting the data and methods together in the first place. Instead of lots of individual instantiated `Model` objects floating around, there are lots of data hashes floating around, and one instantiated object to operate on them all.

The controller is now simply the event hub, blindly passing events between views and models. The event hub can have some logic associated with it, such as being smarter about where to pass events instead of passing them blindly to all listeners. The event hub can also detect events being thrown with no listeners and return an appropriate error message. Beyond event-specific logic, the controller in an event-centered world is just a dumb hub (perhaps upgraded to a slightly smarter switch, exactly like Ethernet hubs and switches).

Views, perhaps the least changed, have data pushed to them via events instead of querying models. Upon a user-initiated event, views "model" the data and throw the appropriate event. Any required UI updates are notified by events.

Event-Based Architectures and Object-Oriented Programming

Storing data along with the methods that operate on it is the basic tenet of object-oriented programming. Another tenet of object-oriented programming is reuse. The theory is that more generic superclasses can be reused by more specific subclasses. Object-oriented methodology introduces another form of coupling: inheritance coupling. There is nothing stopping an event-based programmer from using object-oriented principles when designing her listeners, but she will encounter a few twists.

For starters, the entire application is not based on object-oriented programming. In addition, there are no chains of interconnected objects connected only by inheritance or interface coupling, and the application is not running in a single thread or process, but rather in multiple processes. But the biggest difference is that the data is not stored within the objects. Singleton objects are instantiated with methods that operate on the data, and data is passed to these objects to be operated on.

There are no "public," "private," or "protected" modifiers—everything is private. The only communication with the "outside" world is via the event-based API. As these objects are not instantiated by dependents, there is no need to worry that an external object will mess with your internals. There are no life-cycle issues, as the objects live for the entire life of the application, so constructors (if there are any) are called once at the beginning and destructors are unnecessary.

Event-Based Architectures and Software as a Service

Event-based architectures facilitate Software as a Service (SaaS). Each independent piece can join the event hub to provide a service in isolation from all the other services used to create the application. You can easily imagine a repository of services either available for download or accessible over the Internet for your application to use. Your application would connect to their hub to access their services. The "API" for these services is a unique event name with which to call exposed actions and the data that must be present in the event. Optionally, the service can either fire another event upon completion or use the callback mechanism for responses, if any response is necessary.

Web-Based Applications

Most web-based applications are intractably intertwined with a web server. This is unfortunate, as HTTP servers were never originally built to have the amount of functionality we cram into them today. HTTP servers are built to negotiate Hypertext Transfer Protocol data and to serve static content. Everything else has been bolted on over time and has made web applications unnecessarily complex.

Mixing application logic into the web server and/or relying on a web server to be the central hub of an application not only ties our application to HTTP, but also requires a lot of care and feeding of the web server to keep the application running. Lots of tricks have been created and abused over the years to try to make HTTP support two-way asynchronous communication, but some shortcomings remain. While the `socket.io` library does support running over HTTP, it also supports Web Sockets transparently for when that protocol becomes more widely available.

Web-based applications also suffer from the "same-origin" principle, which severely limits how code can interact with code from differing origins. HTML5 brings `postMes sage` as a workaround, but by using a `socket.io`-based event architecture this can all be easily bypassed.

The event hub in an event-based architecture becomes the hub, not the web server. This is preferable, as the event hub is built from the ground up to be a hub without any unnecessary bits, which web servers have in spades. Additional functionality is built not into the hub itself, but into remote clients, which are much more loosely coupled and significantly easier to test.

Testing Event-Based Architectures

Testing event-based architectures involves merely calling the function that implements the action. Here is an interesting case:

```
// Some handle to a datastore
function DB(eventHub, dbHandle) {
    // Add user function
    eventHub.on('CREATE_USER', addUser);
    function addUser(user) {
        var result = dbHandle.addRow('user', user);
        eventHub.fire('USER_CREATED',
          {
            success: result.success
            , message: result.message
            , user: user
          }
        );
    }
}
```

There are several curious things to note about this piece of code. First, there is no callback, and events are used instead to broadcast the success or failure of this operation. You may be tempted to use a callback so that the caller knows whether this action succeeded, but by broadcasting the response we allow other interested parties to know whether a user was created successfully. Multiple clients may all want to be informed if a new user is created. This way, any browser or server-side client will be notified of this event. This also allows a separate module to handle the results of an attempted user creation event, instead of forcing that code to be within the `addUser` code. Of course, it can live in the same file as the `addUser` code, but it does not have to. This helps tremendously in terms of modularity. In fact, typically a module on the server side and a module on the client side will both want to know whether a user was created and take action because of it. The client-side listener will want to update the UI and a server-side listener can update other internal structures.

Here the eventHub and databaseHandle are injected into the constructor, aiding testing and modularity as well. No object is created; only event listeners are registered to the injected eventHub. This is the essence of event-based architectures: event listeners are registered and no (or few) objects are instantiated.

A browser-based handler could look like this:

```
eventHub.on('USER_CREATED', function(data) {
    dialog.show('User created: ' + data.success);
});
```

A server-side handler could look like this:

```
eventHub.on('USER_CREATED', function(data) {
    console.log('User created: ' + data.success);
});
```

The preceding code would pop up a dialog anytime anyone attempted to create a user from this browser, from any other browser, or even on the server side. If this is what you want, having this event be broadcast is the answer. If not, use a callback.

It is also possible to indicate in the event whether you expect the result to be in a callback or in an event (you could even live it up and do both!). Here is how the client-side code would look:

```
eventHub.fire('CREATE_USER', user);
```

Here is how the server-side code would look:

```
eventHub.fire('CREATE_USER', user);
```

It can't get any simpler than that.

To test this function, you can use a mocked-up event hub and a stubbed-out database handle that verifies events are being fired properly:

```
YUI().use('test', function(Y) {
    var eventHub = Y.Mock()
        , addUserTests = new Y.Test.Case({
            name: 'add user'
            , addOne: function() {
                var user = { user_id: 'mark' }
                    , dbHandle = { // DB stub
                        addRow: function(user) {
                            return { user: user
                                    , success: true
                                    , message: 'ok' };
                        }
```

```
          }
        ;
        DB(eventHub, dbHandle);  // Inject test versions
        Y.Mock.expect(eventHub, 'fire',
            [
              'USER_CREATED'
              , { success: true: message: 'ok', user: user }
            ]
        );
      addUser(user);
      Y.Mock.verify(eventHub);
    });
  Y.Test.Runner.add(addUserTests);
  Y.Test.Runner.run();
});
```

This test case uses both a mock (for the event hub) and a stub (for the DB handle) to test the addUser function. The fire event is expected to be called on the eventHub object by the addUser function with the appropriate arguments. The stubbed DB object's ad dRow function is set to return canned data. Both of these objects are injected into the DB object for testing, and we are off and running.

The end result of all of this is simply testing that the addUser function emits the proper event with the proper arguments.

Compare this with a more standard approach using an instantiated DB object with an addUser method on its prototype:

```
var DB = function(dbHandle) {
    this.handle = dbHandle;
};

DB.prototype.addUser = function(user) {
    var result = dbHandle.addRow('user', user);
    return {
        success: result.success
        , message: result.message
        , user: user
    };
};
```

How would client-side code access this?

```
transporter.sendMessage('addUser', user);
```

A global or centralized message-passing mechanism would post a message back to the server using Ajax or something equivalent. It would do so perhaps after updating or creating an instantiated user model object on the client side. That piece would need to keep track of requests and responses, and the server-side code would need to route that message to the global DB singleton, marshal the response, and send the response back to the client.

Here is a test for this code:

```
YUI().use('test', function(Y) {
    var addUserTests = new Y.Test.Case({
        name: 'add user'
        , addOne: function() {
            var user = { user_id: 'mark' }
                , dbHandle = { // DB stub
                    addRow: function(user) {
                        return {
                            user: user
                            , success: true
                            , message: 'ok'
                        };
                    }
                }
                , result
                ;

            DB(dbHandle); // Inject test versions
            result = addUser(user);
            Y.Assert.areSame(result.user, user.user);
            Y.Assert.isTrue(result.success);
            Y.Assert.areSame(result.message, 'ok');
        }
    })
    ;

    Y.Test.Runner.add(addUserTests);
    Y.Test.Runner.run();
});
```

In this case, as the DB object has no dependencies, the tests look similar.

For a client to add a new user, a new protocol between the client and the server must be created, a route in the server must be created to hand off the "add user" message to this DB object, and the results must be serialized and passed back to the caller. That is a lot of plumbing that needs to be re-created for every message type. Eventually, you will end up with a cobbled-together RPC system that an event hub gives you for free.

That kind of code is a great example of the 85% of boilerplate code you should not be implementing yourself. All applications boil down to message passing and job control. Applications pass messages and wait for replies. Writing and testing all of that boilerplate code adds a lot of overhead to any application, and it is unnecessary overhead. What if you also want a command-line interface to your application? That is another code path you must implement and maintain. Let an event hub give it to you for free.

Caveats to Event-Based Architectures

An event-based architecture is not the answer to all problems. Here are some issues you must keep in mind when using such an architecture.

Scalability

An event hub creates a super single point of failure: if the hub goes down, your application goes down with it. You need to either put a set of event hubs behind a load balancer, or build failing over to another event hub into your application. This is no different from adding more web servers; in fact it's actually simpler, as you do not have to worry about the same-origin policy using `socket.io`.

Broadcasting

A lot of events being broadcast to all clients can potentially result in a lot of traffic. Guards should be put in place to ensure that events that are meant to be consumed locally do not get sent to the hub. Further, the hub itself can act more like a switch than a hub if it knows which client is listening for an event, sending it directly there instead of broadcasting it.

Runtime Checking

Whereas misspelling a function or method name will result in a runtime error, the compiler cannot check string event names for misspellings. Therefore, it is highly recommended that you use enumerations or hashes for event names instead of typing them over and over. A nice way to get runtime checking of your event names is to do something like this:

```javascript
// Return an object with 'on' and 'fire' functions for the specified
// eventName
hub.addEvent = function(eventName) {
    var _this = this;
    this.events[eventName] = {
        on: function(callback) {
            _this.on.call(_this, eventName, callback);
        }
        , fire: function() {
            Array.prototype.unshift.call(arguments, eventName);
            this.fire.apply(_this, arguments);
        }
    };
    return this.events[eventName];
};
```

You would use this code as follows:

```
var clickEvent = hub.addEvent('click');
clickEvent.on(function(data) { /* got a click event! */ });
clickEvent.fire({ button: 'clicked' }); // fired a click event!
```

Now you have runtime checking of event names.

Security

If you're afraid that random unwashed masses will connect to your event hub and inject any events they want, don't be; the event hub implementation requires "trusted" clients to authenticate with the hub.

If you want to encrypt event hub connections, you can build your event hub solution using `socket.io`, which supports encrypted connections.

State

State, which typically is provided by a web server via a session cookie, moves from the web server to a module. Upon web application load, a new session object can be created and persisted completely independently of a web server. The client-side JavaScript writes the session token as a cookie itself, which is then available to the web server if it needs to serve authenticated-only content. The event hub itself injects the session into events, making it impossible for one session to masquerade as another.

Trusted (typically server-side) modules get the session key, and therefore the state, from untrusted (typically client-side) events, passed as a parameter or hash field.

A Smarter Hub: The Event Switch

An event switch enhances event-based architectures by making them more modular and more deployable. If you are willing to add a bit of logic to the event hub and to the events themselves, your applications will be easier to deploy and manage.

By categorizing your events into two groups, broadcast and unicast, you will gain some neat features using an event switch instead of a hub. The biggest win (besides some network bandwidth savings) is fail-safe deployments.

One of the biggest promises of event-based architectures is modularity. A typical monolithic application is replaced with a number of independent modules, which is great for testability; using an event switch instead of a hub is great for deployability too.

An event switch knows the difference between broadcast and unicast events. Broadcast events behave exactly like all events do using an event hub. Unicast events are only sent to a single listener that has registered for the event. This feature makes deployment much simpler, as we shall see in the next section.

Deployment

A monolithic application typically has all the server-side logic intertwined with the HTTP server. Deploying a new version involves pushing the entire application logic at once and restarting the web server. To upgrade a portion of the application, everything must be pushed. The logic for event-based applications is completely separate from the web server; in fact, the logic of the application resides in many different independent modules. This makes pushing new versions of code much simpler, as the modules can be updated and deployed completely independently of one another and of the web server. Although there are more "moving parts" to deal with, you gain much finer-grained control of your deployment and code.

So, how can you safely stop a listener without dropping an event? You can use unicast events and broadcast events. An event switch is necessary for safely shutting down listeners without missing an event.

Unicast events

Unicast events, such as `depositMoney` in the following code, have only one listener. In this case, a listener must notify the event switch that this event is a unicast event and that it is the (only) listener for it. When we're ready to upgrade, we need to start the new version of the module, which announces to the event switch that it is now the sole listener for the event. The event switch will notify the older module that it has been replaced, and that module can now shut down cleanly after handling any outstanding events. No events are lost; the event switch will switch the unicast event over to the new listener, but the switch will remain connected to the original listener to handle any callbacks or events emitted by that listener while it finishes handling any outstanding events. In this way, we have successfully shut down the old listener and brought up a new one with no loss in service:

```
eventSwitch.on('depositMoney', function(data) {
    cash += data.depositAmount;
    eventSwitch.emit('depositedMoney', cash);
}, { type: 'unicast' });
```

When we begin listening for this event, this code informs the event switch that this is a unicast event, and that all events of this name must go only to this listener. All we have done is add a third parameter to the on method with some metadata about the event, which the client passes to the switch.

Meanwhile, the switch will replace the current listener for this event (if there is one) with the new listener, and will send a "hey, someone bumped you" event to the previous listener (again, if there was one). Any listener for this event should have another listener for the "go away" event too:

```
eventHub.on('eventClient:done', function(event) {
    console.log('DONE LISTENING FOR ' + event);
    // finish handling any outstanding events & then safely:
    process.exit(0);
});
```

The `eventClient:done` event signifies that this listener will no longer receive the specified event, and that when it is done processing any outstanding events it can safely shut down or can continue to handle events it is still listening for.

The atomic operation of the event switch ensures that no events are dropped and none are sent to a listener that has been replaced. To understand this more fully, take a look at Figure 3-3. In the figure, time flows from the top of the picture to the bottom. The module on the left registers for the unicast event, and events are delivered to it. Then the updated module on the right registers for that same unicast event. The first module receives the done event; all new event requests are sent to the module on the right, while the module on the left finishes handling any current events and then shuts down. The updated module continues to serve event requests until another updated module notifies the hub that it is now responsible for the unicast event.

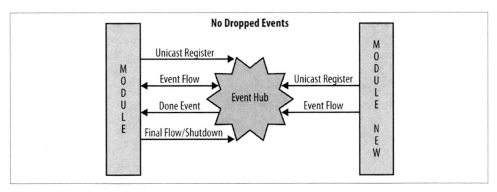

Figure 3-3. Event switch flow for uninterrupted unicast event handling

Broadcast events

Safely shutting down broadcast listeners follows a similar process. However, the event listener itself will broadcast the `eventClient:done` event to signal to all other listeners for the specified event that they should now shut down. The event switch is smart enough to broadcast that event to every listener except the one that emitted the event.

A listener receiving this event will no longer receive messages for the specified event. After processing any outstanding events, the listeners can now shut down safely:

```
eventHub.on('eventClient:done', function(event) {
    console.log('I have been advised to stop listening for event: '
      + event);
    eventHub.removeAllListeners(event);
});
```

Note that the event switch is smart enough to not allow any connected clients to fire `eventClient:done` events and will drop them if it receives one. A rogue client cannot usurp the event switch's authority!

An Implementation

This sample implementation (*http://bit.ly/XUdG0a*) of an event switch with clients for Node.js, YUI3, and jQuery based on `socket.io` can be installed using npm:

```
% npm install EventHub
```

Built on top of `socket.io`, this implementation provides a centralized hub running under Node.js and provides event callback functions for direct responses. Most events do not require a direct callback, so be careful and do not overuse that feature. Think carefully about receiving a direct callback versus firing another event when the action is complete.

After `EventHub` is installed, simply start the hub:

```
% npm start EventHub
```

This starts the event switch listening on port 5883 by default. All clients need to point to the host and port where the hub is listening. Here is a Node.js client:

```
var EventHub = require('EventHub/clients/server/eventClient.js');
    , eventHub = EventHub.getClientHub('http://localhost:5883');
eventHub.on('ADD_USER', function(user) {
    // Add user logic
    eventHub.fire('ADD_USER_DONE', { success: true, user: user });
});
```

These lines of code instantiate an event hub client connecting to the previously started event hub (running on the same machine as this client, but of course it can run on another host). Simply execute this file:

```
% node client.js
```

Now any `ADD_USER` event fired by any client will be routed to this function. Here is a client running in a browser using YUI3:

```
<script src="http://yui.yahooapis.com/3.4.1/build/yui/yui-min.js">
  </script>
<script src="/socket.io/socket.io.js"></script>
<script src="/clients/browser/yui3.js"></script>
<script>
    YUI().use('node', 'EventHub', function(Y) {
```

```
        var hub = new Y.EventHub(io, 'http://myhost:5883');
        hub.on('eventHubReady', function() {
            hub.on('ADD_USER_DONE', function(data) { };

            ... TIME PASSES ...

            hub.fire('ADD_USER', user);
        });
    });
</script>
```

After loading the YUI3 seed, socket.io, and the YUI3 EventHub client, a new Even
tHub client is instantiated, and when it's ready we listen for events and at some point fire
the ADD_USER event. It's that simple.

Here is the same example using jQuery:

```
<script src="http://ajax.googleapis.com/ajax/libs/jquery/1.6.2/jquery.min.js">
  </script>
<script src="/socket.io/socket.io.js"></script>
<script src="/clients/browser/jquery.js"></script>
<script>
    var hub = new $.fn.eventHub(io, 'http://myhost:5883');
    hub.bind('eventHubReady', function() {
        hub.bind('ADD_USER_DONE', function(data) { });
            ... TIME PASSES ...
        hub.trigger('ADD_USER', user);
    });
</script>
```

The process is the same: load up the jQuery seed, socket.io, and the jQuery EventHub
client. The EventHub is provided as a jQuery plug-in and uses the jQuery event syntax
of bind and trigger.

Any event emitted by any client can have an optional callback function as the last parameter in the event arguments:

```
hub.fire('CHECK_USER', 'mark',
    function(result) { console.log('exists: ' + result.exists); });
```

And any responder to this event is given a corresponding function as the last parameter
in the event argument list to pass back any arbitrary data:

```
hub.on('CHECK_USER', function(username, callback) {
    callback({ exists: DB.exists(username) });
});
```

This is slick! The callback will execute the remote function in the caller's space with
the callee's provided data. The data is serialized as JSON, so do not get too crazy, *but* if
necessary you can receive a targeted response to the event you fired!

You can also use the addEvent helper for compile-time checking of event names using
YUI3:

```
var clickEvent = hub.addEvent('click');
clickEvent.on(function(data) { /* got a click event! */ });
clickEvent.fire({ button: 'clicked' }); // fired a click event!
```

This is exactly as outlined earlier. In the jQuery world, you use bind and trigger instead:

```
var clickEvent = hub.addEvent('click');
clickEvent.bind(function(data) { /* got a click event! */ });
clickEvent.trigger({ button: 'clicked' }); // triggered a click event!
```

Finally, you can use event switch features for unicast events:

```
hub.on('CHECK_USER', function(username, callback) {
    callback({ exists: DB.exists(username) });
}, { type: 'unicast' });
```

You can kick off any other listeners for broadcast events, like so:

```
// this goes to everyone BUT me...
hub.emit('eventClient:done', 'user:addUser');
```

To play nicely you must listen for this event:

```
hub.on('eventClient:done', function(event) {
    console.log('DONE LISTENING FOR ' + event);
    hub.removeAllListeners(event);
});
```

This will be fired by the event switch itself when a new unicast listener comes online or by a user module when broadcast modules are being upgraded.

Sessions

Trusted unicast listeners receive session data from thrown events. A "trusted" client connects to the hub using a shared secret:

```
eventHub = require('EventHub/clients/server/eventClient.js')
    .getClientHub('http://localhost:5883?token=secret)
```

Now this client can listen for unicast events. All unicast events receive extra session data in their event callbacks:

```
eventHub.on('user', function(obj) {
    var sessionID =  obj['eventHub:session'];
    ...
});
```

The eventHub:session key is a unique string (a UUID) that identifies this session. Trusted listeners should utilize this key when storing and accessing session data.

Session keys are completely transparent to untrusted clients. Both the YUI3 and jQuery clients persist the session key into a cookie.

The HTTP server, just a trusted event hub client, leverages the session key from the cookie on an HTTP request when deciding to send trusted, authenticated, or personalized content to the browser.

Extensibility

The `socket.io` library has clients in many languages, so services you use are not limited to only JavaScript client implementations. It is relatively trivial (I hope!) for users of other languages supported by `socket.io` to write an `EventHub` client using their language of choice.

 Poke around here (*http://bit.ly/XUdD4I*) to see how a web application works and is transformed by using the event hub implementation versus the standard web server implementation. It really is just a playground for putting event-based web application ideas into practice to see how it all shakes out.

Recap

Event-based architectures are not a panacea. However, their high modularity, loose coupling, small dependency count, and high reusability provide an excellent basis upon which to create testable JavaScript. By taking away a large swath of boilerplate code, event hubs let you focus on the 15% of the application's code that makes your project unique.

The sample event hub implementation has a very small code size, built upon the excellent `socket.io` library. The crux of the event hub code itself consists of fewer than 20 lines. The YUI3, jQuery, and Node.js clients are also vanishingly small. Given the functionality, testability, maintainability, and scalability provided, it is a no-brainer to actively investigate and prove how easy and natural using an event hub can be, instead of locally instantiating objects.

The MVC paradigm is actually enhanced using events. The controller and views are kept separate from the models and themselves. Models are passed around as event data and the logic is encapsulated into independent services. Views are notified via events of changes. The controller is merely the event hub itself. The essence of MVC, separation of concerns, is made more explicit.

Event-based architectures enable the Software as a Service model, whereby small, independent bits of functionality are added and removed dynamically as needed, providing services to the application.

Deploying event-based applications is much easier using an event switch. It allows individual modules to be shut down and new ones started without losing any events. This allows your application to be deployed in piecemeal fashion instead of all at once. Instead of a Big Bang when upgrading, you can upgrade individual modules in isolation, allowing your code and processes to be much more agile.

Testing the already isolated modules is also much more straightforward, and dependency and fan-out counts are greatly reduced. Give an event-based architecture a whirl today!

## CHAPTER 4

Unit Tests

The hardest unit test to write is the first one. That first test requires a nontrivial amount of boilerplate. It also requires that you answer some initial questions. For example, should you use an existing unit test framework, or roll your own? What about an automated build process? How about collecting, displaying, and tracking unit test code coverage? Developers are already barely motivated to write any unit tests, and having to deal with these legitimate questions only makes the process more painful.

Unfortunately, there is no magic bullet when it comes to unit testing. Developers will need to put in the work to get the rewards. Fortunately, the rewards are substantial. Starting with keeping your paycheck and ending with maintainable working code, unit tests provide a lot of value. As a developer, this is typically the only formal testing that is required; luckily, unit testing does not have to be difficult.

A Framework

Just as you would not write any JavaScript without using a sane framework, you cannot write any unit tests until you decide which testing framework to use. Frameworks provide a lot of the boilerplate you do not need to re-create: test suite/case aggregation, assertions, mock/stub helpers, asynchronous testing implementation, and more. Plenty of good open source testing frameworks are available. I will use YUI Test in this chapter, but of course all good practices are applicable across all frameworks—only the syntax (and maybe some semantics) differs.

The most important part of any testing framework is aggregating the tests into suites and test cases. Test suites and test cases are spread across many files, with each test file typically containing tests for a single module. A best practice is to group all tests for a module into a single test suite. The suite can contain many test cases, with each case testing a small aspect of the module. By using `setUp` and `tearDown` functions provided at the suite and test case levels, you can easily handle any pretest setup and post-test teardown, such as resetting the state of a database.

An equally important part of unit testing is assertions. Assertions are the actual tests applied to expected versus received values. This is where the rubber meets the road: is the value under test what you expect it to be? YUI Test provides a full set of assertion functions whose results are tracked by the framework so that when all the tests are done you can easily see which tests passed and which failed.

Nice-to-have framework functionality, such as asynchronous testing, forced failures, ignorable tests, and mock object support, are also provided by the YUI Test framework, which makes it a nice, full-fledged unit testing toolbox.

A final bonus are the events that YUI Test throws at various times during unit test execution and the various output formats that YUI Test supports for test results; these enable you to integrate unit test runs into an automated build.

One final note: the code being tested does *not* have to be written using YUI to utilize the YUI Test framework. You can download the YUI Test framework from here (*http://bit.ly/XUdGxh*).

YUI Test is great for client-side JavaScript, and it can be used for server-side JavaScript unit testing too. However, two popular, behavior-driven development (BDD) testing frameworks are also available for server-side testing: Vows (*http://bit.ly/XUdGNP*) and Jasmine (*http://bit.ly/XUdH4m*). The idea behind BDD is to use "regular language" constructs to describe what you think your code should be doing, or more specifically, what your functions should be returning. Make no mistake: these are unit test frameworks with 100% more fanciness. Most importantly, they also both support asynchronous tests and can be installed and run easily via the command line. Regardless of whether you buy into the BDD nomenclature, these frameworks provide very nice ways to group, execute, and report client- and server-side JavaScript unit tests.

Let's Get Clean

You have to write unit tests, so quit messing around and write some. We will start with this code:

```
function sum(a, b) {
    return a + b;
}
```

Unit tests are all about isolating code and writing tests that only test the chunk of code under test, while factoring out everything else. It sounds simple enough, and with a function such as `sum` (as shown in the preceding code) it is simple indeed:

```
YUI({ logInclude: { TestRunner: true } }).use('test', 'test-console'
  , function(Y) {
    var testCase = new Y.Test.Case(
        {
            name: 'Sum Test'
            , testSimple: function () {
                Y.Assert.areSame(sum(2, 2), 4
                   , '2 + 2 does not equal 4?');
            }
        }
    );
    // Load it up
    Y.Test.Runner.add(testCase);

    (new Y.Test.Console({
        newestOnTop: false
    })).render('#log');

    // Run it
    Y.Test.Runner.run();
});
```

This is the simplest test case possible, so ensure that you can wrap your head around it. A new Y.Test.Case is created, and it is given a name and a set of test functions. Each function is run in turn with the assumption that one or more Y.Assert functions are called to actually test something. The test case is loaded into the local Y.Test.Runner and then all tests are executed.

Given code to test, and code to test that code, we are unfortunately still not quite there, as we need to actually run the tests and view the results. In some server-side-only testing frameworks (e.g., Vows), we would be finished if we were testing server-side-only code. But client-side JavaScript requires an HTML file to tie it all together:

```
<html>
    <head>
        <title>Sum Tests</title>
    </head>
    <body>
        <div id='log' class='yui3-skin-sam'></div>
        <script src='http://yui.yahooapis.com/3.7.3/build/yui/yui-min.js'>
        </script>
        <script src='sum.js'></script>
        <script src='sumTests.js'></script>
    </body>
</html>
```

This HTML ties together YUI3 Test, the code being tested, and the test code. Loading this HTML into a browser will run all the tests and output the test results to log <div>. This represents all the pieces necessary to run client-side unit tests: the code, the test code, and some HTML glue to tie it all together. Load it up in a browser and you will see something similar to Figure 4-1.

Figure 4-1. YUI Test log output

Some pieces are still missing—namely, code coverage and command-line test execution. We will have to revisit those pieces later; first, we must nail down how to write good tests. Fortunately, later we will be able to add those missing pieces for free, so for now let's concentrate on the tests themselves.

Writing Good Tests

Unfortunately, we are rarely called upon to test functions, such as sum, that have no side effects and whose return values are solely a function of their parameters. But even a function as simple as sum has gotchas. What happens if you pass in two strings? What if the parameters are a string and an integer? How about null, undefined, or NaN values? Even the simplest function requires several cases to really run it through its paces.

Even worse, the single unit test metric, code coverage, happily reports 100% code coverage from our single unit test. It's obvious that the single test is not an effective test for the function, but a manager looking at a code coverage report may erroneously conclude that since this function has 100% code coverage it is therefore fully tested and reliable. While unit tests provide value, and code coverage metrics can measure that value to some extent, they obviously do not and cannot tell the whole story.

So, what makes a good unit test? Code coverage, like it or not, is part of the equation. The other part of the equation is the edge and nonedge cases of the parameters. Given that the function's dependencies are mocked out (and are unit-tested themselves to be sane), the parameters and external object stubs are the only knobs you, as a unit tester, have to twist. As an example, let's use our old friend the sum function. This function takes two parameters. Each parameter can be one of six types (number, string, object, undefined, null, or Boolean)—so the perfect set of unit tests will test all combinations of these. But what will it test for? What does it mean, for example, to add null and undefined?

With these questions in mind, perhaps the two most important factors of a good unit test are isolation and scope. As we will see in the following subsections, isolation and scope are closely related.

Isolation

A unit test should load only the bare minimum needed to actually run the test. Any extra code may influence the test or the code being tested, and can cause problems. Typically, unit tests exercise a single method. That method is probably part of a file containing a class or module. That physical unit of code will have to be loaded. Unfortunately, not only does the method under test probably depend on other functions and methods in that file, but it likely has external dependencies (i.e., dependencies in another file) as well.

To avoid loading external dependencies, we can use mocking, stubbing, and test doubles. I will provide details about these strategies later, but for now it's important to note that they are all used in an attempt to keep the code under test isolated from other pieces of code as much as possible.

Unit testing tests the smallest amount of code possible—a method, and nothing else. For that to be feasible, your test code must strive to isolate that method as much as possible.

Scope

The scope of a unit test—what your test is actually testing—must be small. A fully isolated method allows the scope of the test to be as small as possible. Good unit tests test only one method; they should not rely on other methods being called or used. At the bottom level of a single unit test, a single assertion should rely on only the method being tested and any mocks, stubs, or doubles needed for the method to work.

Unit tests are cheap; you should have a lot of them. Just as a "regular" method should not try to do more than one thing, neither should a unit test. Try to test and load the minimal amount of code necessary to successfully execute a unit test for your application. Unit tests typically focus at the level of a single function or method; however, it is up to you to determine the "unit" size that makes the most sense for your testing.

Defining Your Functions

Before we go into further detail, we need to take a step back. It is impossible to write good unit tests unless you know exactly what you are testing and what the result should be. What defines what the result should be? The tests? Having to read and understand tests (if they even exist) to discern how a function should work is not ideal. The comments define what the result should be. This may not be ideal either, if the comments are not kept up to date. So do you have two places to keep up to date—the tests and the comments? Yes, you do. Utilizing test-driven development (TDD) to write tests before code does not obviate the need for comment blocks above functions.

Comment blocks

Our sum function is woefully uncommented, so in this vacuum we have *no idea* what this function should do. Should it add strings? Fractions? Null and undefined? Objects? The function must tell us what it does. So let's try again using Javadoc syntax:

```
/*
 * This function adds two numbers, otherwise return null
 *
 * @param a first Number to add
 * @param b second Number to add
 * @return the numerical sum or null
 */
function sum(a, b) {
    return a + b;
}
```

Now we can actually test this function because we know exactly what to test for: numbers. You cannot write a good unit test for an ill-defined function. It is impossible to write a good unit test in a vacuum. The first rule to writing a good unit test is to have a fully defined function specification.

Does this function actually do what it says? That is what unit tests are for—to determine whether a function behaves properly. And the first step in that regard is to define the function's "proper" behavior. Comments are crucial, and comment bugs are extremely dangerous for both testers and maintainers. Unfortunately, there are no tests to automatically determine whether comments have bugs, but as with code coverage, using a tool such as jsmeter will at least alert you to functions without any comments and to the amount of comments in your code. After code size, the second most telling indicator of bugs in code is missing or incorrect comments, so not only should you have comments, but it is very important that the comments are correct [for more details on this, read this paper (*http://bit.ly/XUdmPf*)].

Ideally, you (or someone else) should be able to write unit tests simply from reading the function comments. These comments will get published from either JSDoc or YUIDoc and Rocco, so make the comments helpful. It is also critical that the function definition is kept up to date. If the parameters or return value change, make sure the comment is also updated.

Writing tests before code, as TDD advocates, may relieve some of the burden of proper commenting. You can utilize the test functions as comments instead of comment blocks, since tests (unlike comments) must stay up to date; otherwise, they will fail. Even if you write tests before any code, a well-commented function header is still beneficial for future maintainers to understand at a glance what your function is up to. Further, having published easily accessible documentation helps in code reuse by allowing other developers to find your code more easily and perhaps use your function instead of writing their own version of that functionality. Other developers need an easily browsable interface to your public methods to help ensure reusability.

Tests

If you write your tests first, they can also be used in the specification for how your functions (or code under test) should function. Since the tests must be maintained to remain in sync with the code under test (otherwise, the tests will fail!), the tests have the final say regarding what the code does, not the comments. In theory, although the comments may fall out of sync, the tests will not, so the tests are to be trusted over the comments. I do not believe you have to fall into this trap: keeping comment blocks up to date should be a normal, standard part of your development practices. The next person to maintain your code will have a much easier time reading your comments while reading your code instead of having to context-switch to another file somewhere else to grok your test code as well.

Positive Testing

Now that we have a well-defined function, let's test the "correct" case. In this instance, we will pass in various flavors of two numbers. Here are the `Y.Assert` statements:

```
Y.Assert.areSame(sum(2, 2), 4, "2 + 2 does not equal 4?");
Y.Assert.areSame(sum(0, 2), 2, "0 + 2 does not equal 2?");
Y.Assert.areSame(sum(-2, 2), 0, "-2 + 2 does not equal 0?");
Y.Assert.areSame(sum(.1, .4), .5, ".1 + .4 does not equal .5?");
```

The preceding code is not earth-shattering; it just tests the basic cases, which is how this function will be called 99% of the time (answering the question, "Does the function do at a very basic level what it claims it does?"). These tests should be the easiest part of your testing, passing in good data and receiving good data back. These should be your first set of tests as these cases are by far the most common. This is where unit tests catch the most bugs; functions that do not fulfill their contract (from the function definition) are obviously broken.

Positive tests should be the first unit tests you write, as they provide a baseline of expected functionality upon which negative and bounds testing can be built. Here, you want to test all the common cases and permutations of how the function is actually supposed to be called and used.

Negative Testing

Negative testing will help locate those hard-to-find bugs typically manifested by the code blowing up somewhere far away from where the bug actually is. Can the code handle values it is not expecting? These tests pass in parameters not expected or wanted by the function under test and ensure that the function under test handles them properly. Here is an example:

```
Y.Assert.areSame(sum(2),null));
Y.Assert.areSame(sum('1', '2'), null));
Y.Assert.areSame(sum('asd', 'weoi'), null));
```

This test quickly reveals that our sum function is not behaving properly. The key is that we know what "properly" is for the sum function: it should be returning null for non-numbers. Without the comment block describing this function's behavior, we would have no idea whether this function was misbehaving.

Negative testing will typically not find the same number of bugs as positive testing, but the bugs negative testing does find are usually nastier. These are the hard-to-find bugs when something is not working at a much higher level. They test corner cases, or cases when unexpected things happen. In such situations, what does the function do? Besides meeting its contract, will it behave sanely with unexpected input or state?

Code Coverage

Code coverage is a measure, typically a percentage, of the lines of code executed versus not executed. It is generally used to view how much code is touched by any given test. More tests can be written to "cover" more uncovered lines of code, typically to a certain percentage. We will discuss code coverage in more depth in Chapter 5, but for now, suffice it to say that code coverage is another key to effective unit tests. While code coverage can be misleading when the percentages are high, it is much more applicable (and scary) when the covered percentage is low. A unit test with less than 50% code coverage is a red flag; 60% to 80% code coverage is the sweet spot, and anything over 80% is gravy. The law of diminishing returns can apply to unit testing when trying to get unit tests above 80% coverage. Remember, unit testing is not the only arrow in your QA quiver, but it is one of the few QA metrics that developers are responsible for. In Chapter 5, we will look at how to measure and visualize code coverage.

It is important that code coverage information be generated automatically, without any human intervention. Once people get involved, things deteriorate rapidly. The process for generating code coverage must be seamless.

Real-World Testing

Unfortunately, while it's an ideal to aim for not all functions are as cut and dried as the sum function. Yet note that even a one-line, zero-dependency function is not as easy to unit-test properly as you might think. This again demonstrates the difficulty of unit testing in general and JavaScript unit testing in particular: if a one-line function has this many gotchas, what about real-world functions?

Dependencies

We touched on the problem with dependencies earlier in the book. Almost every function has external dependencies that unit testing does not want to test. Unit testers can extract dependencies by utilizing mocks and stubs. Note that I said, "Unit testers can extract" here, because the author of the code under test also has several tools to extract dependencies from code, as detailed in Chapter 2. Once all of those avenues have been exhausted, the burden falls on the unit tests to isolate the code in question for testing.

Use of command query separation highlights the differences between mocks and stubs: mocks are used for commands and stubs are used for queries.

Doubles

Test doubles is a generic term for objects used by tests to stub or mock out dependencies (similar to stunt doubles in movies). Doubles can act as stubs and mocks at the same time, ensuring that external methods and APIs are called, determining how many times they have been called, capturing called parameters, and returning canned responses. A test double that records and captures information about how methods were called is called a *spy*.

Mock objects

Mock objects are used to verify that your function is correctly calling an external API. Tests involving mock objects verify that the function under test is passing the correct parameters (either by type or by value) to the external object. In the command query world, mocks test commands. In an event hub world, mocks test events being fired.

Take a look at this example:

```
// actual production code:
function buyNowClicked(event) {
    hub.fire('addToShoppingCart', { item: event.target.id });
}
Y.one('#products').delegate('click', buyNowClicked, '.buy-now-button');

/* ... and in your test code: */
testAddToShoppingCart: function() {
    var hub = Y.Mock();
    Y.Mock.expect(hub,
```

```
            {
              method: "fire"
              , args: [ "addToShoppingCart" , Y.Mock.Value.String]
            }
        );
        Y.one('.buy-now-button').simulate('click');
        Y.Mock.verify(hub);
```

This code tests the flow of a Buy Now button (an element that contains the buy-now-button CSS class). When that button is clicked, the addToShoppingCart event is expected to be fired with a string parameter. Here, the event hub is mocked out and the fire method is expected to be called with a single string parameter (the ID of the Buy Now button).

Stubs

Stubs are used to return canned values back to the tested function. Stubs do not care how the external object's method was called; stubs simply return a canned object of your choosing. Typically this object is something the caller expects for a set of test cases for positive testing and an object with unexpected values during another set of tests for negative testing.

Testing with stubs requires you to substitute the real objects with your stubbed-out replacements, whose only joy in life is to return a canned value to keep the method under test moving along.

Take a look at the following code:

```
    function addToShoppingCart(item) {
        if (item.inStock()) {
            this.cart.push(item);
            return item;
        } else {
            return null;
        }
    }
```

One way to test this is to stub out the item.inStock method to test both paths through the code:

```
    testAddOk: function() {
        var shoppingCart = new ShoppingCart()
        , item = { inStock: function() { return true; } }
        , back = shoppingCart.addToShoppingCart(item)
        ;

        Y.Assert.areSame(back, item, "Item not returned");
        Y.ArrayAssert.contains(item, "Item not pushed into cart!");
    }
    , testAddNok: function() {
        var shoppingCart = new ShoppingCart()
```

```
            , item = { inStock: function() { return false; } }
            , back = shoppingCart.addToShoppingCart(item)
        ;

        Y.Assert.isNull(back, "Item returned is not null");
        Y.ArrayAssert.isEmpty(shoppingCart.cart, "Cart not empty!");
    }
```

This testing captures both branches of the function by stubbing out the `item` object. Of course, it's not just parameters that can can be stubbed; typically, all external dependencies are stubbed or mocked out.

Spies

A test spy wraps the "real" object, overriding some method and letting others pass through. A spy is typically attached to a real object and intercepts some method calls (sometimes even only intercepting method calls with specific parameters) to return a canned response or keep track of the number of times a method has been called. Non-intercepted methods are simply handed off to the real object for normal processing. Spies are great for objects that have some "heavy" operations that you want to mock out and lighter-weight operations that the actual object can easily handle itself.

You are not limited to any of these doubles in your tests! If you need to create a double that has some features of a mock and some of a stub, go for it! Do you want to track how many times an external function was called? Use a spy! Doubles are typically specific to a test or set of tests and are not as reusable as a more limited mock or stub, but in many cases they are necessary for proper testing.

Here is a snippet of test code using a spy for our `sum` function:

```
        , testWithSpy: function() {
            var origSum = sum
                , sumSpy = function(a, b) {
                    Y.Assert.areSame(a, 2, 'first arg is 2!');
                    Y.Assert.areSame(a, 9, 'second arg is 9!');
                    return origSum(a, b);
                }
            ;
            sum = sumSpy;
            Y.Assert.areSame(sum(2, 9), 11
                , '2 + 9 does not equal 11?');
            sum = origSum;  // reset it (or use teardown)
        }
```

This spy is local to this test; it simply verifies that the passed arguments were expected. A spy does not need to call the underlying "real" method if it is a heavyweight operation (perhaps a network call), and instead can just return canned data, both expected and unexpected (e.g., simulating a network failure).

The Jasmine test framework has good support for creating doubles and spies. We will get to play with those features a bit later in this chapter.

Asynchronous Testing

JavaScript relies heavily on events. Asynchronous testing involves suspending the testing flow and waiting for an event to fire, then resuming the flow in the event handler, probably with an assert or two thrown in for good measure.

Using YUI Test

Using YUI Test, an asynchronous test looks like this:

```
testAsync: function () {
    var test = this, myButton = Y.one('#button');
    myButton.on('click', function() {
        this.resume(function() {
            Y.Assert.isTrue(true, 'You sunk my battleship!');
        });
    }
    myButton.simulate('click');
    this.wait(2000);
}
```

This code will simulate a button click and wait two seconds. If the test is not resumed by then, the test will fail; otherwise; the test is resumed and a (hopefully successful) assertion is tested. Clearly, we can do far more interesting things than simulating a click on a button and verifying that a handler was called.

If your code does a lot of Cascading Style Sheets (CSS) manipulation in response to events, asynchronous testing is the way to go. However, for any hardcore UI testing, integration testing using a tool such as Selenium is preferable to unit tests, which can be more brittle and incomplete in these situations. Further, not all DOM events can be simulated; in those cases other types of testing are required.

Regardless, asynchronous testing is necessary when testing event-based code such as the following:

```
hub.on('log', function(severity, message) {
    console.log(severity + ': ' + message);
});
```

Testing this code requires mocking out the global `console` object (it's a command, not a query):

```
console = Y.Mock();
testLogHandler: function () {
    var sev = 'DEBUG', message = 'TEST';
    Y.Mock.expect(console, { method: log
        , arguments: [ sev, message ] });
    hub.fire('log', sev, message);
```

```
    this.wait(function() {
        Y.Mock.verify(console);
    }, 1000);
}
```

We can use a "real" event hub, as we are not testing hub functionality here. This test merely verifies that the mocked-out object's log method was called with the expected arguments, which is what mock objects are for: testing that the interface is being used correctly.

Running Tests: Client-Side JavaScript

Once you have written a set of test cases and event-aggregated them into a set of test suites, then what? Running tests in your browser by loading up the HTML glue code is amusing and necessary while developing your code, but it does not lend itself at all to automation. There are several strategies that you can use to make your tests part of an automated build process.

PhantomJS

PhantomJS (*http://bit.ly/XUdEp4*) is a *headless* WebKit browser—that is, a browser that is accessed programmatically. This is an excellent sandbox within which to run unit tests without having a browser up and running somewhere. Note that unit tests typically focus on core functionality abstracted from the UI. Obviously, PhantomJS cannot and does not attempt to handle all the various CSS levels as they are implemented in each browser (although it is very up to date with most standards). Testing fancy CSS or browser-specific CSS requires that browser, and it is unclear whether a unit test is even a valid way to test this type of functionality. That being said, PhantomJS/WebKit can handle a ton of modern features; only the latest cutting-edge CSS 3D transformations, local storage, and WebGL are not supported. Of course, what is supported all depends on the version of WebKit used when building PhantomJS, which is constantly evolving and adding new features.

PhantomJS no longer requires an X server running anywhere, so setup cannot be easier! Simply download the binary for your operating system and you are ready to go. You can also compile phantomjs from source, but prepare to wait awhile, as a good chunk of Qt must be compiled as well. The actual phantomjs binary is tiny compared to the giant chunk of required Qt.

Here is our complex JavaScript file to test in *sum.js*:

```
YUI().add('sum', function(Y) {
    Y.MySum = function(a, b) { return a + b };
});
```

Once you are set up, running your YUI tests through PhantomJS is easy with one little trick. Here again is our HTML glue for the sum tests, with a single addition:

```html
<html>
    <head>
        <title>Sum Tests</title>
    </head>
    <body class="yui3-skin-sam">
        <div id="log"></div>
        <script src="http://yui.yahooapis.com/3.4.1/build/yui/yui-min.js">
        </script>
        <script src="sum.js"></script>
        <script src="phantomOutput.js"></script>
        <script src="sumTests.js"></script>
    </body>
</html>
```

And here's another JavaScript file to be loaded, *phantomOutput.js*, which defines a small YUI phantomjs module:

```javascript
YUI().add('phantomjs', function(Y) {
    var TR;
    if (typeof(console) !== 'undefined') {
        TR = Y.Test.Runner;
        TR.subscribe(TR.COMPLETE_EVENT, function(obj) {
            console.log(Y.Test.Format.JUnitXML(obj.results));
        });
    }
});
```

The sole purpose of this module is to output test results, in JUnit XML format, to the console upon test completion (YUI supports other output formats that you can use instead; use whatever your build tool understands—for example, Hudson/Jenkins understands JUnit XML). This dependency must be declared in your test file. Here is *sumTests.js*:

```javascript
YUI({
    logInclude: { TestRunner: true },
}).use('test', 'sum', 'console', 'phantomjs', function(Y) {

    var suite = new Y.Test.Suite('sum');
    suite.add(new Y.Test.Case({
        name:'simple test',
        testIntAdd : function () {
            Y.log('testIntAdd');
            Y.Assert.areEqual(Y.MySum(2 ,2), 4);
        },
        testStringAdd : function () {
            Y.log('testStringAdd');
            Y.Assert.areEqual(Y.MySum('my', 'sum'), 'mysum');
        }
```

```
        }));

        Y.Test.Runner.add(suite);

        //Initialize the console
        var yconsole = new Y.Console({
            newestOnTop: false
        });

        yconsole.render('#log');
        Y.Test.Runner.run();
    });
```

PhantomJS will pick up the console output and can then persist it to a file for later processing. Unfortunately, including the phantomjs module in your tests is not ideal. In Chapter 8 we will make this process more dynamic.

Here is the PhantomJS script to grab the test output:

```
var page = new WebPage();
page.onConsoleMessage = function(msg) {
    console.log(msg);
    phantom.exit(0);
};
page.open(phantom.args[0], function (status) {
    // Check for page load success
    if (status !== "success") {
        console.log("Unable to load file");
        phantom.exit(1);
    }
});
```

That was quite simple! This PhantomJS script takes the URL to the "glue" HTML test file as the only command-line parameter, loads it up, and, if successful, waits to capture the console output. This script just prints it to the screen, but if you're running it as part of a larger process you can redirect the standard output from this script to a file, or this PhantomJS script itself can write the output to a file.

PhantomJS has no access to the JavaScript running on the loaded page itself, so we utilize the console to pass the test output from the page being loaded back to PhantomJS-land, where it can be persisted.

Here is how I ran the whole thing against some tests for a sample Toolbar module in the JUTE repository (more on that later) on my Mac:

```
% phantomjs ~/phantomOutput.js sumTests.html
```

Here is the output I received (although not fancily formatted):

```
<?xml version="1.0" encoding="UTF-8"?>
  <testsuites>
    <testsuite name="simple test" tests="2" failures="0" time="0.005">
```

```
        <testcase name="testIsObject" time="0"></testcase>
        <testcase name="testMessage" time="0.001"></testcase>
      </testsuite>
    </testsuites>
```

This is the JUnit XML output for the two unit tests that were executed.

Adding snapshots, so you can actually see what happened, is easy. Here is the whole script with snapshot support added. The only difference is that here we "render" the output after any console output:

```
var page = new WebPage();
page.viewportSize = { width: 1024, height: 768 };

page.onConsoleMessage = function(msg) {
    console.log(msg);
    setTimeout(function() {
        page.render('output.png');
        phantom.exit();
    }, 500);
};

page.open(phantom.args[0], function (status) {
    // Check for page load success
    if (status !== "success") {
        console.log("Unable to load file");
        phantom.exit(1);
    }
});
```

First I set the viewport size, and after getting the test results the page is rendered into a PNG file (this needs to be wrapped in a timeout block to give the render step time to finish before exiting). This script will generate snapshots after each test. PhantomJS can also render PDF and JPG files. Figure 4-2 shows our lovely snapshot.

Mighty beautiful! By default, PhantomJS backgrounds are transparent, but we can clearly see the YUI Test output as it went to the <div id="log"> element in the HTML.

But wait! What about those awesome log messages YUI is outputting to the logger? We want to capture those too! We need to revisit the phantomjs YUI module:

```
YUI().add('phantomjs', function(Y) {

    var yconsole = new Y.Console();
    yconsole.on('entry',
        function(obj) {
            console.log(JSON.stringify(obj.message));
        }
    );

    if (typeof(console) !== 'undefined') {
        var TR = Y.Test.Runner;
```

```
    TR.subscribe(TR.COMPLETE_EVENT, function(obj) {
        console.log(JSON.stringify(
            { results: Y.Test.Format.JUnitXML(obj.results) }));
    });
  }
}, '1.0', { requires: [ 'console' ] });
```

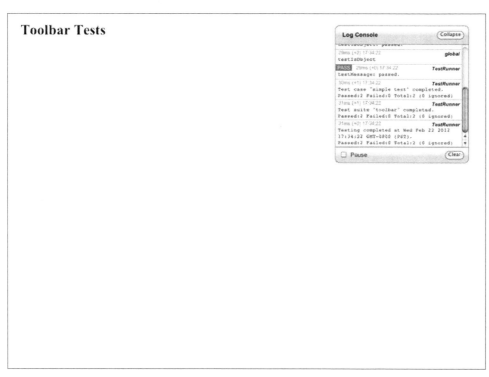

Figure 4-2. PhantomJS screenshot

The biggest addition is the `Y.Console` object we've created solely to capture YUI Test's logging messages. Listening for the `entry` event gives us all the messages in an object, which we stringify using JSON (note that the JSON object is included in WebKit; this JavaScript is running the PhantomJS WebKit browser).

Now two types of messages emitted to the console are passed "back" to our PhantomJS script: logging messages and the final JUnit XML results. Our PhantomJS server-side code must keep track of both types of messages.

Here is the first message:

```
{
    "time":"2012-02-23T02:38:03.222Z",
    "message":"Testing began at Wed Feb 22 2012 18:38:03 GMT-0800
      (PST).",
```

```
            "category":"info",
            "sourceAndDetail":"TestRunner",
            "source":"TestRunner",
            "localTime":"18:38:03",
            "elapsedTime":24,
            "totalTime":24
    }
```

It's not too exciting by itself, but the entire list of messages together is a great resource to dump into a log for each test suite. Details of message properties are available at the YUI (*http://bit.ly/XUdHRN*) website.

Here is the updated onConsoleMessage function from the PhantomJS script (that function is the only thing that has changed in the script):

```
page.onConsoleMessage = function(msg) {
    var obj = JSON.parse(msg);
    if (obj.results) {
        window.setTimeout(function () {
            console.log(obj.results);
            page.render('output.png');
            phantom.exit();
        }, 200);
    } else {
        console.log(msg);
    }
};
```

Besides parsing the JSON from the console output, the script now only exits when it gets the final test results. Of course, you need to ensure that nothing else (such as your tests or the code you are testing) is writing to console.log! You could also get crazier and take a snapshot before/during/after each test to view the actual test progress (you will know what stage each test is at due to the log messages).

PhantomJS is an excellent way to run your unit tests during an automated build process. During a build, you can feed this script a list of files/URLs for PhantomJS to execute in the WebKit browser. But you should also run your unit tests in "real" browsers at some point before pushing code out to your production environment. We'll look at that next.

Selenium

Using Selenium Remote Control (RC) or Selenium2 (WebDriver), you can farm out your unit tests to real browsers: either a browser running on your local machine or one running remotely. Running the Selenium JAR on a machine with Firefox, Safari, Chrome, or IE installed, you can easily launch your unit tests in that browser and then capture the results to be persisted locally. Selenium2/WebDriver is the preferred/current tool provided by Selenium; do not choose Selenium RC if you are just getting started with Selenium.

Here is how it works. Start Selenium somewhere where the browser in which you want to run your tests is installed. To do this you must download the latest version of the Selenium JAR from the SeleniumHQ website (*http://bit.ly/XUdI8k*). You want the latest version of the Selenium server, which at the time of this writing is version 2.28. Now fire it up:

```
% java -jar ~/selenium-server-standalone-2.28.0.jar
```

This will start the Selenium server on the default port of 4444. You will need to reach this port from whatever machine you run the Selenium client on, so keep that firewall open. You can change this port with the `-port` option.

Now that the Selenium server is up and running, you need to tell it to open a browser and fetch a URL. This means you need a web server running somewhere to serve your test files. It doesn't need to be anything fancy—remember, these are only unit tests; you are not serving up your entire application. However, it is easiest to have your test code under the same document root as your production code to make serving the tests easier during development. Keep in mind that you probably do not want to actually push your tests into production. Therefore, a nice setup is a *test* directory under your document root containing a mirror of your production directory structure with the tests for the corresponding modules in the same place in the mirrored hierarchy. When bundling for production, simply do not include the *test* directory. The structure looks like Figure 4-3.

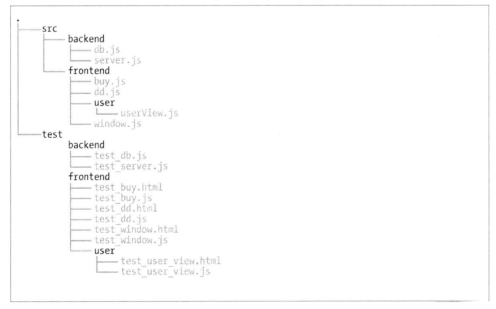

Figure 4-3. Source code directory layout for testability

As you can see in Figure 4-3, the *test* tree mirrors the *src* tree. Each leaf in the test hierarchy contains (at least) two files: the JavaScript tests and the HTML glue file for those tests. The HTML glue file for *test_user_view.html* looks like this:

```html
<!DOCTYPE HTML PUBLIC "-//W3C//DTD HTML 4.01 Transitional//EN">
<html lang="en">
    <head>
        <meta http-equiv="Content-Type"
          content="text/html; charset=ISO-8859-1">
        <title>User View Tests</title>
    </head>
    <body class="yui3-skin-sam">
        <h1>Test User View</h1>
        <div id="log" />
        <script src="http://yui.yahooapis.com/3.4.0/build/yui/yui-min.js">
        </script>
        <script src="../../../src/frontend/user/userView.js"></script>
        <script src="test_user_view.js"></script>
    </body>
</html>
```

This HTML uses relative paths to pull in the file/module to be tested: *user_view.js*. When the local web server serves, this file all the local files are found and the tests are run.

We now have a URL to feed to Selenium so that the remote browser controlled by Selenium can fetch and run our test(s). Using the `webdriverjs` (*http://bit.ly/XUdKgq*) Node.js npm package, we can easily send URLs to a Selenium server to be executed:

```js
var webdriverjs = require("webdriverjs")
    , url = '...';

browser = webdriverjs.remote({
    host: 'localhost'
    , port: 4444
    , desiredCapabilities: { browserName: 'firefox' }
});
browser.init().url(url).end();
```

This code will contact the Selenium server running on port 4444 at `localhost` and tell it to fire up Firefox and load the specified URL. We're halfway there! All we need to do now is capture the test output—those useful log messages that YUI Test emits—capture a snapshot, and persist it all locally.

As in the PhantomJS case, we need to somehow communicate all of that output (test results, logging messages, and snapshot data) back to the Selenium driver. Unlike PhantomJS, Selenium cannot read the console remotely, so we have to perform another trick to manage this communication. Here is the equivalent to the `phantomjs` module included by our test JavaScript for Selenium:

```js
YUI().add('selenium', function(Y) {
```

```
        var messages = [];
            , yconsole = new Y.Console();

        yconsole.on('entry', function(obj) { messages.push(obj.message); });

        var TR = Y.Test.Runner;
        TR.subscribe(TR.COMPLETE_EVENT, function(obj) {
            // Data to dump
            var data = escape(JSON.stringify(
                {
                    messages: messages
                    , results: Y.Test.Format.JUnitXML(obj.results)
                }
            ));

            // Create a new Node
            var item = Y.Node.create('<div id="testresults"></div>');
            item.setContent(data);

            // Append to document
            Y.one('body').append(item);
        });
    }, '1.0', { requires: [ 'console', 'node' ] });
```

OK, did you spot the trick? Instead of writing the data we want to capture to con
sole.log, we save all the messages we get from YUI Test into an array. When the tests
are complete, we create a <div> with a specific ID and dump the JSON-ified version of
all the messages and results in there. Finally, we append this new element to the current
document. The two most important points about this are that the <div> must be visible
and we must escape the entire contents of the resultant JSON string, as the JUnit XML
output is—surprise, surprise—XML. We do not want the browser to attempt to parse it;
otherwise, it will get lost since it is not valid HTML.

Now let's look at the other half to see how it all fits together. Here is the entire client-
side Selenium runner:

```
var webdriverjs = require("webdriverjs")
    , url = '...'
    , browser = webdriverjs.remote({
        host: 'localhost'
        , port: 4444
        , desiredCapabilities: { browserName: 'firefox' }
    })
;

browser.init().url(url).waitFor('#testresults', 10000, function(found) {
    var res;
    if (found) {
        res = browser.getText('#testresults',
            function(text) {
                // Do something smarter than console.log!
```

```
                console.log(JSON.parse(unescape(text.value)));
            }
        );
    } else {
        console.log('TEST RESULTS NOT FOUND');
    }
}).end();
```

Using the same outline from earlier, after we load the URL we `waitFor` the element with the ID `testresults` to show up in the DOM (here we will wait for up to 10 seconds; your mileage may vary). When it shows up, we pull out its text.

The first thing we have to do is to `unescape` it to get our XML back. Now we can re-create the hash containing a `messages` property, which is the array of YUI Test messages, and a `results` property that contains the JUnit XML output for this test run.

Using this runner, you can run your tests in a real Firefox, Chrome, or IE browser from the command line, as long as the Selenium server is running somewhere reachable on the same host as one of those browsers.

To utilize the Chrome browser, you need to add an extra executable (the Chrome driver) somewhere in your path. You can download the latest version of the Chrome driver for your operating system from the Chromium open-source project site (*http://bit.ly/ XUdKwX*). Just add it somewhere in your `PATH` and use `chrome` as the `browserName` in the `desiredCapabilities` hash.

Finally, what about snapshots? Selenium conveniently provides snapshot support. So let's take some pictures! Unlike PhantomJS, our simplistic Selenium runner only knows when the tests end, so we will take the snapshot then.

Here is the full script with snapshot support. Note that Selenium only supports the PNG format. After we get the test results, we grab the snapshot and write it to a local file named *snapshot.png*:

```
var webdriverjs = require("webdriverjs")
    , url
    , browser = webdriverjs.remote({
        host: 'localhost'
        , port: 4444
        , desiredCapabilities: { browserName: 'firefox' }
    })
;

browser.init().url(url).waitFor('#testresults', 10000, function(found) {
    if (found) {
        var res = browser.getText('#testresults'
            ,function(text) {
                // Get log messages and JUnit XML results
                console.log(JSON.parse(unescape(text.value)));
```

```
                            // Now take the snapshot
                            browser.screenshot(
                                function(screenshot) {
                                    var fs = require('fs')
                                        , filename = 'snapshot.png'
                                        , imageData
                                    ;

                                    try {
                                        imageData  =
                                            new Buffer(screenshot.value
                                                , 'base64');
                                        fs.writeFileSync(filename, imageData);
                                    } catch(e) {
                                        console.log('Error getting snapshot: '
                                            + e);
                                    }
                                }
                            );
                        }
                    );
                } else {
                    console.log('TEST RESULTS NOT FOUND');
                }
            }).end();
```

Again, during your build, you will use a smarter way to pass all your tests to these drivers rather than having the URL or filename hardcoded into them.

An issue with the use of Selenium concerns speed: starting up a browser session for each test or set of tests can be a very slow process. Something to keep an eye on is the Ghost Driver project (*http://bit.ly/XUdKNA*). This driver, similar to the Chrome driver, allows Selenium to use PhantomJS as a backend. This, of course, significantly speeds up Selenium backend startup and teardown times. Not all Selenium primitives are supported at the time of this writing, but most if not all of the basic ones are. If the speed of Selenium tests is important to you, help the project along!

Another option for speeding up Selenium tests is to farm out your tests to a lot of runners in parallel using the Selenium grid. We will examine better ways to run tests in an automated and distributed fashion in Chapter 5, where we will discuss code coverage, and in Chapter 6 and Chapter 8, where we will discuss other types of testing and automation, respectively.

Mobile

You can also run your unit tests on your phone or tablet using Selenium, as, yes, there is a driver for that.

iOS. The iOS Selenium driver runs either in the iPhone simulator or on an iPhone device itself. The details are available at the code.google selenium project site (*http://bit.ly/XUdL43*). The driver uses a UIWebView application to encase your web application and accept Selenium commands. To run Selenium tests on an actual device you will need a provisioning profile from Apple, which means you must be a member of the iOS Developer Program; an individual membership (*http://bit.ly/XUdJck*) costs $99 at the time of this writing.

Install at least version 4.2 (4.5 is the newest version available at the time of this writing) and you can check out and build the iPhone driver from this Subversion repository (*http://bit.ly/XUdLB0*).

After following the instructions you will have built the WebDriver application, which can then be installed either in the simulator or on an iDevice. You connect to it just like any other remote Selenium driver, so the simulator running the WebDriver application does not need to be on the host where you execute your tests. Here is how it looks using `webdriverjs`:

```
var browser = webdriverjs.remote({
    host: 'localhost'
    , port: 3001
    , desiredCapabilities: { browserName: 'iPhone' }  // or 'iPad'
});
```

And now your Selenium tests are running in iOS. Note that the default port of the iPhone WebDriver is 3001. Alternatively, you can specify `iPhone` or `iPad` to target devices individually. Unfortunately, there is no headless option, but you can keep an emulator up and running with the WebDriver application running within it so that you can be connected and can run tests anytime.

Android. Details of running a Selenium WebDriver on Android are available on the code.google selenium site (*http://bit.ly/XUdLRE*). After downloading the Android SDK and setting up the emulator, you have two choices: run the stock Selenium Android driver in Android or run an Android-specific test framework. If you are running these same tests on multiple operating systems you will want to stick with the standard Selenium Android WebDriver. Only if all your tests are specific to Android can you choose to use the Android test framework.

Let's investigate the Selenium driver further. First, you need to build the driver application bundle (*.apk* file) and install it on your device or in the simulator.

At this point, connecting is easy:

```
var browser = webdriverjs.remote({
    host: 'localhost'
    , port: 8080
    , desiredCapabilities: { browserName: 'android' }
});
```

This assumes the emulator is running on your local host. Of course, it does not have to be, and if you are connecting directly to an actual device you will need to be on the same network and know your Android's IP address. If you have issues, refer to the URL at the beginning of this subsection, which has lots of great information.

An even better option is to run the Android simulator headlessly so that you can run all your tests remotely from almost anywhere. If you run the emulator using the -no-window option, you can start the WebDriver application using this code (all on one line):

```
$ adb shell am start -a android.intent.action.MAIN -n
org.openqa.selenium.android.app.MainActivity
```

Now you can connect to it locally or remotely to run your tests.

Running Tests: Server-Side JavaScript

The process for server-side JavaScript unit testing is not much different from the process for unit-testing any other server-side code. Your tests and code all reside and run on the same host, making this much simpler than client-side unit testing. I will demonstrate how this works using Jasmine for server-side JavaScript unit testing.

Although you could cook up your own assertions and test framework, you could probably also build your own airplane; do not reinvent the wheel with an inferior version. There are plenty of other test frameworks you can utilize if you do not like Jasmine, so pick one.

Jasmine

Installing Jasmine is easy:

```
% npm install jasmine-node -g
```

Jasmine gives us a nice way to run tests from the command line and output test results in a number of interesting ways: namely, for human or automated consumption.

The idea is that you write a bunch of unit tests using Jasmine-provided syntax and semantics and then point the Jasmine command line to the root directory (or any subdirectory) where those tests live. Jasmine will recurse down the directory tree and run all the tests found within.

By default, Jasmine expects your test files to contain the string *spec*, as in *sum-spec.js*—this convention is a BDD artifact and you can override it with the --matchall option.

Go to the Jasmine website (*http://bit.ly/XUdJJo*) to see all of what Jasmine can do. For now, we will look at some short examples, starting with our favorite piece of code: the sum function! Here is the *mySum.js* file:

```
exports.sum = function(a, b) { return a + b };
```

Exciting stuff! Here is some Jasmine code to test integer addition:

```
var mySum = require('./mySum');

describe("Sum suite", function() {
  it("Adds Integers!", function() {
    expect(mySum.sum(7, 11)).toEqual(18);
  });
});
```

And finally, here is how the test is run:

```
% jasmine-node .
.


Finished in 0.009 seconds
1 test, 1 assertion, 0 failures
```

The test passed! We are definitely on to something. Jasmine matchers (`toEqual` in the previous example) are equivalent to YUI Test assertions. Plus, you can write your own custom matchers. Jasmine's `describe` is equivalent to YUI Test suites and the specs (the `it` functions) are similar to YUI Test's test cases. Jasmine also supports `beforeEach` and `afterEach` functions that are executed before and after each spec, similarly to YUI Test's `setUp` and `tearDown` functions.

Dependencies

Factoring out dependent objects of the Node.js code under test can become more demanding as dependencies are pulled in via the `require` function. You'll need to either change your source code for testing (not good), or mock out the `require` function itself (painful). Fortunately, the latter option has already been done for us in a very nice npm package called Mockery (*http://bit.ly/XUdMoI*). Mockery intercepts all calls to `require`, allowing easy insertion of mocked versions of your code's dependencies instead of the real deal.

Here is our modified sum function, which now reads a JSON string from a file and adds the a and b properties found therein:

```
var fs = require('fs');
exports.sum = function(file) {
    var data = JSON.parse(fs.readFileSync(file, 'utf8'));
    return data.a + data.b;
};
```

Here is a simple Jasmine test for this:

```
var mySum = require('./mySumFS');

    describe("Sum suite File", function() {
        it("Adds Integers!", function() {
        expect(mySum.sum("numbers")).toEqual(12);
    });
});
```

where the content of the file numbers is:

```
{"a":5,"b":7}
```

Fair enough—Jasmine runs the test, it passes, and all is good. But we are simultaneously testing too much—namely the fs dependency is being pulled in and utilized and unit testing is all about dependency isolation. We do not want anything brought into the fs dependency to affect our tests. Granted, this is an extreme case, but let's follow through with the logic.

Using Mockery as part of our Jasmine test we can handle the require call and replace the fs module with a mocked-out version of our own. Here is our new Jasmine script:

```
var mockery = require('mockery');
mockery.enable();

describe("Sum suite File", function() {

    beforeEach(function() {
        mockery.registerAllowable('./mySumFS', true);
    });

    afterEach(function() {
        mockery.deregisterAllowable('./mySumFS');
    });

    it("Adds Integers!", function() {

        var filename = "numbers"
            , fsMock = {
                readFileSync: function (path, encoding) {
                    expect(path).toEqual(filename);
                    expect(encoding).toEqual('utf8');
                    return JSON.stringify({ a: 9, b: 3 });
                }
            }
        ;

        mockery.registerMock('fs', fsMock);

        var mySum = require('./mySumFS');
```

```
        expect(mySum.sum(filename)).toEqual(12);

        mockery.deregisterMock('fs');
    });
```

Here, we have added the mockery object, enabled it, and told Mockery to ignore the requireing of the object under test. By default, Mockery will print an error message if *any* module being required is not known to it (via registerAllowable or register Mock); since we do not want to mock out the object under test, we tell Mockery to load it without complaining.

Because we're creating new mocks for the fs module for each test (as we will see shortly, instead of reusing the same one for each test), we have to pass the true second parameter to registerAllowable so that the deregisterAllowable method will clean up properly.

Finally, there is the test itself. It now tests that the fs.readFileSync method was called correctly and returns canned data back to the sum function. The code under test is blissfully unaware that any of this is happening as it plows forward.

Here is a test for string addition:

```
it("Adds Strings!", function() {

    var filename = "strings"
      , fsMock = {
            readFileSync: function (path, encoding) {
                expect(path).toEqual(filename);
                expect(encoding).toEqual('utf8');
                return JSON.stringify({ a: 'testable'
                                      , b: 'JavaScript' });
            }
        }
    ;

    mockery.registerMock('fs', fsMock);

    var mySum = require('./mySumFS');
    expect(mySum.sum(filename)).toEqual('testableJavaScript');

    mockery.deregisterMock('fs');
});
```

Again, here we're registering a new mock for the fs object that will return a canned object for string concatenation after checking the parameters to readFileSync.

Alternatively, if we wanted to actually read the JSON objects off the disk, before we enabled Mockery we could have required the real fs object and delegated the calls from the mocked-out readFileSync method to that object—this would be a test spy. However, keeping the test data within the tests themselves is useful, especially for small tests like these.

If your mocked objects are large or you would like to keep a library of them, you can also tell Mockery to substitute your mocked object for the original using this code:

```
mockery.registerSubstitute('fs', 'fs-mock');
```

As shown in the Mockery documentation, now every require('fs') call will actually require('fs-mock').

Mockery is an excellent tool. Just remember that after you enable it *all* require calls will be routed through Mockery!

Spies

Spies in Jasmine are most useful for code injection. They are essentially a stub and a mock, all rolled into one zany object.

So, we have decided that our sum function that reads JSON from a file and our sum function that reads operands from the parameter list can be combined like so:

```
exports.sum = function(func, data) {
    var data = JSON.parse(func.apply(this, data));
    return data.a + data.b;
};

exports.getByFile = function(file) {
    var fs = require('fs');
    return fs.readFileSync(file, 'utf8');
};

exports.getByParam = function(a, b) {
    return JSON.stringify({a: a, b: b});
};
```

We have generalized the data input and now only have the sum operation in one place. This not only lets us add new operations (subtract, multiply, etc.), but also separates operations for getting the data from operations performed on the data.

Our Jasmine spec file for this (without the Mockery stuff for clarity) looks like this:

```
mySum = require('./mySumFunc');

describe("Sum suite Functions", function() {
    it("Adds By Param!", function() {
        var sum = mySum.sum(mySum.getByParam, [6,6]));
        expect(sum).toEqual(12);
    });

    it("Adds By File!", function() {
        var sum = mySum.sum(mySum.getByFile, ["strings"]));
        expect(sum).toEqual("testableJavaScript");
    });
});
```

And of course, the strings file contains the following:

```
{"a":"testable","b":"JavaScript"}
```

But something is not quite right. We are not doing a good job of isolating the mySum functions for testing. Of course, we need individual tests for the various mySum inputters: getByParam and getByFile. But to test the actual sum function, we need those functions. So we would like to mock and stub out those functions when testing the sum function so that it is tested in isolation.

This scenario is a good time to break out Jasmine spies. Using spies, we can test those two helper functions to ensure that they are called with the correct parameters, and allow the test code to either return called values or let the call pass through to the underlying function.

Here is a modified version of the test function with getByParam using a spy:

```
it("Adds By Param!", function() {
    var params = [ 8, 4 ]
        , expected = 12
    ;

    spyOn(mySum, 'getByParam').andCallThrough();
    expect(mySum.sum(mySum.getByParam, params)).toEqual(expected);
    expect(mySum.getByParam).toHaveBeenCalled();
    expect(mySum.getByParam.mostRecentCall.args).toEqual(params);
});
```

After setting up the spy on mySum.getByParam and directing it to call through to the actual implementation, we can verify that the helper function has been called and that the correct arguments were used.

Replacing the andCallThrough line with:

```
spyOn(mySum, 'getByParam').andReturn('{"a":8,"b":4}');
```

lets our test code return canned data and skips the call to getByParam completely. You can also supply an alternate function to be called whose return value will be passed back to the caller if you must calculate a canned return value—very handy!

Jasmine has more tricks up its sleeve, including easy test disabling, mocking setTimer and setInterval for easier testing, and asynchronous test support, so go to its home page and check it all out. Also, Jasmine is not just for server-side JavaScript testing! It can run within a browser for client-side JavaScript unit testing as well; however, extracting test output while running Jasmine in a browser is not as easy as using YUI Test for automated builds. Jasmine does support custom test reporters that can export results, unlike YUI Test, which supports that out of the box.

Output

By default, Jasmine will dump test results to the screen, which is great for developing tests but not so great for automated runs. By using -junitreport, however, you can instruct Jasmine to dump test results in the widely supported JUnit XML output format. By default, all test results are dumped into a *reports* directory and are named with the test suite name (the first parameter to the describe method). For example:

```
% ls reports
TEST-Sumsuite.xml     TEST-SumsuiteFile.xml
% cat reports/TEST-SumsuiteFile.xml
<?xml version="1.0" encoding="UTF-8" ?>
<testsuites>
<testsuite name="Sum suite File" errors="0" tests="2" failures="0"
time="0.001" timestamp="2012-07-25T15:31:48">
  <testcase classname="Sum suite File" name="Adds By Param!" time="0.001">
  </testcase>
  <testcase classname="Sum suite File" name="Adds By File!" time="0">
  </testcase>
</testsuite>
</testsuites>
```

The output is now ready to be imported into something that understands that format, as we shall see in Chapter 8. Note that the number of tests reported by Jasmine is the number of it functions, not the number of times you call expect.

Recap

Unit-testing your JavaScript is not burdensome. With all the great tools available for both writing and running unit tests, there is a lot of flexibility for getting the job done. We investigated two such tools, YUI Test and Jasmine. Both provide full-featured environments for JavaScript unit testing, and at the time of this writing both are active projects, with the developers regularly adding new features and fixing bugs.

The process begins by defining your functions precisely so that you know what to test for. Any comments sprinkled throughout the code greatly enhance testability. Loose coupling of objects makes mocking and stubbing them out much simpler.

After picking a full-featured unit test framework, writing and running the tests should be relatively painless. Different frameworks provide different features, so make sure that whatever you choose is easily added to an automated build process and supports the different modes of testing you require (probably asynchronous testing, and mocking, and stubbing of dependencies).

Running your tests locally or remotely, headlessly or not, is easy using PhantomJS or Selenium. PhantomJS provides a full-featured headless WebKit browser, while Selenium provides a very basic headless browser plus access to almost any "real" browser, including iOS and Android for mobile devices.

Generating code coverage reports to measure the scope and effectiveness of your tests and running the tests automatically in a build environment will be covered in upcoming chapters, so stay tuned!

## CHAPTER 5

Code Coverage

Even though code coverage metrics can be misleading, they are still vital. While code coverage is typically associated with unit tests, it is equally easy to generate code coverage metrics from integration tests. And it is trivial to combine multiple code coverage reports into a single report that includes all your unit and integration tests, thereby providing a complete picture of exactly what code is covered by your full suite of tests.

Regardless of the coverage tools you utilize, the flow is similar: instrument JavaScript files for code coverage information, deploy or exercise those files, pull the coverage results and persist them into a local file, potentially combine coverage results from different tests, and either generate pretty HTML output or just get the coverage numbers and percentages you are interested in for upstream tools and reporting.

Coverage Basics

Code coverage measures if, and if so, how many times, a line of code is executed. This is useful for measuring the efficacy of your test code. In theory, the more lines that are "covered", the more complete your tests are. However, the link between code coverage and test completeness can be tenuous.

Here is a simple Node.js function that returns the current stock price of a given symbol:

```
/**
 * Return current stock price for given symbol
 *     in the callback
 *
 * @method getPrice
 * @param symbol <String> the ticker symbol
 * @param cb <Function> callback with results cb(error, value)
 * @param httpObj <HTTP> Optional HTTP object for injection
 * @return nothing
 **/
```

```
function getPrice(symbol, cb, httpObj) {
    var http = httpObj || require('http')
        , options = {
            host: 'download.finance.yahoo.com'  // Thanks Yahoo!
            , path: '/d/quotes.csv?s=' + symbol + '&f=l1'
        }
    ;

    http.get(options, function(res) {
        res.on('data', function(d) {
            cb(null, d);
        });
    }).on('error', function(e) {
        cb(e.message);
    });
}
```

Given a stock ticker symbol and a callback, this function will fetch the current price of the symbol. It follows the standard callback convention of providing the error as the first callback argument, if there was one. Also note that this function allows the `http` object to be injected to ease testing. Doing this allows for looser coupling between this function and the `http` object, greatly increasing testability (you could also use Mockery for this; see Chapter 4). In a general production scenario, this value defaults to the system-provided HTTP object while allowing for a stubbed or mocked value for testing. Whenever a function has a tightly coupled relationship with external objects it is usually worthwhile to allow for injection of that object, for both testability and loose coupling.

We discussed dependency injection in detail in Chapter 2, and here is another example where dependency injection makes testing easier. Besides testability, what if the host providing the stock price service required HTTPS? Or even HTTPS for some symbols and HTTP for others? The flexibility provided by injection is almost always a good thing, and it's easy to take advantage of it.

Writing a test for maximum code coverage is an almost trivial process. First we stub out the `http` object:

```
/**
 * A simple stub for HTTP object
 */
var events = require('events').EventEmitter
    , util = require('util')
    , myhttp = function() {  // Dummy up NodeJS's 'http' object
        var _this = this ;
        events.call(this);

        this.get = function(options, cb) {
            cb(_this);
            return _this;
```

```
        };
    }
    ;
    util.inherits(myhttp, events);
```

It is important to realize that we are not testing the http module that is supplied by Node.js (nor do we want to). Yes, there may be bugs in it, but our tests are not trying to find them. We only want to test the code in this function, not any other external object, regardless of who wrote it or where it came from. Integration tests will (hopefully) find any bugs due to interactions between our code and its dependencies.

This stubbed-out http object will make testing possible. Here is how we can use it using YUI Test's asynchronous testing methods (I am omitting the YUI Test boilerplate for clarity):

```
    testPrice: function() {
        var symbol = 'YHOO'
            , stockPrice = 50  // Wishful thinking??
            , _this = this
            , http = new myhttp()
        ;
        getPrice(symbol, function(err, price) {
            _this.resume(function() {
                Y.Assert.areEqual(stockPrice, price, "Prices not equal!");
            }, http);  // Inject our 'http' object
        http.fire('data', stockPrice);  // Our mock data
        this.wait(1000);
    }
```

This is a basic test for a successful case. To test an error case, we just fire the error event on our http object:

```
    testPriceError: function() {
        var symbol = 'YHOO'
            , _this = this
            , http = new myhttp()
        ;
        getPrice(symbol, function(err, price) {
            _this.resume(function() {
                Y.Assert.areEqual(err, 'an error', "Did not get error!");
            }, http);
        http.fire('error', { message: 'an error'} );
        this.wait(1000);
    }
```

With these two tests, code coverage data will show 100% code coverage—awesome! This means there could not possibly be any more testing to do and the getPrice function works exactly as expected, right? Well, of course not. This is why large code coverage percentages can be misleading. This function is not fully tested, but coverage numbers indicate otherwise.

What is also interesting is the sheer amount of test code versus the amount of code under test. We have written almost three times the amount of code to test this function as the function itself contains—maybe more, if we count the YUI Test boilerplate that is not included in these listings. While we did achieve 100% code coverage, we can't say with confidence from just these tests that the `getPrice` function is 100% reliable. This is the crux of a complaint sometimes made about unit testing: it hinders and slows down development. Unfortunately, with time to market being so important for web applications, unit testing—and testing in general—is typically given short shrift. At best, unit tests are created later, after the code has shipped; at worst, they are never created. This is problematic, as testing after the fact is neither as helpful nor as productive as testing while (or even before) developing the code. An ounce of prevention is absolutely better than a pound of cure.

While large coverage percentages can be misleading, low coverage percentages are not. Even if most (or even all) lines are executed by a test or set of tests, this does not necessarily mean that all edge cases have been tested, or even that the general case has been tested. However, low code coverage percentages show clearly those lines that are not being exercised or tested at all. This is a very strong indication of what your testing resources should target next.

Code Coverage Data

Code coverage data typically comes in two pieces, line coverage and function coverage, both of which are most easily expressed as percentages. These numbers are easily understood for individual unit tests. When testing either an individual function or a method within an object, the total number of functions and lines in the file loaded serves as the denominator for the percentage calculation. So, if you spread your testing across multiple files for a single module, unit test coverage will be low for each individual test. Aggregation of all the coverage numbers from each individual test will give the complete coverage picture for that file.

Similarly, when trying to ascertain the total coverage percentages of your entire application (or even a single directory of files), your totals, by default, will *not* include any files for which there are no tests. Coverage metrics are completely blind to any files that do not have tests associated with them, so be careful with the "final" aggregated numbers.

To get the full picture of your test's code coverage you must generate "dummy" or "empty" test files to account for files without any tests, and therefore without any coverage. We will investigate this technique later in this chapter.

A Hands-on Example

In this section, I will demonstrate coverage using YUI's coverage tools (*http://bit.ly/ XUdNc5*). Unzip the latest version and you'll see that the *java/build* directory contains the two necessary JAR files: *yuitest-coverage.jar* and *yuitest-coverage-report.jar*. Of course, you will need a recent version of the Java runtime (1.5 or later) installed somewhere convenient, such as in your PATH.

The first JAR is used to transform plain JavaScript files into instrumented files for code coverage, and the second generates reports from the extracted coverage information.

Instrumenting Files

Instrumenting a file is simple:

```
% java -jar yuitest-coverage.jar -o coveraged.js instrument-me.js
```

The file *coveraged.js* is now a fully working copy of *instrument-me.js* with embedded coverage tracking. If you look at the file you will see how it was transformed: interspersed between each statement is a new statement that increments a counter belonging to a global variable that tracks whether the line was executed. This instrumented file is a drop-in replacement for the original file. After exercising the code, the counts can be extracted from the global variable _yuitest_coverage.

Obtaining code coverage information from unit tests is a simple matter of instrumenting the code tested by the unit tests, running the tests, and then extracting the coverage information.

Extracting code coverage information from integration tests requires instrumenting all application JavaScript files, deploying the bundle exactly as you would the regular code, running your Selenium (or manual[1]) tests against the instrumented build, and then extracting the coverage information. You can usually instrument all your code in one shot by using a single find operation (this must all be on one line, of course):

```
% find build_dir -name "*.js" -exec echo "Coveraging {}" \;
-exec java -jar yuitest-coverage.jar -o /tmp/o {} \;
-exec mv /tmp/o {} \;
```

Here we just start at the root of the deployment directory, find all JavaScript files, and replace them in place with their coveraged versions. We can then package and deploy the application as normal. However, as code coverage deals with lines of code, not statements, make sure you run the coverage tools on noncompressed JavaScript.

---

1. But of course, all your tests are automated, right?

Anatomy of a Coveraged File

The YUI coverage tool takes a plain JavaScript file and morphs it into a file that tracks which lines and functions are executed. To see this in action, let's revisit the sum function:

```
function sum(a, b) {
    return a + b;
}
```

Converting this file to its coveraged version:

```
% java -jar yuitest_coverage sum.js -o sum_cover.js
```

yields a 37-line file! The first 18 lines are boilerplate defining global variables and functions that YUI Test Coverage uses to track its information, if they are not already defined. The remaining 19 lines are as follows:

```
_yuitest_coverage["sum.js"] = {
    lines: {},
    functions: {},
    coveredLines: 0,
    calledLines: 0,
    coveredFunctions: 0,
    calledFunctions: 0,
    path: "/home/trostler/sum.js",
    code: []
};
_yuitest_coverage["sum.js"].code=["function sum(a, b)
  {","    return a + b;","}"];
_yuitest_coverage["sum.js"].lines = {"1":0,"2":0};
_yuitest_coverage["sum.js"].functions = {"sum:1":0};
_yuitest_coverage["sum.js"].coveredLines = 2;
_yuitest_coverage["sum.js"].coveredFunctions = 1;
_yuitest_coverline("sum.js", 1); function sum(a, b) {
    _yuitest_coverfunc("sum.js", "sum", 1);
    _yuitest_coverline("sum.js", 2); return a + b;
}
```

The first block of lines defines the _yuitest_coverage["sum.js"] object, which will hold the counts for line and function coverage and well as some other bookkeeping.

Setup continues in the last block, which defines the line counts (there are two countable lines in the file, line 1 and line 2, and one function at line 1, called sum).

The actual counting of lines happens with each call to _yuitest_coverline or _yuitest_coverfunc. Those functions are defined in the boilerplate, but all they do is increment the count for either the function or the line number.

So, in this example, when this file is loaded `_yuitest_coverline("sum.js", 1)` is executed, as every file has the first line executed. When the `sum` function is actually called `_yuitest_coverfunc` is executed first, meaning that our `sum` function is called, then `_yuitest_coverline` is executed, incrementing this line's count, and finally the actual `return a+b` is executed and we are done.

In this way, at the beginning of every file, between every statement, and at the beginning of every function, YUI Test Coverage is tracking the lines and functions executed.

It is important to note that each time this file is loaded the counts are reset. Caching may prevent this, but be aware that if a file is loaded multiple times, any previous coverage information will be lost. It is always best to extract the coverage results after each test is run.

Exercise/Deploy

Different strategies are required for generating coveraged versions of JavaScript files for client- versus server-side code. An HTTP server can dynamically serve coveraged versions of certain JavaScript files based on a query string or other method. Dynamically generating server-side coveraged versions of JavaScript files can be accomplished by spying on Node.js's loader.

Client-Side JavaScript

For unit testing, the HTML glue file can now include the coveraged version of the file to be tested instead of the regular version. There are several strategies for doing this, and we will discuss a fully automated method in Chapter 6. The simplest method is to instrument all your code before you run your unit tests. The HTML will pick up the instrumented version of your code when running the test. A fancier way, if you are using Apache, is to dynamically instrument the code based off a `mod_rewrite` rule. In this scenario, you must tag which JavaScript files you want coverage information for in the HTML file. Using a query string for this purpose is most convenient:

```
<script src="/path/to/file/myModule.js?coverage=1"></script>
```

A matching `mod_rewrite` rule will redirect requests of this type to a script that picks up the original file, generates the coveraged version of it, and then returns that instead of the plain version:

```
RewriteEngine On
RewriteCond %{QUERY_STRING} coverage=1
RewriteRule ^(.*)$ make_coverage.pl?file=%{DOCUMENT_ROOT}/$1 [L]
```

This will pass off any request for a file with a `coverage=1` query string to a script that returns the coveraged version of the requested file.

The script can be as simple as:

```perl
#!/usr/bin/perl
use CGI;
my $q    = CGI->new;
my $file = $q->param('file');
system("java -jar /path/to/yuitest_coverage.jar -o /tmp/$$.js $file");
print $q->header('application/JavaScript');
open(C, "/tmp/$$.js");
print <C>;
```

There is no need to instrument the test code itself; the only code you should be instrumenting is the JavaScript actually being tested. If your module has external dependencies that also must be included to run your tests, you may be tempted to instrument those as well in order to see the connectedness of your code. However, I advise against this. You presumably also have unit tests for the dependencies, and further, any code your tests cover in an external module does not count as being "covered," as the tests for this module are not intended to test that other module. Unit testing is all about isolation, not seeing what other modules your module may use.

In fact, in an ideal world, no external dependencies should even be loaded to test a single module; they should be stubbed or mocked out from your test code. Few things are worse than having to debug another module beyond the one you are currently trying to test. Isolation is key.

As for deploying coveraged code for integration/Selenium-type testing, the setup could not be simpler. Here, all code must be instrumented and then deployed as usual. Note that instrumented code will run more slowly because it has double the number of statements, so do not performance-test against a coveraged deployment!

Once you have deployed the code, run your tests, but note that coverage information is not persisted across reloads. If you reload the browser between every test, or if you jump to another page, you will need to extract and persist the coverage information before moving on.

Fortunately, Selenium makes this easy, as each test case or suite has a `tearDown` function within which you can accomplish this.

Also, a deployed instrumented build is fun for manual testing. Load the page in your browser and click around; when you're finished you can dump the coverage information to the console (view the `_yuitest_coverage` global variable) and cut and paste that into a file for transformation into HTML. You can now see exactly what code was exercised during your random clicking.

It is important to note that you are not actually "testing" anything when you manually click around a coveraged build. You are merely satisfying your curiosity about what code is executed when you click around.

Server-Side JavaScript

Mucking about with the Node.js loader is a not-too-hideous way to dynamically inject coveraged versions of JavaScript under test into the mix. If this proves too scary (it involves overriding a private method), fear not, as there is another option.

The scary but more transparent technique is to override Node.js's Module_load method. Yes, this is an internal method that can change at any moment, and all will be lost, but until then, this method is very transparent.

Here is the basic code:

```
var Module = require('module')
  , path = require('path')
  , originalLoader = Module._load
  , coverageBase = '/tmp'
  , COVERAGE_ME = []
;

Module._load = coverageLoader;

// Figure out what files to generate code coverage for
//        & put into COVERAGE_ME
// And run those JS files thru yuitest-coverage.jar
//      and dump the output into coverageBase

// Then execute tests
//    All calls to 'require' will filter thru this:
function coverageLoader(request, parent, isMain) {
    if (COVERAGE_ME[request]) {
        request = PATH.join(coverageBase, path.basename(request));
    }

    return originalLoader(request, parent, isMain);
}

// At the end dump the global _yuitest_coverage variable
```

First we determine which JavaScript files we want to have code coverage associated with, and generate the coveraged versions of those files—this will drop them all into the */tmp* directory without any other path information.

Now we execute our tests using whatever framework we like. While our tests execute, their calls to require will filter through the coverageLoader function. If it is a file we want code coverage information for, we return the coveraged version; otherwise, we delegate back to the regular Node.js loader to work its magic and load the requested module normally.

When all the tests are finished, the global _yuitest_coverage variable will be available to be persisted, and will be converted to LCOV format and optionally HTML-ized.

In the preceding code, the client-side JavaScript told the HTTP server to generate coverage information for it using a query parameter—but what about for server-side JavaScript? For this, I like to add an extra parameter to the `require` call. Like the query string for the client-side JavaScript, the extra parameter to `require` is transparent. This may be overkill, so another option is to regex-match the `required` file, if it exists in your local development area (as opposed to native, external, third-party modules that return a coveraged version).

Note that all of this requires two passes: the first pass determines which files need code coverage generated for them, and the second pass actually runs the tests, dynamically intercepts the `require`'s calls, and potentially returns coveraged versions of the requested files. This occurs because the `yuitest_coverage` code requires spawning an asynchronous external process to create the coveraged files, yet the `require` call is synchronous. It's not a deal-breaker, but it is something to be aware of. If Node.js ever releases a synchronous spawning method, or if a pure synchronous JavaScript coverage generator becomes available, the coveraged versions of the files could be generated in the overridden `_load` method.

So, how does adding an extra parameter to `require` to request code coverage work? For starters, your test code looks like this:

```
my moduleToTest = require('./src/testMe', true);
```

This statement in your test file that requires the module you are testing simply adds a second parameter (`true`) to the `require` call. Node.js ignores this unexpected parameter. A simple regex will catch this:

```
/require\s*\(\s*['"]([^'"]+)['"]\s*,\s*true\s*\)/g
```

It looks nastier than it is. The idea is to suck in the source of your test JavaScript file and run this regex on it, which will capture all instances of modules required with the extra `true` parameter. You are free to get crazier using an abstract syntax tree walker (using a tree generated by JSLint or Uglify.js) or a JavaScript parser, but in practice this regex has been 100% solid (If you have a `require` statement that breaks it, let me know how ugly it is!).

Once you have collected the list of modules for which you want to generate code coverage metrics, the following code will generate the coveraged versions of them:

```
var tempFile = PATH.join(coverageBase, PATH.basename(file));
    , realFile = require.resolve(file)
;

exec('java -jar ' + coverageJar + " -o " + tempFile + " " + realFile
    , function(err) {
        FILES_FOR_COVERAGE[keep] = 1;
});
```

This code is looped over the results of the regular expression, asking Node.js where the file exists and then running that through the YUI code coverage tool and stashing the result where `coverageLoader` can find it later when the file under test is `required`.

The last bit is to run the tests and then persist the coverage results. The `_yuitest_cov erage` variable is a JavaScript object that needs to be converted to JSON and persisted. Finally, it can be converted to LCOV format and pretty HTML can be generated, and you are done:

```
var coverOutFile = 'cover.json';
fs.writeFileSync(coverOutFile, JSON.stringify(_yuitest_coverage));
exec([ 'java', '-jar', coverageReportJar, '--format', 'lcov', '-o'
  , dirname, coverOutFile ].join(' '), function(err, stdout, stderr) {
  ...
});
```

Earlier, I alluded to another way to get coverage information using Node.js. Of course, there are probably several ways, many that I have never imagined, but the one I alluded to utilizes suffixes. The Node.js loader by default knows about three kinds of file extensions—*.js*, *.json*, and *.node*—and deals with them accordingly. When the Node.js loader is searching for a file to load, if no extension is provided the loader will tack on these extensions to continue its search. Due to the synchronous nature of the loader, we unfortunately cannot dynamically generate the coverage information at load time, so we still need the `require('module', true)` trick to determine which files need code coverage and pregenerate them.

Also, this method, unlike using the second parameter to `require`, forces us to load a specific coveraged version of the file under test. In this instance, we could just use the full path to a coveraged version of the file instead, but using the extension is cleaner. We also must be sure to dump the generated coveraged file into the same directory as the original and give it our new extension so that the original loader will load it for us.

Let's take a look in our test file:

```
require('./src/myModule.cover');
```

This will load the coveraged version of the file. Our regex changes to match this:

```
/require\s*\(\s*['"]([^'"]+)\.cover['"]\)/g
```

When we generated the coveraged version of the file, instead of dumping it into `cover ageBase` (*/tmp*, typically) we just put it right next to the original file, but we ensured that it has a *.cover* extension:

```
var realFile = require.resolve(file)
    , coverFile = realFile.replace('.js', '.cover');
;
exec('java -jar ' + coverageJar + " -o " + coverFile + " " + realFile,
  function(err) {});
```

We no longer need to keep track of which files are covered, as the loader will do the right thing due to the *.cover* extension.

Finally, we just tell the loader what to do when it encounters a file with a *.cover* extension:

```
require.extensions['.cover'] = require.extensions['.js'];
```

Conveniently, this is exactly what the loader should do with files with a *.js* extension.

There are several ways to generate code coverage information for your server-side Java-Script. Pick the one that works best for you. And fear not: if the steps covered here are too terrible to contemplate, Chapter 8 will provide a fully automated solution for dynamically incorporating code coverage generation and reporting without all the fuss.

Persisting Coverage Information

Persisting coverage information means taking it from the browser's memory and saving it locally to disk. "Locally" is where the web server that is serving the test files is running. Each page refresh will clear out any coverage information for the JavaScript loaded on the page, so before a page refresh, coverage information must be stored on disk somewhere or it will be lost forever.

Unit Tests

This is all fun and games until you are able to persist coverage information locally. For unit testing, persisting coverage information, presents the exact same problem as persisting unit test results—namely, POST-ing or Ajax-ing the data back to the server for persistence. Normally you can run unit tests without a web server: simply load the HTML glue file into your browser and your tests will run. However, to persist test results and coverage information you will need the help of a web server.

YUI Test provides helper hooks to get this information in various formats:

```
var TestRunner = Y.Test.Runner;
TestRunner.subscribe(TestRunner.TEST_SUITE_COMPLETE_EVENT, getResults);
TestRunner.run();

function getResults(data) {
  var reporter = new Y.Test.Reporter(
    "http://www.yourserver.com/path/to/target",
    Y.Test.Format.JUnitXML);
  reporter.report(results);
}
```

Use this snippet at the bottom of each of your test suites, and unit test reports will be sent to your server in JUnit XML format, which is recognized by Hudson/Jenkins and many other build tools. YUI also provides output in XML, JSON, and TAP formats. The XML and JSON formats you will have to deal with yourself, but the TAP format, from the Perl world, is also recognized by a host of tools.

When passing the test results back you can also piggyback the coverage results:

```
function getResults(data) {
      // Use JUnitXML format for unit test results
      var reporter = new Y.Test.Reporter(
        "http://www.yourserver.com/path/to/target",
        Y.Test.Format.JUnitXML);
      // Toss in coverage results
      reporter.addField("coverageResults",
        Y.Test.Runner.getCoverage(Y.Coverage.Format.JSON));
      // Ship it
      reporter.report(results);
}
```

The addField method on the reporter object allows you to pass back arbitrary data to the server. In this case we are grabbing the coverage results, encoding them as JSON, and passing them back along with the unit test results. Note that JSON is the only sane output for coverage information; it is the format the YUI coverage reporting tool expects.

The end result of this is a POST to our server with results and coverageResults parameters. These two chunks of data can now be persisted to the local filesystem.

Integration Tests

Persisting coverage information from integration tests using Selenium follows a similar pattern. After running the Selenium test(s) but before navigating away from the current page, you must grab the coverage information and pass it back to the server. Selenium provides tearDown and after hooks where this code should be placed to ensure that it is captured.

This is best done in Selenium using the global variable _yuitest_coverage, where all the coverage information is kept. Using Selenium1, the code looks like this:

```
String coverage = selenium.getEval(
  "JSON.stringify(window._yuitest_coverage)");
```

Using Selenium2/WebDriver, the code is as follows:

```
String coverage = (String)((JavaScriptExecutor) driver)
  .executeScript("return JSON.stringify(window._yuitest_coverage);");
```

Then simply dump the coverage string out to a file, ideally named after your test, such as *testClick.coverage.json*.

Keep in mind that if your application incorporates iframes, coverage information from code in the iframe will not be gathered from the top-level _yuitest_coverage variable. After grabbing the code coverage from the top-level main window, you will need to tell Selenium1 to use it like so:

```
selenium.SelectFrame("src=foo.html");
```

Use this code if you are using Selenium2/WebDriver:

```
driver.SwitchTo().Frame(driver.FindElement(By.CssSelector(
    "iframe[src=\"foo.html\"]")));
```

With this code you can grab the contents of the _yuitest_coverage variable. Of course, you can use any Selenium selector to pick the iframe that you want to extract code coverage from.

Be sure to aggregate the _yuitest_coverage data from each iframe into the total coverage report. We will examine how to do that in depth in the "Aggregation" (page 129) section.

Generating Output

While the JUnit XML format is understood by most if not all build tools, the YUI JSON coverage format is not. Fortunately, it is a simple step to convert the YUI JSON coverage output to the industry- and open source standard LCOV format (all on one line):

```
% java -jar yuitest-coverage-report.jar --format LCOV
-o <output_directory> coverage.json
```

In the preceding code, *coverage.json* is the JSON file dumped from the coverageResults POST parameter (or grabbed directly from _yuitest_coverage for integration tests). Now in *<output_directory>* there is the LCOV-formatted coverage information file, suitable for use with the lcov and genhtml (which is distributed along with LCOV) commands. Hudson/Jenkins will accept this file format natively and generate the pretty HTML coverage automatically, or you can roll your own HTML using the genhtml command. Information on lcov, genhtml, and friends is available here (*http://bit.ly/XUdNsB*). Sample genhtml output is available here (*http://bit.ly/XUdNJn*). Very snazzy! You can see line by line which lines and functions were covered and which were not (and how many times each line was executed).

Figure 5-1 shows what some sample output looks like.

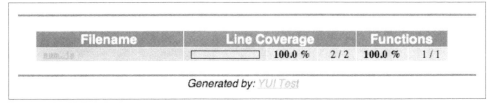

Figure 5-1. Code coverage results for sum.js

Figure 5-2 shows the file containing our sum function. Two out of two lines were covered and one out of one function was reached.

```
1        1 : function sum(a, b) {
2        1 :     return a   b;
3          : }
4          :
```

Generated by: YUI Test

Figure 5-2. Code coverage breakdown for sum.js

Although it's not terribly exciting, we can see that each line was executed once, giving us 100% code coverage. It's great motivation watching the graph and code coverage counts increase while developing code!

The genhtml command accepts many options to customize the HTML output, if you are the tinkering kind who just is not happy with the look of the default output.

Aggregation

For both the unit test and integration test pieces we were able to persist coverage information for individual tests or suites, but how can we see the whole picture? For this, the lcov command comes to the rescue!

The lcov -a command aggregates multiple LCOV files into one large file. So, a command like this:

```
% lcov -a test.lcov -a test1.lcov -a test2.lcov ... -o total.lcov
```

will merge together the set of LCOV files. This can be used to merge all unit tests as well as all integration tests together.

In order to be merged, all LCOV files must share the same root directory. This is not a problem when merging all unit test coverage results or all integration test coverage results independently of each other, but when trying to merge unit and integration tests this can become an issue.

Looking at the format of LCOV files, the first line of each new file coverage section begins with the full path to that source file (a JavaScript one, in our case). If the two roots do not match, lcov will not be able to merge them.

We need a simple shell script to ensure that the roots are the same (also, the machine where the merge is happening must have the source tree rooted at that location). Most likely, one of the sets of roots will be correct and the other will be wrong. Since LCOV files are just plain tests, it's simply a matter of rerooting the incorrect LCOV file to match where the source code actually resides.

If your source code on the box where you want to generate the coverage HTML is rooted at /a/b/c but the LCOV file from the integration tests has the source rooted at /d/e/f, write a script in your favorite language to convert /d/e/f to /a/b/c. In Perl the script looks like this:

```
my $old = '/a/b/c';
my $new = '/d/e/f';
open(F, "wrong.lcov");
open(G, ">right.lcov");
while(<F>) {
    s#^$old#$new#;
    print G;
}
close(G);
close(F);
```

In the preceding code, *wrong.lcov* is converted to be merged with another LCOV file rooted at /d/e/f. Once you have a total LCOV file you are happy with, generating pretty HTML is easy:

```
% genhtml -o /path/to/docRoot/coverage total.lcov
```

Now point your browser to *coverage* on that host and watch your coverage numbers grow!

The generated output—either a single or an aggregated LCOV-formatted file—can then be easily fed into an automated build tool such as Hudson/Jenkins. Conveniently, older versions of Hudson natively understand LCOV-formatted files and only need a pointer to the aggregated file to be included in the build output. Figure 5-3 shows how this is configured.

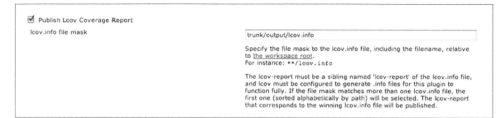

Figure 5-3. The "configure" screen in Hudson

Hudson handles the HTML-izing and persisting of coverage data across builds to easily track your code coverage over time. On the front page of your Hudson build you will now have the button shown in Figure 5-4.

Figure 5-4. Close-up of Hudson coverage report overview

When this button is clicked, the Hudson build will show the coverage tables. According to the figure, 24,979 out of 50,844 lines were covered.

More recent versions of Jenkins do not have this functionality. We will investigate what to do about that in Chapter 8.

Hidden Files

What about files that do not have any code coverage data? These files are hidden from the total report and are not accounted for. What we need are "dummy" empty LCOV files for these modules so that they can be aggregated with the rest of the LCOV files to give a clearer picture of our test coverage.

The simplest method to account for these otherwise hidden files is to ensure that *all* of your application files have at least one empty test for them. Then run the empty test against the coveraged version of the file to generate the (0%) LCOV output. You can now persist and process this LCOV data as you normally would, and all your code will be accounted for in the aggregated coverage rollup.

Here is the HTML of an empty test of the kind that all application files must have. Once you are ready to write tests for this code, you can remove this HTML glue and replace it with the actual tests:

```
<html lang="en">
<body class="yui3-skin-sam">
    <div id="log"></div>
    <h3>Running dummy unit test for APP_FILE</h3>
    <script src="http://yui.yahooapis.com/3.4.0/build/yui/yui.js">
     </script>
    <script src="/path/to/coveraged/file/without/tests.js"></script>
    <script>
        YUI().use('test',  function(Y) {
            Y.Test.Runner.add(
                new Y.Test.Suite('no test').add(
                    new Y.Test.Case({
                        name: 'dummy_NOTESTS'
                        , 'testFile': function() {
                            Y.Assert.areEqual(true, true);
                        }
                    })
                )
            );
            Y.TestRunner.go();
        });
    </script>
</body>
</html>
```

This empty test is enough to load up the coveraged version of the file and have the empty coverage information be persisted along with all the nondummy coverage numbers, and be included in the aggregated rollup.

When looking at the total report, it will be quite obvious which files do not have any tests covering them.

In larger environments, these dummy test files should be autogenerated by comparing what the HTML glue code includes with all the code in your application and determining where the gaps are. The autogenerated version of this file will be created dynamically and be included in your test runs.

A nice way to accomplish this is to iterate through all your test HTML files and look to see what JavaScript files are being loaded, then compare that list with the list of all the JavaScript files in your project.

Let's look at a quick Perl script that does just that. This script is called like so (all on one line):

```
% perl find_no_unit_tests.pl --test_dir test --src_dir dir1
--src_dir dir2 ... --src_base /homes/trostler/mycoolapp
```

The idea is to pass in the root of where all your tests live (in this case, in a directory called *test*) and a list of source directories from which to pull JavaScript files. The `src_base` option is the root directory of your project. This script will create a list of all your JavaScript source files and a list of all JavaScript files included by your tests, and then output the difference between those two sets:

```perl
#!/usr/local/bin/perl

use Getopt::Long;
use File::Find;
use File::Basename;

my($debug, $test_dir, @src_dir, $src_base);
my $src_key = 'src';   // root of source tree
GetOptions (
    "test_dir=s" => \$test_dir,
    "src_dir=s"  => \@src_dir,
    "src_base=s" => \$src_base,
) || die "Bad Options!\n";;

my $src_files = {};

find(\&all_src_files, @src_dir);
find(\&all_tested_files, $test_dir);
```

We ingest the command-line options, traverse all the source directories, and pull out the names of all the JavaScript files:

```perl
sub all_src_files {
    return unless (/\.js$/);
    foreach my $src_dir (@src_dir) {
        $File::Find::name =~ s/^\Q$src_base\E//;
    }
    $src_files->{$File::Find::name}++;
}
```

The `%src_files` hash now contains all your JavaScript source files. Here is the code to blow through the test files:

```perl
sub all_tested_files {
    return unless (/\.html?$/);

    open(F, $_) || die "Can't open $_: $!\n";
    while(my $line = <F>) {
        if ($line =~ /["']([^"]+?\/($src_key\/[^"]+?\.js))["']/) {
            my($full_file_path) = $2;
            print "Test file $File::Find::name is coveraging
                $full_file_path\n" if ($debug);
            delete $src_files->{$full_file_path};
        }.
    }
}
```

The nastiest thing here, by far, is the regex looking for script tags of the form:

```
<script src="/path/to/JS/file"></script>
```

Once a filename is pulled that file is deleted from the `%src_files` hash, which marks it as "covered."

The `%src_files` hash contains only JavaScript files without unit tests. Now it is simple to use your favorite templating system to generate an empty unit test for each of these files. You can save these empty tests somewhere in your *test* directory tree to be run later by your automated unit test running tool (we will investigate one such tool in Chapter 8), so now your entire project's code coverage will be accounted for regardless of whether a file has unit tests associated with it or not.

When these empty tests are run the code coverage for these files will stick out like a sore thumb (hopefully), as the coverage will be very close to 0% (it probably will not be exactly 0%, as any code not nested in a function will get executed by just loading the file itself).

Coverage Goals

Typically, unit test coverage goals are different from integration coverage goals. Since integration tests cover larger swaths of code, it is harder to determine the correlation between what has been covered and what has been tested. Unlike unit tests, which are tightly focused on a particular piece of code such as a function or a small piece of functionality, feature tests cover significantly more lines. This is a manifestation of the exact same problem seen with code coverage and unit tests: just because a line of code is executed by a test does not mean that code is "tested."

Therefore, the already tenuous connection between a line of code being executed and a line of code being tested for unit tests is even more pronounced for integration tests and code coverage tests. After all, the desired result of testing is not "code coverage," it is correct code.

Of course, to have any confidence that your code is correct, the code must be executed during a test and must perform as expected. Simply executing a line of code from a test is not sufficient, but it is necessary.

So, where does that leave code coverage?

The sane consensus, which I also advocate, is to strive for unit test code coverage results of approximately 80% line coverage. Function coverage is not important for unit-testing purposes, as ideally, your unit tests are only testing one function or method (other than to know which functions have any tests associated with them). Other code, especially initialization code when unit-testing methods, gets covered incidentally. Your unit tests should cover at least 80% of the function under test. But be careful how you achieve that level of coverage, as that number is not the real goal. The true goal is good tests that exercise the code in expected and unexpected ways. Code coverage metrics should be the by-product of good tests, not the other way around! It is easy, but useless, to write tests just to obtain larger coverage. Fortunately, professional developers would never do that.

As for integration tests, which test at the feature level, code coverage metrics are relatively useless by themselves. It is instructive to see and understand all the code that is necessary for a feature. Typically you will be surprised by what code is being executed or not—and initially, that is interesting information to have. But over time, code coverage metrics for feature testing are not too meaningful. However, aggregated coverage information about all feature testing is very useful. In fact, the aggregated coverage metrics for any and all kinds of testing, including performance, integration, and acceptance testing, are very nice numbers to have to check the thoroughness of your testing.

What percentage of code is executed by your acceptance tests? Your integration tests? Your performance tests? These are good numbers to know. Interestingly, there is no standard, as with unit test line coverage, to shoot for. These are numbers that should increase over time, so you should start by aiming for the most common code paths. Concentrate your feature tests on the most-used features. Clearly, you want higher coverage there first. Between unit testing and feature testing, line coverage should approach 100%, but remember that code coverage metrics are not the ultimate goal of your testing. Exercising your code under many different conditions is. Do not put the cart before the horse.

Recap

Generating and viewing code coverage information is crucial for unit testing and important for aggregated integration testing. While code coverage numbers do not tell the whole tale, code coverage information does provide a nice single number to use to track the progress of your tests.

Large percentages can be misleading, but small percentages are not. You, your boss, and anyone else can clearly see at a glance how much code is covered by tests, whether unit tests or otherwise. Small line coverage percentages provide obvious signposts for where to focus future testing efforts.

It is relatively straightforward to capture code coverage results from both unit and integration tests and merge them into a single report. This provides a handy metric for tracking test progress. In Chapter 8 we will discuss how to automate this process even further using the open source JavaScript Unit Test Environment.

Along with static code analysis, tracking the code coverage of your tests gives you another metric to analyze your code. No number can give a complete picture of your code or your tests, good or bad, but gathering and tracking these numbers over time provides insight into how your code is evolving.

Reaching code coverage goals must be a by-product of good testing, not the goal itself. Do not lose track of why you are writing all these tests: to ensure that your code is correct and robust.

## CHAPTER 6

Integration, Performance, and Load Testing

In addition to unit testing, it is also important for you to conduct integration, performance, and load testing on your applications. Writing integration tests that run either against "real" browsers or headlessly in an automated build environment is surprisingly simple. As is true of most things, once the boilerplate code and configuration are in place, it's easy to add tests. For the tests we conduct in this chapter, we will generate a standard waterfall graph of web application load times. Generating and integrating a waterfall graph is also surprisingly simple!

The Importance of Integration

All test types rely on your entire application being up and running. Whether in a testing environment or in production, all the pieces of the application must fit together. Testable JavaScript mandates small pieces of code with minimal dependencies; the piper gets paid when all those pieces are combined. An event-based architecture is an example of lots of loosely coupled pieces that must work in concert when combined. Therefore, it is imperative that automation is present to deploy and bring up the system. Once the system is up, testing can proceed.

Integration Testing

Conducting an integration test on a web application requires running your application in a browser and ensuring that its functionality works as expected. Testing pieces in isolation through unit testing is a nice start, but you must follow this up with integration testing. Integration testing tests how your code fits together in the larger scheme of things. There is no mocking or stubbing out of dependencies at this level; you are testing at the application level.

Selenium

Testing JavaScript in a browser typically involves Selenium. Testing with Selenium usually requires a chunk of Java code running on the same box as the browsers you want to spawn to run your tests, and a client-side API for controlling the remote browser. Selenium2/WebDriver can control Firefox, Chrome, and Internet Explorer for Mac OS X and Windows.

You can write Selenium tests in a variety of languages, or you can use a Firefox plug-in that will generate your tests in various languages by following your mouse movements and keystrokes. Selenium also provides a set of assertion and verification functions that test the current page to ensure the current state is valid.

Using the Selenium IDE is the quickest way to get something to play with. While in any version of Firefox, go to the SeleniumHQ site (*http://bit.ly/XUdI8k*) and get the latest version of the IDE (1.10.0 as of this writing), and let Firefox install the add-on.

Now load your website and open the Selenium IDE (Tools→Selenium IDE). Set the Base URL to the URL of the page where your web application resides. Click on the record button on the upper right of the Selenium IDE and Selenium will start tracking your mouse and keyboard movements as you click and type around your application. Click the record button again to stop recording.

Select File→Export Test Case As and you can save your clicking and typing in a variety of languages for Selenium2/WebDriver, or for original Selenium (Remote Control), which you should not use if you're new to Selenium.

You can rerun these tests from within the Selenium IDE by clicking the green play button. The log at the bottom of the Selenium IDE window will let you know what is going on.

A common problem with Selenium is that it uses element IDs by default to identify the elements you are interacting with, and using a JavaScript framework that dynamically generates IDs will cause your test to fail, as the elements with these dynamic IDs will not be found during subsequent runs. Fortunately, the Target text field in the Selenium IDE lets you remedy this situation by using XPath or CSS expressions to locate elements, instead of the IDs used by default (of course, if you are setting element IDs yourself you will not have this problem). Click the find button next to the Target text field to locate elements you want to target when changing selectors.

You can also run saved test cases from the command line using JUnit. Export your test case as a JUnit 4 (WebDriver Backend) file and name it something interesting. The IDE will put the following declaration at the top of your file:

```
package com.example.tests;
```

Change the declaration to match your environment, or just delete that line.

Now you'll need both the current version of the Selenium server and the client drivers. From the SeleniumHQ site (*http://bit.ly/XUdI8k*), download the current version of the Selenium server (version 2.28 as of this writing) and the Java Selenium client driver (version 2.28.0 as of this writing). You will need to unzip the Java Selenium client.

To compile your exported Selenium script you need the *selenium-server* JAR:

```
% java -cp path/to/selenium-server-standalone-2.28.0.jar test.java
```

This will compile your exported Selenium test case. To execute the test you need to start the Selenium server, like so:

```
% java -jar path/to/selenium-server-standalone-2.28.0.jar
```

And now you can run your JUnit test case (all on one line):

```
% java -cp path/to/selenium-server-standalone-2.28.0.jar:Downloads/
selenium-2.20.0/libs/junit-dep-4.10.jar:.
org.junit.runner.JUnitCore test
```

You need the path to the Selenium server JAR and the JUnit JAR (which is supplied by the Java Selenium client code if you do not already have it somewhere). The preceding code assumes you deleted the package declaration. If not, you need something like this (again, all on one line):

```
% java -cp selenium-server-standalone-2.28.0.jar
:selenium-2.20.0/libs/junit-dep-4.10.jar:.
org.junit.runner.JUnitCore com.example.tests.test
```

The compiled Java program must reside in *com/example/tests* for the Java interpreter to find it (or you can change the class path).

Using the Selenium IDE is clunky; you are better served by handwriting the test cases yourself (you can use JUnit for this). But note that this becomes an exercise in learning XPath or CSS selectors and/or using ID attributes judiciously throughout your HTML so that Selenium can "grab" them and manipulate your application: clicking links and buttons, dragging and dropping, editing form elements, and so on.

You can use either the `assert` or the `verify` family of Selenium functions to verify your application's functionality. Note that the `assert` family of functions will fail the test immediately and skip to the next test function, while the `verify` family of functions will fail the assertion but continue running further code within the test function. You should almost always use the `assert` family of functions in your Selenium tests.

Fortunately, there are JavaScript bindings for Selenium (both Remote Control and WebDriver) by way of npm packages for NodeJS, so we can write Selenium integration tests using our beloved JavaScript.

WebDriver

Using the webdriverjs npm module (*http://bit.ly/XUdKgq*) to drive Selenium2 is straightforward:

```
var webdriverjs = require("webdriverjs")
    , browser = webdriverjs.remote({
        host: 'localhost'
        , port: 4444
        , desiredCapabilities: { browserName: 'firefox' }
    })
;

browser
    .testMode()
    .init()
    .url("http://search.yahoo.com")
    .setValue("#yschsp", "JavaScript")
    .submitForm("#sf")
    .tests.visible('#resultCount', true, 'Got result count')
    .end();
```

With the Selenium server started locally, the preceding code will start a Firefox browser, search for "JavaScript" at the Yahoo! search page (*http://yhoo.it/XUdP3S*), and ensure that an element whose id is resultCount is visible.

Generating a screenshot is equally easy. Simply add the saveScreenshot call:

```
var webdriverjs = require("webdriverjs")
    , browser = webdriverjs.remote({
        host: 'localhost'
        , port: 4444
        , desiredCapabilities: { browserName: 'firefox' }
    })
;

browser
    .testMode()
    .init()
    .url("http://search.yahoo.com")
    .setValue("#yschsp", "javascript")
    .submitForm("#sf")
    .tests.visible('#resultCount', true, 'Got result count')
    .saveScreenshot('results.png')
    .end();
```

And now you have a beautiful screenshot, as shown in Figure 6-1. Note that although the Yahoo! Axis ad appears in the middle of Figure 6-1, it is actually positioned at the bottom of the visible page. But since Selenium is taking a snapshot of the entire page, it appears in the middle. When you view this page in a browser, the ad appears at the bottom of the visible area.

Figure 6-1. Generating a screenshot with Selenium

To run this example in Chrome, you need to download the Chrome driver (*http://bit.ly/XUdRsv*) for your operating system and install it somewhere in your PATH. Then you simply change this line:

```
, desiredCapabilities: { browserName: 'firefox' }
```

to this:

```
, desiredCapabilities: { browserName: 'chrome' }
```

and your tests will run in Google Chrome.

How about Internet Explorer? You can download the latest IE driver for your platform from the code.google selenium site (*http://bit.ly/XUdRZF*). Then put the executable in your PATH and fire it up. It starts up on port 5555 by default:

```
, port: 5555
, desiredCapabilities: { browserName: 'internetExplorer' }
```

Remote Control

A nice npm module for Selenium Remote Control (Selenium1) is soda (*http://bit.ly/XUdSwp*). Here is the same example as before, this time running against Safari using the soda module:

```
var soda = require('soda')
    , browser = soda.createClient({
        url: 'http://search.yahoo.com'
        , host: 'localhost'
        , browser: 'safari'
    })
;

browser
    .chain
    .session()
    .open('/')
    .type('yschsp', 'JavaScript')
    .submit('sf')
    .waitForPageToLoad(5000)
    .assertElementPresent('resultCount')
    .end(function(err) {
        browser.testComplete(function() {
            if (err) {
                console.log('Test failures: ' + err);
            } else {
                console.log('success!');
            }
        })
    });
```

The soda module chains Selenium commands ("Selenese") similarly to the webdriverjs module, but instead of WebDriver commands, you now use the Selenium1 commands (*http://bit.ly/XUdUEL*). The main difference is that Selenium1 supports a wider range of browsers because it is all just JavaScript running in each browser, whereas WebDrivers are external processes that allow more control over the browsers than Selenium1 does. Note that the standalone Selenium server JAR understands both Selenium1 and Selenium2 commands, so that part does not change. Only the client-side commands change.

Grid

Selenium also supports a "grid" configuration comprising one central "hub" and many distributed "spokes" that actually spawn browsers and feed commands to them. This is great for parallel processing of Selenium jobs or for acting as a central repository for Selenium runners that provide developer and QA access to Selenium without requiring each person to run and maintain his own Selenium instance.

Each spoke connects to the central hub with the browser(s) it can spawn, and the hub hands Selenium jobs to a spoke when a matching capability list comes in. A single hub can service Mac, Windows, and Linux clients running different browsers.

Conveniently, the latest version of the Selenium standalone server supports both Web-Driver and Remote Control for grids. To start a grid hub, simply use this command:

```
% java -jar selenium-server-standalone-2.28.0.jar -role hub
```

Once the hub is started, start up the nodes that connect to the hub and spawn browsers using the following code (all on one line)—the nodes can run on the same host as the hub, or on a remote host:

```
% java -jar selenium-server-standalone-2.28.0.jar
-role node -hub http://localhost:4444/grid/register
```

This node assumes the hub is running on port 4444 (the default) and on the same machine as the node.

The best part about this setup is that your client-side code does not change! Using webdriverjs you can take advantage of the extra nodes for parallelization; whereas a single standalone server can handle one request at a time, each node can handle multiple requests simultaneously. Pointing a browser to *http://localhost:4444/grid/console* (on the host where the hub is running) will provide a nice visual of the number of nodes connected to the hub and the number of jobs they can each handle in parallel. The older Selenium1 Remote Control–backed grids could only handle one Selenium job per node. The newer WebDriver-based grids can handle several. Five is the default, but you can change this using the -maxSession <*num*> command-line switch for each node.

You can now batter the Selenium hub with nodes and jobs to support all your testing, regardless of the language the tests are written in and which browsers you want to test on (which, I hope, is all of them).

CasperJS

Selenium is not the only browser integration-testing framework around. Built on top of PhantomJS, CasperJS provides similar functionality as Selenium but in a completely headless environment. Using pure JavaScript or CoffeeScript, you can script interactions with your web application and test the results, including screenshots, without any Java. When using CasperJS with the latest version of PhantomJS (1.7.0 as of this writing) you no longer need X11 or Xvfb running to start up the PhantomJS WebKit browser, as PhantomJS is now built on the Lighthouse Qt 4.8.0 device-independent display framework. This means truly headless integration testing is now possible on your servers.

To use CasperJS, first you must install the latest version of PhantomJS from the code.google phantomjs site (*http://bit.ly/XUdSNb*). Downloading the binary version for your operating system is easiest, but building from source is not much more difficult (unless you have an older version of Linux; I had to make some changes when compiling for Red Hat Enterprise 4/CentOS 4, due to my lack of Thread Local Storage, and to remove some SSE optimizations).

Now grab the latest version of CasperJS (*http://bit.ly/XUdVs6*); 1.0.0-RC6 as of this writing.

Here is the CasperJS version of the earlier Yahoo! search test:

```
var casper = require('casper').create();

casper.start('http://search.yahoo.com/', function() {
    this.fill('form#sf', { "p": 'JavaScript' }, false);
    this.click('#yschbt');
});

casper.then(function() {
    this.test.assertExists('#resultCount', 'Got result count');
});

casper.run(function() {
    this.exit();
});
```

Here's how to run this CasperJS script:

```
% bin/casperjs yahooSearch.js
PASS Got result count
%
```

Sweet, that was easy enough. And it is significantly quicker than connecting to a possibly remote Selenium server and having it spawn and then kill a browser. This is running in a real WebKit browser, but note that the version of WebKit that Apple uses in Safari and the version of WebKit that Google uses in Chrome are different from what is running here with PhantomJS.

How about a screenshot?

```
var casper = require('casper').create();

casper.start('http://search.yahoo.com/', function() {
    this.fill('form#sf', { "p": 'JavaScript' }, false);
    this.click('#yschbt');
});

casper.then(function() {

    this.capture('results.png', {
        top: 0,
        left: 0,
        width: 1024,
        height: 768
    });

    this.test.assertExists('#resultCount', 'Got result count');
});

casper.run(function() {
    this.exit();
});
```

The capture code can also capture a given CSS selector instead of the entire page; see Figure 6-2.

Figure 6-2. Generating a screenshot with CasperJS

This looks very similar to the Firefox screenshot captured by Selenium! The biggest difference between the two concerns specifying the exact size of the screenshot you want; CasperJS does not capture the entire browser area, whereas Selenium does.

CasperJS has other tricks up its sleeve, including automatic export of test results to a JUnit XML-formatted file. Here is the full script:

```
var casper = require('casper').create();

casper.start('http://search.yahoo.com/', function() {
    this.fill('form#sf', { "p": 'JavaScript' }, false);
    this.click('#yschbt');
});

casper.then(function() {
    this.capture('results.png', {
        top: 0,
        left: 0,
        width: 1024,
        height: 768
    });

    this.test.assertExists('#resultCount', 'Got result count');
});

casper.run(function() {
    this.test.renderResults(true, 0, 'test-results.xml');
});
```

Besides outputting test results to the console, the *test-results.xml* file will now contain the JUnit XML test output, a format well understood by build tools including Hudson/Jenkins. Here are the contents of that file after running this test:

```
<testsuite>
    <testcase classname="ss" name="Got result count">
    </testcase>
</testsuite>
```

Here is the console output:

```
PASS 1 tests executed, 1 passed, 0 failed.
Result log stored in test-results.xml
```

Of course, you will want to test your code in Internet Explorer, as (unfortunately) the bulk of your users are probably using it, and for that you will have to use Selenium. But CasperJS is a great addition for quick testing in a headless environment.

Performance Testing

A central aspect of performance testing concerns knowing how your web application loads. The HTTP Archive (HAR) format is the standard for capturing this information;

the specification is available at Jan Odvarko's blog (*http://bit.ly/XUdVIH*). A HAR is a JSON-formatted object that can be viewed and inspected by many tools, including free online viewers. To monitor your web application's performance, you'll want to generate a HAR of the application's profile and inspect the data for issues. Capturing and monitoring this data over time will give you insight into how your application is performing.

Generating HAR Files

Several tools are capable of generating HAR files. One of the most flexible is a programmable proxy that intercepts HTTP requests and responses. The proxy can work with any browser, including mobile ones, giving it maximum flexibility.

Another option is to use a packet-sniffing tool such as tcpdump (*http://bit.ly/XUdVZh*) to capture HTTP traffic in PCAP format, and to then use a tool such as pcap2har (*http://bit.ly/XUdWfL*) to generate the HAR. This arguably gives "truer" performance numbers, as there is no proxy between your server and the client. Although this method is messier, I encourage you to check it out if the proxy method does not work for you. For instance, mobile browsers do not allow you to set proxies, so generating HARs for mobile devices requires a packet sniffer. Visit this code.google webpage (*http://bit.ly/XUdU7K*) for more details.

Using a proxy

To investigate how proxies work, we will play with the open source programmable proxy browsermob (*http://bit.ly/XUdWMJ*). Written in Java, this proxy is easily integrated into Selenium WebDriver scripts and has some nice programmable features, as well as a REST interface. Unfortunately, as of this writing not all features are available via the REST interface. But enough are available to do some damage!

To use browsermob, you simply start up the proxy and get it ready to start capturing a HAR, start Selenium WebDriver and set the proxy to the browsermob proxy, use Selenium to connect and do whatever else needs to happen, and then collect the HAR from browsermob and dump it out to a file.

 browsermob is actually more full-featured than is strictly necessary to just get a HAR. It can run multiple simultaneous proxies, set upload and download speeds, blacklist and whitelist sites, and even add custom DNS.

browsermob starts on port 8080 by default. This is not a proxy port, it is the port the REST interface communicates on, so there's no reason to change it, but you can if you want to.

After you download browsermob-proxy, start it up:

```
% /bin/sh bin/browsermob-proxy
```

Now you can communicate with it to start up and tear down a proxy (or multiple proxies) and take advantage of its other functionality. I've hacked up JavaScript bindings for the browsermob-proxy that are available as an npm package:

```
% npm install browsermob-proxy
```

At this point, you're ready for some serious HAR file generation in JavaScript!

For starters, HARs can only be generated automatically using Selenium WebDriver with Firefox or Internet Explorer, as those are the only browsers whose proxy settings Selenium WebDriver can alter programmatically. Since HARs measure network time, this is not a big issue, unless each browser requests radically different resources on launch. This means you must have the Selenium server running somewhere to start Firefox or Internet Explorer (standalone or grid).

The browsermob-proxy npm module will generate a HAR using one of two methods:

- The easy method
- The advanced method

Let's start with the easy method, which is advisable if you just have one URL whose waterfall graph you want to view. The following code generates the HAR file for Yahoo.com (*http://yhoo.it/XUdX3p*):

```
var Proxy = require('browsermob-proxy').Proxy
  , fs = require('fs')
  , proxy = new Proxy()
  ;

proxy.doHAR('http://yahoo.com', function(err, data) {
    if (err) {
        console.error('ERROR: ' + err);
    } else {
        fs.writeFileSync('yahoo.com.har', data, 'utf8');
    }
});
```

In the preceding code, we loaded the browsermob-proxy module and created a new Proxy object. As this object has no parameters, it assumes browsermob-proxy is running on *localhost* or port 8080. Next, we simply passed inu the URL and a callback; if there were no errors, the second parameter to the callback will be the HAR data for that site. Dump this data to a file, and you're done.

If your browsermob-proxy is not running on *localhost* or port 8080 (the defaults), just specify where it is in the constructor:

```
  , proxy = new Proxy( { host: 'some.other.host', port: 9999 } )
```

Remember also that this requires the 2.x version of the Selenium server to be running somewhere; the default configuration assumes it is running on localhost port 4444. If that is not the case, you must specify where it is in the Proxy constructor:

```
, proxy = new Proxy( { selHost: 'some.other.host', selPort: 6666 } )
```

Now let's take a look at the advanced method of generating HAR files. You would use this method if you wanted a HAR file for more advanced web interaction than just loading up a page. With this method, you set up the proxy, it starts to capture the data, and the browsermob-proxy module calls back into your Selenium code with the proxy to use. You then instantiate a Selenium object using that proxy with whatever browser and page you want, and you use the provided callback to generate the HAR file, which calls your provided callback with the HAR data.

For this example, we'll use the earlier Selenium webdriverjs example of loading up a Yahoo! page (*http://yhoo.it/XUdP3S*) and then searching for "JavaScript". First we generate a HAR for all of that interaction, like so:

```
var Proxy = require('browsermob-proxy').Proxy
    , webdriverjs = require("webdriverjs")
    , fs = require('fs')
    , proxy = new Proxy()
;

/*
 * Call into the proxy with a 'name' for this session, a Selenium
 *      function to run the interaction we want to capture, and
 *      finally a callback that will contain either the HAR data or
 *      an error
 */
proxy.cbHAR('search.yahoo.com', doSeleniumStuff, function(err, data) {
        if (err) {
            console.error('Error capturing HAR: ' + err);
        } else {
            fs.writeFileSync('search.yahoo.com.har', data, 'utf8');
        }
});

/*
 * This is the Selenium function that gets passed the proxy webdriverjs
 *      should use and a callback to call when the interaction is done
 */
function doSeleniumStuff(proxy, cb) {
    var browser = webdriverjs.remote({
        host: 'localhost'
        , port: 4444
        , desiredCapabilities: {
            browserName: 'firefox'
            , seleniumProtocol: 'WebDriver'
            , proxy: { httpProxy: proxy }
        }
```

```
        });

        // Just run our regular Selenium stuff - note this can just
        //     be your regular test code or something special you want
        //     to capture with a HAR
        // Just pass the browsermob-proxy callback to 'end()'
        browser
            .testMode()
            .init()
            .url("http://search.yahoo.com")
            .setValue("#yschsp", "JavaScript")
            .submitForm("#sf")
            .tests.visible('#resultCount', true, 'Got result count')
            .saveScreenshot('results.png')
            .end(cb);
    }
```

This method assumes browsermob-proxy is running on the same host (*localhost*) and default port (8080) as this script. You can change these values by passing in a configuration object to the Proxy constructor. This method also enables you to control the Selenium interaction, so you no longer need to pass in selHost and selPort to the Proxy constructor if the Selenium standalone server or grid is not running on *localhost* port 4444.

Also, do not forget that Selenium dynamic proxy injection only works with Firefox and Internet Explorer using WebDriver (not Selenium1/Remote Control), so your Selenium webdriverjs object must specify one of those two browsers.

The browsermob-proxy npm package also allows you to specify bandwidth and latency. This is useful for not only HAR generation, but also slow-connection testing in general, enabling you to experience your site from a 56k modem with 200 ms of latency, like a dial-up connection from halfway around the world. You specify these values to the Proxy constructor using the downloadKbps, uploadKbps, and latency keys, like so:

```
    , proxy = new Proxy({
        downloadKbps: 56
        , uploadKbps: 56
        , latency: 200
    })
```

This will slow everything down significantly, which is necessary for testing low-bandwidth situations.

The browsermob-proxy allows further advanced interaction as well. I strongly encourage you to check it out. Other alternatives, such as Fiddler (*http://bit.ly/XUe0vY*) and Charles (*http://bit.ly/XUe0MF*), can do similar things, but browsermob-proxy is free and works great.

But why should Selenium have all the fun? PhantomJS and CasperJS are equally adept at generating HAR files. All you need to do is to set the proxy, which is easy to do in both PhantomJS and CasperJS.

The browsermob-proxy module is written for Node.js, and PhantomJS/CasperJS is an entirely different beast, even though they look very similar. Therefore, we first must set up the proxy using Node.js, then spawn off a CasperJS process with the correct proxy information, and finally collect the HAR and output it back in Node.js-land.

Basically, the process is very similar to the advanced method we used earlier, except the passed function callback for the Selenium piece will spawn a CasperJS script to do the driving. Once that is done, we can grab the HAR. Someday perhaps PhantomJS and Node.js will play nicely together, or PhantomJS will gain HTTP request code. Until then, we need Node.js.

Here is how it looks from the Node.js side:

```
var Proxy = require('browsermob-proxy').Proxy
  , spawn = require('child_process').spawn
  , fs = require('fs')
;

var proxy = new Proxy();
proxy.selHAR('MyCoolHARFile', doCasperJSStuff, function(err, data) {
    if (err) {
        console.error('ERR: ' + err);
    } else {
        fs.writeFileSync('casper.har', data, 'utf8');
    }
});

function doCasperJSStuff(proxy, cb) {
    casperjs = spawn('bin/casperjs'
      , [ '--proxy=' + proxy, process.argv[2] ]);
    casperjs.on('exit', cb);
}
```

We are using `proxy.selHAR` just like in the earlier example, but the passed-in Selenium function is actually spawning off a CasperJS job (namely, the one passed into this script on the command line) with the proxy set to browsermob. Once the CasperJS process exits, we call back to generate the HAR file. Here is how to use it:

```
% node casperHAR.js casperScript.js
```

In the preceding code, *casperHAR.js* is the file from the previous code sample and *casperScript.js* is any CasperJS script (such as the one demonstrated earlier for searching Yahoo!). As with the Selenium examples, you can pass in the location where the browsermob-proxy is actually running (host and port) and any bandwidth limitations you would like to inspect. Pretty easy!

This demonstrates that *any* program can "drive" web interaction when generating a HAR file. Here we saw how Selenium and CasperJS do it, but any other tool you have that can drive a browser and set a proxy will work well too.

Viewing HAR Files

So, thus far we have generated HAR files, which are just JSON, and you know that you can get arbitrarily fancy, perhaps sticking their values in a database or storing the files to watch trends in your application profile. But at some point you are going to want to view the things.

Visualizing the data in HAR files is easy. The simplest method is to go to the canonical web-based viewer (*http://bit.ly/XUdYEu*); simply drag a HAR file onto the page (go HTML5!) and drop it into any moderately modern browser, and you will see a waterfall graph of the HAR data. Make sure you uncheck the "Validate data before processing" checkbox before uploading your HAR. I have yet to come across a HAR file that validates correctly! Figure 6-3 shows a HAR file for our *search.yahoo.com* (*http://yhoo.it/XUdP3S*) search example.

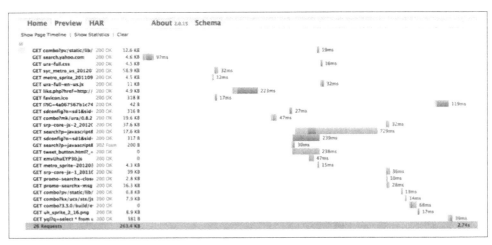

Figure 6-3. Waterfall graph for the search.yahoo.com (http://yhoo.it/XUdP3S) example

This is pretty snazzy! From this graph, we can see that 26 requests were made; hovering over any bar will reveal a specific breakdown of the amount of time each request took, in order: DNS Lookup, Connecting, Sending, Waiting, and Receiving.

A much more involved example comes from Yahoo.com (*http://yhoo.it/XUdX3p*). In this example, shown in Figure 6-4, 81 requests were made to download the page, and the download time was 4.39 seconds (actually, the page was visible much sooner than that; the data that was downloaded at the end of the process comprised a big Flash ad). The perceived performance and the initial time until the page looks ready are the most important bits of information to pay attention to, not the total amount of time all the pieces take to download.

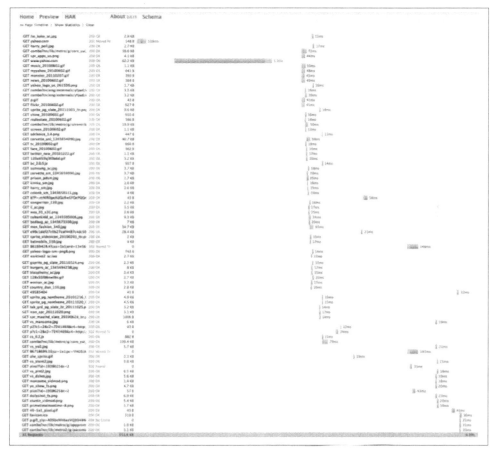

Figure 6-4. Waterfall graph for the Yahoo.com (http://yhoo.it/XUdX3p) example

Other options are also available for viewing HAR files without having to upload them to a remote website. For starters, download the source code for the HAR Viewer (*http:// bit.ly/XUe27h*). You can also easilyembed HAR graphs (*http://bit.ly/XUe5zG*) generated by the HAR Viewer into your own pages (the HAR files themselves can be grabbed remotely).

Another way to interrogate HAR files is with YSlow (*http://yhoo.it/XUe3rK*). Besides being a browser plug-in that gives grades on load performance, YSlow is also available as a command-line tool that can read HAR files and export YSlow output (*http://yhoo.it/ XUe3YM*). You can run YSlow from the command line or from within a Node.js script via the following command:

```
% npm install yslow -g
```

The YSlow output can be in XML, plain text, or JSON format. To graphically view the YSlow output, a beacon can be sent to a YSlow visualizer (*http://bit.ly/XUe4fd*), which you can also install locally (*http://bit.ly/XUe6nu*) if you do not want to send your precious YSlow data to a third party.

Let's take a look at how this all fits together. After installing YSlow, we'll feed it a HAR file and use the beacon to view the results at Showslow.com (*http://bit.ly/XUe4Mf*):

```
% yslow -i all -b http://www.showslow.com/beacon/yslow/ yahoo.com.har
```

This will send our HAR output from Yahoo.com (*http://yhoo.it/XUdX3p*) to be visualized. Then we cruise over to Show Slow (*http://bit.ly/XUe4Mf*) and find our URL in the list of recent beacons to see the full graphical output (*http://bit.ly/XUe8eQ*).

In this case, a lot of people have YSlow'ed Yahoo.com (*http://yhoo.it/XUdX3p*), so there are nice history graphs, and of course all the grades are A's! At the bottom of the page is a link back to the HAR Viewer for Yahoo.com (*http://yhoo.it/XUdX3p*)—the circle is complete!

You can generate visualizations yourself using the -`beacon` feature (*http://yhoo.it/ XUebr3*)—all the data provided by the beacon is detailed.

Or you can leverage the Showslow code and run your own local Showslow server.

HAR files are very interesting, but of course they do not represent the complete performance picture. Entire books are dedicated to this topic, and with good reason!

Browser Performance Testing

HAR files are amusing and easy to generate, but they do not tell the entire story. Beyond network performance, browsers must also parse HTML, parse and execute JavaScript, and lay out and paint the browser window, and that all takes time. How much time? There are tools to measure what exactly the browser is doing while your web application is running. dynaTrace AJAX Edition (*http://bit.ly/XUe92y*) for Firefox and Internet Explorer (Windows only) and Speed Tracer (*http://bit.ly/XUeceE*) for Chrome are two such tools. Both accomplish the same basic tasks. While a page is loading, the tools are collecting timing information that can be graphed immediately, or saved and graphed and inspected later. By inspecting the graphed output, you can identify performance issues and then fix them. The process of collecting these low-level timings is very specific to each browser; hence, there can be no generic collector like a HAR proxy.

In this section we will take a quick look at Speed Tracer. Speed Tracer (*http://bit.ly/XUea6v*) is an extension for Google Chrome.

Install the extension, and then click on its little green stopwatch icon to bring up the Speed Tracer UI. Clicking the red record button will start tracing browser internals, which mostly consists of fetching resources from the network, parsing HTML and JavaScript, and laying out and painting the browser window. This is all presented in the familiar waterfall graph. At the top of the UI are a Sluggishness graph and a Network graph. The Network graph is essentially identical to the HAR graphs we saw earlier. The Sluggishness graph is more interesting and visualizes how responsive (or not) the user interface is at the specified time. The taller peaks indicate that the browser's single UI thread was blocked—a bad thing!

Speed Tracer provides hints regarding problem areas in your application (as does YSlow); for instance, Speed Tracer will flag an event lasting longer than 100 ms. Event handling blocks the main UI thread while events are being serviced, so handlers longer than 100 ms can make the UI seem sluggish.

Finally, Speed Tracer provides a save button to save the data so that you can load and examine it again at a later time—this is a great feature to leverage during an automatic build process. To wit, as part of our build we can automatically generate the Speed Tracer data for our application to ensure that no changes are impacting performance (we will investigate this further in Chapter 8). Figure 6-5 provides a peek at the Speed Tracer UI analyzing Yahoo.com (*http://yhoo.it/XUdX3p*).

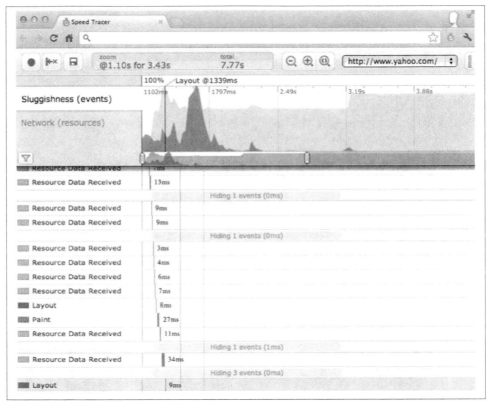

Figure 6-5. Speed Tracer UI as it analyzes Yahoo.com (http://yhoo.it/XUdX3p)

Load Testing

Performance testing identifies bottlenecks in your code that hinder performance at the application level, basically answering the question, "How fast can your application go?" Load testing attempts to identify how much your application can handle. This is very similar to performance testing. In fact, you could argue that performance testing is a subset of load testing. Performance testing determines what your application does under the smallest loads, while load testing determines how your application performs under maximum loads—both what the maximum load is and how your application reacts as the maximum is approached. The "maximum" is not necessarily the number of requests per second until the whole thing crashes, but rather how much load your application can handle before the response time becomes unacceptable. You get to define what the response time is.

Although being able to handle huge loads and still respond within a reasonable amount of time is nice, the end goal of load testing is not only to attempt to wring out low response times in the face of heavy loads, but also to know what your maximum acceptable response time is. Perhaps it is easier to scale servers horizontally when the maximum is reached rather than rewriting your codebase to handle the load itself. Eventually there will be a point where scaling horizontally or vertically will be necessary, and identifying that point is very helpful.

But load testing is not just for entire applications. Individual functions can be load-tested as well to determine their performance. Load testing is also not just about "time"; memory, disk, and CPU usage are also important to consider when testing a system or function under load. The end result of maxing out one (or more) of those resources is increased response time, so knowing which of those values has hit the wall is crucial.

Browser Load Testing

Load testing a web application in a browser usually involves sending your application as much traffic as possible and measuring its performance. Measuring performance typically means response time: you GET a page or POST a form multiple times and track how long the application takes to respond.

The canonical tool for this type of testing is Apache Bench (*http://bit.ly/XUefXO*). The command-line ab tool takes many options to GET, POST, PUT, or DELETE pages, and dumps out a CSV file of the results. In this chapter, we will work with the Node.js version, called nodeload (*http://bit.ly/XUedzr*).

nodeload has lots of great features beyond just hitting URLs repeatedly, so let's get started. Begin by installing the tool:

```
% sudo npm install nodeload -g
```

As a basic example we will use the nl.js utility, which acts similarly to the ab Apache Bench executable:

```
% nl.js
1 Aug 20:28:52 - nodeload.js [options] <host>:<port>[<path>]

Available options:
  -n, --number NUMBER          Number of requests to make.
Defaults to value of --concurrency unless a time limit is specified.
  -c, --concurrency NUMBER     Concurrent number of connections.
Defaults to 1.
  -t, --time-limit NUMBER      Number of seconds to spend running
test. No timelimit by default.
  -e, --request-rate NUMBER    Target number of requests per
seconds. Infinite by default
  -m, --method STRING          HTTP method to use.
  -d, --data STRING            Data to send along with PUT or
POST request.
```

```
    -r, --request-generator STRING    Path to module that exports
getRequest function
    -i, --report-interval NUMBER      Frequency in seconds to report
statistics. Default is 10.
    -q, --quiet                       Supress display of progress
count info.
    -h, --help                        Show usage info
```

A typical usage of this utility looks like this:

```
% nl.js -c 10 -n 1000 http://yhoo.it/XUdX3p
```

Do not try this at home, as this will hit Yahoo.com (*http://yhoo.it/XUdX3p*) 1,000 times, with 10 requests happening at a time. Here is what I got when I did not try this at home:

```
% nl.js -c 10 -n 1000 http://yahoo.com
http.createClient is deprecated. Use `http.request` instead.
Completed 910 requests
Completed 1000 requests

Server:                                yahoo.com:80
HTTP Method:                           GET
Document Path:                         /
Concurrency Level:                     10
Number of requests:                    1000
Body bytes transferred:                207549
Elapsed time (s):                      11.19
Requests per second:                   89.37
Mean time per request (ms):            111.23
Time per request standard deviation:   147.69

Percentages of requests served within a certain time (ms)
   Min: 86
   Avg: 111.2
   50%: 94
   95%: 113
   99%: 1516
   Max: 1638
```

These 1,000 requests averaged 111.2 milliseconds round trip, with one request taking 1.638 seconds to return. This kind of testing works best when also generating server-side statistics. Normally you would let this test run much longer, not only for "endurance testing" (can your application sustain a lot of hits over a long time?) but also to watch CPU, RAM, and disk utilization on the web server, as well as on any other backend machine that is providing services to your web application. Conveniently, nodeload can also generate those values.

nodeload also has a great reporting function. To see it, let's look at a full example. First we will put a long-running load on our web application. While our web server is servicing those hits, we will measure its CPU, disk, and RAM load. Finally, while the test is running, we can watch a live-updated graph of web server performance.

The first step is to send lots of hits. Here we're sending 100,000 of them:

```
% nl.js -c 10 -n 100000 -i 2 http://localhost:8080
```

While this is running, nodeload runs a web server on port 8000 to display the request activity (see Figure 6-6).

Upon completion, the final HTML and JSON values are saved into the current directory —pretty snazzy.

Meanwhile, you can monitor what is happening on the server side using your favorite statistics generator (vmstat, iostat, uptime, ps, etc.), using nodeload to graph and persist the values. Using Linux and the /proc filesystem, you can report and graph server-side values easily.

nodeload also provides a handy Loop class that will execute code at a specified frequency. As an example, this construct will execute the getMemory and getCPU functions once every five seconds, at most:

```
var myLoop = new loop.Loop(
    function(finished, args) {
        getMemory();
        getCPU();
        finished();
    }
    , []   // No args
    , []   // No conditions
    , .2   // Once every 5 seconds
);

myLoop.start();
```

The last parameter in the preceding code is the maximum number of times per second that the loop should execute.

Figure 6-6. nodeload graphical output

The header of this script sets up all our variables:

```
var reporting = require('nodeload/lib/reporting')
    , report = reporting.REPORT_MANAGER.getReport('System Usage')
    , memChart = report.getChart('Memory Usage')
```

```
    , cpuChart = report.getChart('CPU Usage')
    , loop = require('nodeload/lib/loop')
    , fs = require('fs')
;
```

Here I am defining a single report ('System Usage') with two charts, 'Memory Us
age' and 'CPU Usage'. The getMemory function uses the Linux */proc* filesystem to get
memory usage data:

```
function getMemory() {
    var memData = getProc('meminfo', /\s*kb/i);

    memChart.put({ 'Free Memory': memData['MemFree']
      , 'Free Swap': memData['SwapFree'] });
    report.summary['Total Memory'] = memData['MemTotal'];
    report.summary['Total Swap'] = memData['SwapTotal'];
}
```

We can, of course, pick out any value we like. The getProc utility function is not shown;
it simply takes a file in the */proc* filesystem and objectifies it. The interesting bits are
adding the current data point to the memory chart we defined in the header and adding
it to the report summary, which is displayed in the righthand column on the reporting
web page.

The getCPU function is similar:

```
function getCPU() {
    var meminfo   = fs.readFileSync('/proc/loadavg', 'utf8')
        , vals     = meminfo.split(/\s+/)
        , cpuInfo = getProc('cpuinfo')
    ;

    cpuChart.put( {
        '1 Min': vals[0]
        , '5 Min': vals[1]
        , '15 Min': vals[2]
    });

    report.summary['CPU'] = cpuInfo['model name'];
}
```

Again, we grab some values and add them to the CPU chart. Fire up the script and go
to port 8000 to view the live results.

The summary information is displayed on the right, and live-updating graphs are in the
main column. When the script ends, by whatever means necessary, a file will be available
in the local directory with the HTML of the graph.

nodeload has a lot of other tricks up its sleeve, including multiple loops for parallel execution of loops; a statistics package for further analysis of data sets; and a very flexible, programmatic way to specify requests (you do not have to just send vanilla HTTP requests). Of course, you can wrap any testing, hitting of web pages, or anything else within a loop, and easily graph the result.

Finally, the monitoring package allows for easy monitoring and collection of runtime data to prod your code for slowness and bottlenecks.

Tracking Resource Usage

Tracking the memory and CPU usage of your application is especially interesting in two scenarios: a single-page client-side JavaScript application and a server-side daemon. If the user does not stay on a single page for any length of time, JavaScript memory usage probably (of course, there are exceptions) does not matter; CPU usage may be a factor if a lot of processing is happening in the browser. Newer versions of modern browsers, such as Chrome, also do an excellent job of isolating memory- and CPU-hungry pages from one another. However, a single-page web application should be mindful of CPU and, especially, memory usage. Any long-running server-side process also must take care not to peg the CPU and to ensure that its memory footprint will not continue to grow until the program crashes (or worse).

Using modern browsers, the only way to leak memory in JavaScript is to keep references to objects you no longer need. This typically happens within a closure that references objects (potentially large objects) that you either no longer need or use, or do not even realize the closure is referencing. Here is an example:

```
function createClosure() {
    var bigHairyVariable = { ... }, wow = 'wow';
    return {
          a: bigHairyVariable
        , b: wow
        , c: 87
        , d: function() { return bigHairyVariable; }
    };
}

// never use global.a - wasted a lot of memory - a leak?
var global = createClosure();
```

Of course, rarely, if ever, will the code look so basic; moreover, this does not fit the typical idea of a memory "leak" from languages such as C, where memory is explicitly allocated. In fact, this may not be a leak at all if using bigHairyVariable at some point in the future is what is intended.

JavaScript object and function variables are references. In the preceding example, bigHairyVariable goes out of scope when the function returns, but the memory it points to is still being referenced by two other variables, `global.a` and the function `glob al.d`. Setting `global.a = null` frees that reference to whatever `bigHairyVariable` was originally pointing to, but that memory cannot be freed yet as `global.d` still references it. The only way to free this memory is to set `global.d` to `null`:

```
global.d = null;  // or global = null
```

The memory is not freed right away; not until the next time the garbage collector runs will the chunk of memory that `bigHairyVariable` was pointing to be freed.

Calling `createClosure` again will allocate a brand-new memory chunk for `bigHairy Variable` and keep that memory allocated until all references are released.

Note that if we called this function from within another function, when the return value went out of scope (when that function returned) all the memory associated with it would be marked as free (unless, of course, that function returned a closure referencing that variable!).

Client-Side Tracking

The WebKit Developer Tools provide excellent support for tracking the memory usage of your client-side JavaScript. As you will see in this section, the Profile panel is your friend for both memory and CPU tracking.

Memory usage

First, to get a look at overall memory usage, fire up your Chrome browser and go to *chrome://memory-redirect/*. There is a lot of data here, a summary of which you can find by selecting Wrench→Tools→Task Manager or Windows→Task Manager. This output is similar to that of the `top` utility but within the browser, including CPU usage, I/O, and network status information for each plug-in and tab, as well as overall browser activity (see Figure 6-7).

You can alter the columns that are shown by right- or context-clicking on a column header. For now, JavaScript memory is most useful. Other potentially interesting values are current cache sizes (see Figure 6-8) and, of course, "Goats Teleported."

There is a lot of good overall information here. Let's take a closer look at our application.

The heavy memory user here is Gmail. This is not surprising, as Gmail is a single-page web application with lots of JavaScript (like Google Calendar).

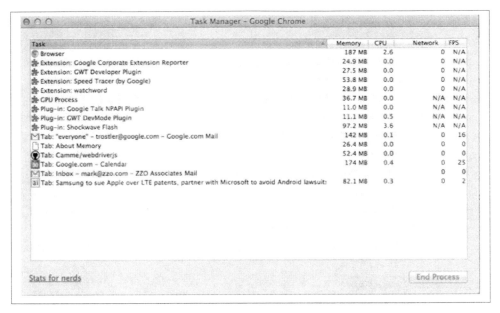

Figure 6-7. Chrome Task Manager

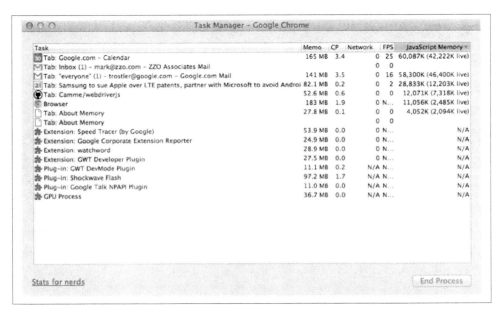

Figure 6-8. JavaScript memory per tab/process

As all recent browser versions use mark-and-sweep for garbage collection instead of reference counting, cycles can now be freed properly. But there are still plenty of other ways for your application to consume memory! A good overview is available on the Mozilla Developer Network site (*http://mzl.la/XUeeDg*).

To determine whether an application is leaking memory, our first stop is the Memory graph in the Timeline panel (see Figure 6-9).

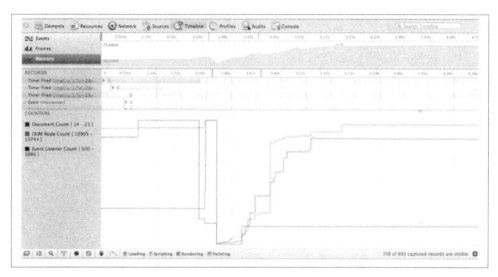

Figure 6-9. Memory graph in the Timeline panel

Memory usage can go up as long as it comes back down. As Figure 6-9 shows, this is a well-behaved application in terms of memory usage—usage goes up and down as the application requests and then releases memory. If your memory usage always increases and never decreases, you may have a memory leak.

In our case, the Profiles tab in the WebKit Developer Tools comes to our rescue! (See Figure 6-10.)

Figure 6-10. The Profiles tab in the WebKit Developer Tools

A heap snapshot makes it very easy to see how much memory a set of JavaScript objects is using. When you take a heap snapshot, the application runs the garbage collector first so that you are getting a "clean" view of actual memory usage (see Figure 6-11). Use the Class Filter text box to filter the resultant objects into the ones you are concerned about.

Figure 6-11. Heap memory used by RegExp objects

According to Figure 6-11, there are more than 1,200 regular expression objects; drilling down, you can inspect every one of them. Besides your own objects, you can also filter on DOM objects. If you are concerned that a certain action is leaking memory, take multiple snapshots. In the Summary view, shown in Figure 6-12, you can see which objects were allocated between each snapshot (note the pull-down at the bottom where I have selected "Objects allocated between Snapshots 1 and 2").

Figure 6-12. The Summary view

Finally, you can compare two heap snapshots for another view of what has changed between the two (see Figure 6-13).

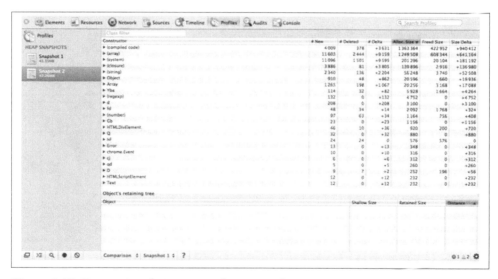

Figure 6-13. Comparison between two heap snapshots

Here, I used a lot of memory between Snapshot 1 and Snapshot 2. According to the Comparison view, more than 1,000 new array objects were created between the two snapshots. To determine whether this was intended, you can drill down into each object to see what they contain.

Interestingly, there currently is no way to trigger a heap snapshot programmatically. One solution to this issue is to insert a debugger statement into your code, and manually trigger a heap snapshot once the interpreter stops.

You can read about Gmail's approach to finding and squashing memory leaks (*http://bitly.com/PzCbfm*) in its code. Also, the Chrome Developer Tools team has created a leak finder (*http://bit.ly/XUehir*).

CPU usage

Collecting a JavaScript CPU profile from the Profiles tab shows similar information from the CPU usage angle. You can easily inspect how much time (real or a percentage) your program spends in each function, and how many times each function was executed. Click Start to begin capturing CPU information; you can click around or perform some actions and then click Stop to see what happened.

Figure 6-14 shows that the YUI function to add a node was the heavy hitter (although it was called many times, it still only took 40 ms to decorate the page). This displays the call stack to that function, and clicking on the link on the right will take you to the actual code.

Figure 6-14. JavaScript CPU usage

Clicking the % button will toggle the display between real time and percentage time spent in each function.

By taking heap snapshots and collecting CPU profiles, you can gain a very intimate understanding of what exactly your application is up to while it is running.

If you are interested in tracking noninteractive code paths, use console.profile:

```html
<html>
    <script>
        var Cache = function() {
            this.cache = {};
            this.add = function(key, val) {
                var now = new Date().getTime();
                cache[key] = { val: val, time: now };
            };
        }

        var cache = new Cache();
        console.profile('squared');
        for (var i = 0, l = 1000000; i < l; ++i) {
            cache.add(i, i ^ 2);
        }
        console.profileEnd('squared');
    </script>
</html>
```

Loading this code in a WebKit-based browser and opening the Profiles tab will produce output similar to that shown in Figure 6-15.

Figure 6-15. CPU usage from console.profile

The Profiles tab has captured the "squared" profile report, and now it is available for inspection.

Server-Side Tracking

Node.js exposes the V8 profiler, which you can use to gather CPU and memory usage data beyond console.trace. Using the webkit-devtools-agent npm package (*http://bit.ly/XUehiH*) makes profiling Node.js server-side applications almost as easy (and pretty) as profiling client-side ones. So, install it, and get ready to rumble!:

```
% sudo npm install webkit-devtools-agent -g
```

This package allows your Node.js application to utilize the Heap Snapshot and JavaScript CPU Profiles tabs in a WebKit-based browser (such as Chrome or Safari). To use the package, simply require it at the top of your program and then signal your Node.js process with a USR2 signal:

```
var agent = require('webkit-devtools-agent');
process.kill(process.pid, 'SIGUSR2');
```

Of course, you can also send the USR2 signal externally from your program. This starts up a local daemon listening for connections from a WebKit browser that will then fire up the Developer Tools to analyze your program.

To get all this to work, you will need to start a copy of Chrome with the -remote-debugging-port=9222 option. On a Mac, from a shell issue the following command (all on one line):

```
% /Applications/Google\ Chrome.app/Contents/MacOS/Google\ Chrome
--remote-debugging-port=9222 -user-data-dir=/tmp
```

Another WebKit-based browser can use this copy of Chrome to connect to debug the Node.js application. Once your application has started and you have signaled it with USR2, you can now connect to the following URL from another WebKit browser: *http://localhost:9222/devtools/devtools.html?host=localhost:1337&page=0*.

This loads the Developer Tools as served by the first WebKit browser, which speaks the Web Sockets protocol to the webkit-developer-agent spawned by your Node.js program. While the entire set of Chrome Developer Tools appears, only the Profiles tab actually works (see Figure 6-16).

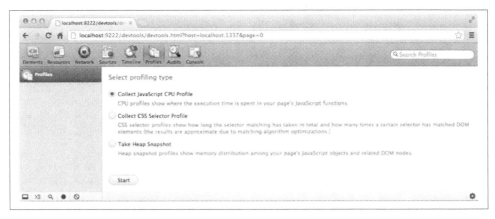

Figure 6-16. Profiles tab from webkit-developer-agent

Programmatic heap snapshots

Using the UI, you can also collect a JavaScript CPU profile or take a heap snapshot of your Node.js program. Alternatively, you can programmatically take a heap snapshot using the heapdump package (*http://bit.ly/XUehz9*):

```
% sudo npm install heapdump -g
```

Using this package is simple, but it does require an addition to your code. First, you must `require` the module:

```
require('heapdump');
```

When you're ready to take a heap snapshot, simply send the USR2 signal to your Node.js process:

```
% kill -USR2 <NodeJS process ID>
```

This will dump into the current directory a heap snapshot file that can be viewed using Chrome Canary (*http://bit.ly/XUehPC*), the developer build of Chrome.

To programmatically trigger a heap dump, signal yourself:

```
process.kill(process.pid, 'SIGUSR2');
```

After requiring heapdump, the preceding statement will trigger a heap dump to the application's directory.

To see the dump in all its glory, open the Developer Tools in Chrome Canary and click the Profiles tab. Then right-click Profiles to load the snapshot, and select the heapdump-snapshot file output by your Node.js process. The heap snapshot will appear in the list of snapshots—click on it to check it out.

Programmatic CPU usage

Capturing CPU usage in Node.js is similar to taking a heap snapshot. To profile the entire application, simply issue this command:

```
% node --prof myapp.js
```

When your application exits, the file *v8.log* will be written to the application's directory. If you build Node.js from source, you can use your operating system's `*-tick-processor` execute command to visualize this file, but it is simpler to just install the profiler npm package (*http://bit.ly/XUefHm*):

```
% sudo npm install profiler -g
```

Now you can build the nprof command-line tool. First find the *node_modules* directory where the package was installed. In that directory will be a *profiler* directory; change into that directory and issue the following command:

```
% /bin/sh tools/build-nprof
```

This will create an *nprof* JavaScript executable in the *profiler* directory. Execute it either with the path to your *v8.log* file or from a directory with a *v8.log* file in it:

```
% .../node_modules/profiler/nprof path/to/v8.log
```

You will be greeted by output similar to Chrome's JavaScript CPU Profile output (but in glorious text).

Recap

Your job does not end with writing code and unit-testing it. Especially for web-based applications, integration and rudimentary performance testing are also necessary. Integration testing is not just for QA people anymore. Using pure JavaScript, developers can easily create integration tests that integrate into Selenium.

By leveraging Selenium or CasperJS, you can easily generate and view HAR files for your web applications, all in pure JavaScript. Keeping track of the code you are writing and the effects the code is having on the entire application is a required activity for all well-rounded JavaScript developers. Now that you know how to do it—both in "real" browsers and in PhantomJS—it's easy to include this in your development workflow.

In addition to network issues, performance testing is also concerned with digging deep into the browser to determine exactly what it is doing and how long it is taking, as this is what provides the deepest understanding of an application. Tools such as dynaTrace AJAX Edition and Speed Tracer provide this highly browser-dependent data to be analyzed.

Load and runtime monitoring are also easy to accomplish using nodeload or similar tools. Of course, the monitoring and testing processes are relatively straightforward, and the results will provide lots of detail regarding what is happening with your application, but tracking down the actual underlying issues can require patience and perseverance!

Finally, you can stay completely on top of your application's memory and CPU usage using Chrome Developer Tools and Node.js modules. These tools will help you to optimize your code as well as find memory and CPU bottlenecks.

Tools for JavaScript are continuing to increase in quantity and robustness. As the number of tools increases, it is important to understand JavaScript's memory model and code hot spots so that you will be productive regardless of which tool you choose.

## CHAPTER 7

Debugging

Debugging sucks. I heartily recommend not doing it. For those rare times when you must, however, there are many great tools and techniques to assist you.

In-Browser Debugging

Debugging client-side JavaScript invariably leads to using the debuggers provided by the various browsers themselves, or extensions to the browsers. You can view the current market share of each browser worldwide, or in your region, at the StateCounter website (*http://bit.ly/XUefHw*). Figure 7-1 shows the graph as of October 2012.

Of course, your web server logs will provide the most accurate assessment of browser usage for your application, but according to the global statistics shown in Figure 7-1, usage of Google Chrome is on the rise while all other browsers are either declining or stagnant. In terms of specific browser versions, Figure 7-2 shows that as of October 2012, use of Chrome 17 and IE 9.0 was rising, while use of all other major browser versions, representing only about a 15% share of the market, was falling. The scariest part of the graph in Figure 7-2 is the dotted line. This line represents mobile and tablet browsers, and its position in the graph indicates that these browsers are used more than the others.

We will discuss debugging on mobile and tablet browsers later in the chapter. In the meantime, let's take a quick look at the various debuggers each major desktop browser provides. I will highlight some basics and differences between them, but for the most part they are similar and are constantly evolving. You will find a wealth of information about the current features of each debugger online.

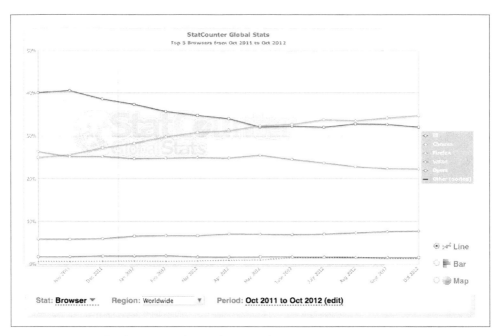

Figure 7-1. Worldwide market share of the top five browsers

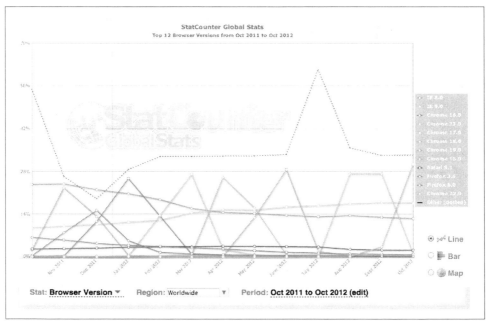

Figure 7-2. Top 12 browser versions worldwide

Firefox

The granddaddy of them all, Firebug (*http://bit.ly/XUeiD4*) is a Firefox extension that provides all the debugging bells and whistles expected in a JavaScript debugger. After installing the latest version (1.11.1 as of this writing) and restarting Firefox, start Firebug by selecting Tools→Web Developer→Firebug→Open Firebug. The Firebug window will open by default at the bottom of the browser; alternatively, you can "detach" it from the browser and place it in its own window if you like. Figure 7-3 shows the Firebug window while browsing Yahoo.com (*http://yhoo.it/XUdX3p*).

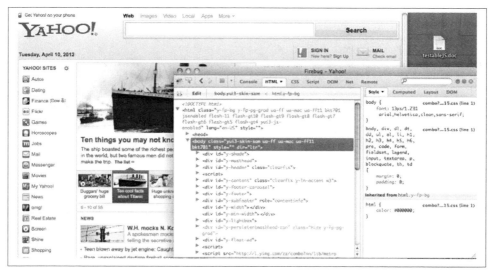

Figure 7-3. Firebug window while browsing Yahoo.com (http://yhoo.it/XUdX3p)

With Firebug, you can manipulate HTML and CSS, step through JavaScript, and set breakpoints. The Net panel will show you the familiar waterfall graph of loading elements. You will see gaps in this graph after JavaScript loads while it is being parsed—holes that Speed Tracer (in Chrome) and dynaTrace (on Windows) can fill in.

Firebug also provides the `window.console` object that you can use to log messages to the console. In addition to printing strings, you can pass any object to the console output methods and Firebug will dereference it for you to display its fields. You can display basic timing information using the `console.time(<STRING>)` and `console.time End(<STRING>)` methods (yes, the strings have to match, allowing you to have multiple overlapping timings simultaneously). Firebug will also display the time that has elapsed between the two calls. You can view more detailed timings using the `console.pro file()` and `console.profileEnd()` methods. Firebug will display complete timing information for each function that was called between those two invocations. Firebug also provides the `console.trace()` method to generate a stack trace, including all parameters that were passed to each function within the trace. Objects can be inspected using `console.dir(<object>)` and HTML nodes can be inspected using `console.dirxml(<node reference>)`. Finally, `console.assert(<boolean condition>)` will display a red error message in the console if the condition does not evaluate to `true`.

You can execute arbitrary JavaScript in Firebug or place `console.*` statements in your code to track it as it runs, and you can insert a `debugger` statement to set a breakpoint, but be careful to take them out when you are done debugging!

Finally, Firebug allows the naming of anonymous functions using the `displayName` property. This is easiest to see with an example. Imagine debugging this function:

```
function getIterator(countBy, startAt, upTill) {

    countBy = countBy || 1;
    startAt = startAt || 0;
    upTill  = upTill || 100;

    var current = startAt;

    return function() {
        current += countBy;
        return (current > upTill) ? NaN : current;
    };
}
```

The simple function in the preceding example creates an iterator. The following code demonstrates its usage:

```
var q = getIterator(10, 0, 200);
console.log(q());
```

That's simple enough, but debug this in Firebug and look at the stack, as shown in Figure 7-4.

The stack reveals a function named (?). Firebug does not know what to call this anonymous function, so you can tell it what to call it using the `displayName` property of the anonymous function, like so:

```
function getIterator(countBy, startAt, upTill) {

    countBy = countBy || 1;
    startAt = startAt || 0;
    upTill  = upTill || 100;

    var current = startAt
        , ret = function() {
            current += countBy;
            return (current > upTill) ? NaN : current;
        }
    ;
```

```
        ret.displayName = "Iterator from " + startAt + " until "
          + upTill + " by "  countBy;

        return ret;
    }
```

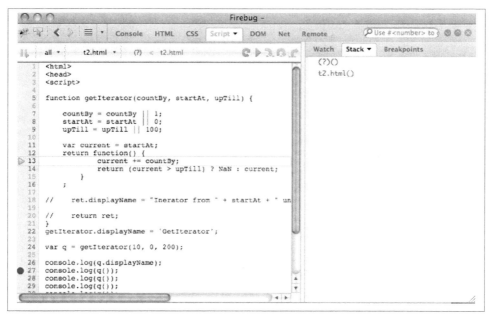

Figure 7-4. Anonymous functions in Firebug

Here I added the `displayName` property to the anonymous function—and a pretty descriptive `displayName` at that! Now when we use Firebug to step through this code, we'll see something similar to Figure 7-5.

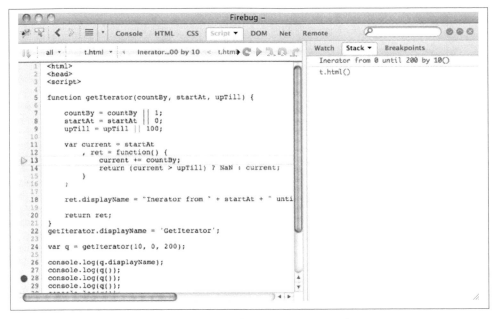

Figure 7-5. Anonymous function with displayName set in Firebug

That's much better! We have transformed (?) into something very descriptive and helpful. You can add the `displayName` property to any function, and it can be anything you like. Obviously, it is especially useful for anonymous functions, such as those typically used in event callbacks or, as in this example, ones you generate yourself.

Chrome

Chrome has an equally useful set of developer tools (*http://bit.ly/XUejaf*), including a debugger. Accessed from the View→Developer menu, the Chrome Developer Tools can also be attached to the bottom of the main Chrome window or detached as a separate window. Figure 7-6 shows the window for Yahoo.com (*http://yhoo.it/XUdX3p*).

Awaiting you here is a set of tabs that are similar to those in Firebug. However, Chrome's Timeline tab includes much of the same data as Speed Tracer, showing not only network traffic, but also what the UI thread is up to, including painting, events, and layout. The Timeline graph also displays when the main resource has finished loading (a purple line) and when the main resource DOM document is finished parsing (a red line). These events represent the initial load time and the first time when the user sees the initial HTML and can start interacting with it—both important measurements. The Timeline panel also has a memory graph. For longer-lived applications with just one page you do not want to see the number forever climbing upward, as such a condition indicates a memory leak in your code. Figure 7-7 shows a peek at the Timeline panel.

Figure 7-6. Chrome Developer Tools window while browsing Yahoo.com

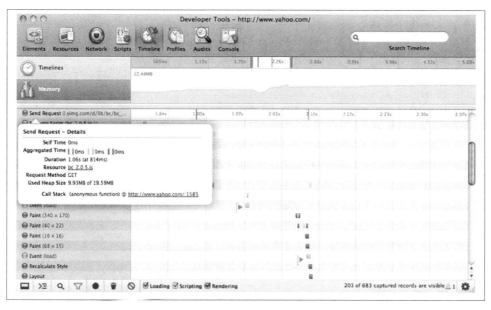

Figure 7-7. Chrome Developer Tools Timeline panel

The Chrome debugger also supports all of Firebug's console methods, and for minified code the debugger has a nice "prettifier" that renders the JavaScript code readable again. Once the code is prettified, you can set breakpoints as normal—a very handy feature! Obfuscated and minified code requires more work to prettify, and we will investigate how to do this using source maps later in this chapter.

The Chrome debugger also supports the "naming" of eval blocks. As you are not using eval, this hopefully will not affect you. However, some tools—especially tools that manipulate JavaScript, such as the CoffeeScript compiler—use eval generously. The following format:

```
//@ sourceURL=<any string without spaces>
```

will make your eval appear in the Scripts drop-down, where you can select it to jump immediately to the eval statement. Here is a quick example:

```
var two = eval('1 + 1; //@ sourceURL=addedOnePlusOne!');
```

Figure 7-8 shows what this looks like in the Scripts panel of the Chrome debugger.

Figure 7-8. sourceURL set in Chrome Developer Tools

As you can see in the figure, addedOnePlusOne! is available in the list of scripts to select to jump directly to—and the evaled expression will be available to examine and breakpoint, as it is in the earlier example. The name is also visible in the stack trace.

Chrome also allows you to easily change the User Agent string it sends when fetching web pages. You can access this capability in the Settings menu, where you can pretend to be any browser you want (see Figure 7-9).

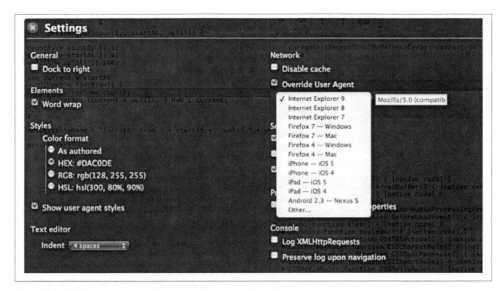

Figure 7-9. Changing the User Agent string in Chrome

Finally, Chrome allows you to break on all errors, even errors that were caught in a `try/catch` block, as shown in Figure 7-10.

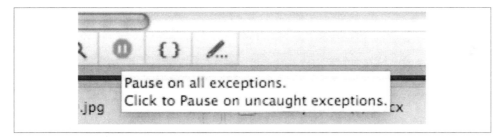

Figure 7-10. "Pause on exceptions" toggle in Chrome Developer Tools

You can toggle this feature on and off. I recommend that you leave it on initially, to ensure that the errors and exceptions you are catching are acceptable.

Safari

Like Chrome, Safari is based on WebKit (*http://bit.ly/XUejH2*), and its debugger is very similar to the Chrome debugger. To use the tools, you begin by enabling the Develop menu in Safari. The checkbox for doing so is hidden under Preferences→Advanced→"Show Develop menu in menu bar" (see Figure 7-11).

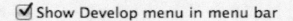

Figure 7-11. Enabling the Develop menu in Safari

Now you have a Develop top-level menu with a lot of options. Go ahead and open the Web Inspector, and you'll see something similar to Figure 7-12.

Figure 7-12. Safari Web Inspector

Chrome has added some bells and whistles that are not available in the standard WebKit —namely, the remote debugging JSON protocol (even though it was ported back to WebKit, the feature is not yet available in Safari) and other advanced options—but typically Safari and Chrome behave in virtually the same manner when rendering pages, so choose whichever one you enjoy developing with the most. Of course, there are differences between the two browsers, but they are not as pronounced as are those between Safari/Chrome and Firefox, and especially between Safari/Chrome and Internet Explorer. Like Chrome, Safari also offers easy access to changing the User Agent string it sends to masquerade as different browsers. You can enter an arbitrary string to trick websites into sending content optimized for other browsers. This is most useful for pretending to be a mobile iOS browser, as the iPhone, iPad, and iTouch User Agent strings are all available. Figure 7-13 shows what happens after selecting the iPhone User Agent string and visiting LinkedIn (*http://linkd.in/XUemmk*).

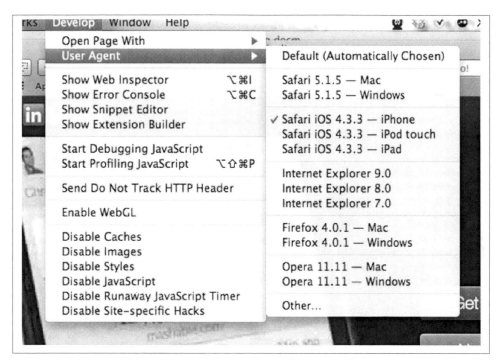

Figure 7-13. Changing the User Agent string in Safari

Safari also supports the `displayName` property on functions for display in its debugger.

Internet Explorer

I cannot say much about Internet Explorer that has not been said already. Unfortunately, most of your users may be using IE. Fortunately, use of IE 8 and earlier versions is waning; however, IE 8 and later versions do provide a nice debugger (*http://bit.ly/XUemCY*). You access the IE debugger by pressing the F12 key on your keyboard (hence the name "F12 Developer Tools") or via the Tools menu. The debugger provides similar tools to Firefox and WebKit-based browsers, including rudimentary profiling information.

IE 8 also provides the `console` object, but with very limited functionality: only `log`, `info`, `warn`, `error`, and `assert` are supported. At some point you will have to use the IE debugger, but fear not, it is not ridiculously hideous.

Node.js Debugging

Node.js ships with a decent command-line debugger (*http://bit.ly/XUemTp*). Starting the debugger is easy:

```
% node debug myscript.js
```

The debugger has a small set of commands, which you can review using the help command:

```
% node debug chrome.js
< debugger listening on port 5858
connecting... ok
break in chrome.js:1
  1 var webdriverjs = require("webdriverjs")
  2     , fs = require('fs')
  3     , WebSocket = require('faye-websocket')
debug> help
Commands: run (r), cont (c), next (n), step (s), out (o),
backtrace (bt), setBreakpoint (sb), clearBreakpoint (cb),
watch, unwatch, watchers, repl, restart, kill, list, scripts,
breakpoints, version
debug>
```

These commands are detailed in the aforementioned documentation, but all the basics are there: starting, stopping, and stepping through code; setting and clearing breakpoints; and watching variables.

An interesting twist is the repl command: this switches into REPL (read-evaluate-print-loop) mode, where you can evaluate JavaScript (including inspecting variables) in the current context and scope of the debugger at that moment. Exiting out of REPL mode brings you back into debugger mode, where you can issue the commands listed earlier.

You can also use the familiar debugger statement somewhere in your code to trigger a breakpoint.

The watch commands are not terribly useful, but they are amusing, as you can "watch" a variable and at each breakpoint the debugger will dump the variable's contents—not only at explicit breakpoints, but also after each step, next, or out command. There is currently no support for conditional breakpoints.

Running node debug *<script>* to interactively debug your Node.js script is useful, if clunky. V8, the JavaScript engine upon which Node.js runs, provides a JSON-based protocol for debugging code. You can access this mode using the --debug and --debug-brk switches. There currently can be only one debugger connected to a session at a time; running node debug ... immediately utilizes that single debugger connection. The --debug and --debug-brk flags start your Node.js script and either wait or allow a single connection from a remote debugger (at a time).

Details regarding the V8 JSON debugging protocol are available at the code.google V8 website (*http://bit.ly/XUekL9*). To use it, simply connect to the debugger port (5858 by default) and pass and accept the JSON objects. The bit the developers conveniently forgot to document is the required presence of a Content-Length header. Regardless, a bare-bones implementation using the protocol is available (*http://bit.ly/XUenqz*). You can install it via npm:

```
% npm install pDebug -g
```

Now you can write programs to debug and exercise your applications. First, start a Node.js program you want to inspect or debug:

```
% node -debug-brk myProgram.js
```

This will load the debugger but will not start your program. Attach to it and start issuing debugger commands:

```
var pDebug = require('pDebug').pDebug
    , debug = new pDebug({ eventHandler: function(event) {
        console.log('Event'); console.log(event); } })
    ;

debug.connect(function() {
    var msg = { command: 'continue' };
    debug.send(msg, function(req, resp) {
        console.log('REQ: ');
        console.log(req);

        console.log('RES: ');
        console.log(resp);
    });

});
```

You can also start your program running and attach to it later using:

```
% node -debug myProgram.js
```

Using the API specified on the V8 wiki, you can programmatically send requests and get responses and events from a local or remote debugger running your program. I'll leave it up to your imagination how to leverage such power—a good start would be conditional breakpoints!

You can also use WebKit's debugger and developer tools to debug your Node.js application using an npm module such as node-inspector (*http://bit.ly/XUeqCx*):

```
% npm install node-inspector -g
```

Now you can fire up your Node.js program under the debugger:

```
% node -debug-brk myProgram.js
```

start the inspector in the background:

```
% node-inspector &
```

and point Chrome or Safari to this URL: *http://localhost:8080/debug?port=5858*.

As if by magic, the debugger will open and you will be debugging your Node.js program! Very, very awesome! And funny you should ask, but *yes*, since PhantomJS is built on WebKit, you can feed this URL to it and open the debugger console in PhantomJS. Figure 7-14 shows a screenshot of PhantomJS running the WebKit debugger.

Figure 7-14. PhantomJS running the WebKit debugger

Once PhantomJS exposes the debugger server interface, the details of which we will discuss shortly, you can manipulate the debugger remotely—mind-bendingly zany! For now, you should stick with Chrome or Safari to visually debug your Node.js applications.

Remote Debugging

Debugging JavaScript remotely is easy. This situation is more common and more useful than you may originally think. Remote debugging is either necessary or useful in the following scenarios:

- Debugging mobile browsers
- Debugging server-side JavaScript
- Debugging browser tools

- Programmable debugging

First we will look at the nuts and bolts of remote debugging in two environments (Chrome and Firefox), and then we will visit each of the aforementioned scenarios in turn to see how it works. Remote debugging allows the debugger to run in a separate process (or even another host) from the JavaScript being debugged.

Chrome

Chrome/WebKit has, by far, the most mature remote development environment. Versions 18 and later of Chrome have the latest version of the JSON-based remote debugging API, version 1.0 (*http://bit.ly/XUenXw*). Note that this is *not* the same API as the V8 debugger API. Chrome allows its debugger to be used on remote code and allows a remote debugger to connect to Chrome to debug JavaScript running within it. That's service!

To debug JavaScript running in Chrome remotely, you need to start the Chrome executable with a port for the debugger to listen on. Here's the code if you're using Windows:

```
% chrome.exe --remote-debugging-port=9222
```

Here it is if you're on a Mac (all on one line):

```
% /Applications/Google\ Chrome.app/Contents/MacOS/Google\ Chrome
--remote-debugging-port=9222
```

You should also start Chrome with this option:

```
--user-data-dir=<some directory>
```

This is equivalent to starting Chrome with a fresh profile, such as your Firefox profile. Now you can attach to port 9222 and interact with the 1.0 debugger profile.

Here is an example of how to use this functionality to pull out timing statistics—the same statistics as those that Speed Tracer and the Chrome debugger's Timeline panel visualize. We will use Selenium to automatically spawn a Chrome instance listening on port 9222 for debugger connections. You may find it interesting that the JSON debugging API runs over Web Sockets, not HTTP; use of Web Sockets makes event propagation trivial. Using `EventHub` or `socket.io` would provide the same functionality over plain HTTP.

Let's take a look at a Node.js script using webdriverjs, the Node.js package discussed in Chapter 6 for Selenium WebDriver, which leverages Chrome's remote debugging capabilities. This script is a bit longer, so we will look at it in two parts. This first part starts up Selenium with the appropriate Chrome command-line options and exercises the browser with the flow we want to capture:

```
var webdriverjs = require("webdriverjs")
    , browser = webdriverjs.remote({
```

```
            host: 'localhost'
            , port: 4444
            , desiredCapabilities: {
                browserName: 'chrome'
                , seleniumProtocol: 'WebDriver'
                , 'chrome.switches': [
                    '--remote-debugging-port=9222'
                    , '--user-data-dir=remote-profile'
                ]
            }
        }
    );

    browser.addCommand("startCapture", startCapture);

    browser
        .init()
        .url('http://search.yahoo.com')
        .startCapture()
        .setValue("#yschsp", "JavaScript")
        .submitForm("#sf")
        .saveScreenshot('results.png')
        .end();
```

This is mostly standard webdriverjs stuff we have seen before. However, there are two additions. The first addition is the `chrome.switches` desired capability. The Chrome driver conveniently allows us to provide command-line switches to the Chrome executable. Here we are telling Chrome to start listening for remote debugger connections on port 9222 and to use a profile from a specific directory. We do not need any specific Chrome extensions or settings to use remote debugging, so this is pretty much just a blank profile.

The second addition is the `startCapture` function. webdriverjs allows us to define a custom method that can be chained along with all the standard webdriverjs methods. Any custom method receives a callback function to be invoked when the custom function is finished. Here we have defined a `startCapture` method that will start capturing all Chrome-supplied timing information—network times, painting times, layout times, everything that is available. There is no corresponding `stopCapture` function in this example, as we will just capture everything until the browser is closed.

Here is the `startCapture` function:

```
    function startCapture(ready) {

        var http = require('http')
            , options = {
                host: 'localhost'
                , port: 9222
                , path: '/json'
            }
```

```
;

    http.get(options, function(res) {
        res.on('data', function (chunk) {
            var resObj = JSON.parse(chunk);
            connectToDebugger(resObj[0], ready);
        });
    }).on('error', function(e) {
        console.log("Got error: " + e.message);
    }
```

Visiting *http://localhost:9222/json* (or whatever host Chrome is now running on) will return a JSON response, which is an array of tabs that can be attached to for remote debugging. Since we just opened this Chrome instance with Selenium there is only one tab, and hence only one object in the array. Note that webdriverjs passed `startCap ture` a callback function to be called when our `startCapture` step is finished. So, this function connects to the local (or remote) Chrome instance, gets the JSON data about the current tab we want to debug, and then hands off this information to the `connect ToDebugger` function, shown here:

```
function connectToDebugger(obj, ready) {

    var fs = require('fs')
        , WebSocket = require('faye-websocket')
        , ws = new WebSocket.Client(obj.webSocketDebuggerUrl)
        , msg = {
            id: 777
            , method: "Timeline.start"
            , params: {
                maxCallStackDepth: 10
            }
        }
        , messages = ''
    ;

    ws.onopen = function(event) {
        ws.send(JSON.stringify(msg));
        ready();
    };

    ws.onmessage = function(event) {
        var obj = JSON.parse(event.data);

        if (obj.method && obj.method === 'Timeline.eventRecorded') {
            obj.record = obj.params.record;   // Zany little hack
            messages += JSON.stringify(obj) + '\n';
        }
    };

    ws.onclose = function(event) {
        var header = '<html isdump="true">\n<body><span id="info">'
```

```
           + '</span>\n<div id="traceData" isRaw="true" version="0.26">'
           , footer = '</div></body></html>'
         ;

         ws = null;
         fs.writeFileSync('DUMP.speedtracer.html', header + messages
           + footer, 'utf8');
     };
```

OK, this is the meat of the whole thing! Remember, the debugger protocol runs over a web socket connection. The faye-websocket npm module provides an excellent client-side web socket implementation, which we leverage here. The object provided by `start Capture` contains the `webSocketDebuggerUrl` property, which is the web socket address to connect to for this tab—which was just spawned by Selenium.

After connecting to the specified web socket address, faye-websocket will issue a callback to the onopen function. Our onopen function will send a single JSON-encoded message:

```
msg = {
    id: 777
    , method: "Timeline.start"
    , params: {
        maxCallStackDepth: 10
    }
};
```

The specification for this message is available at the Chrome Developers Tools website (*http://bit.ly/XUer9D*). This tells Chrome to send us web socket messages, which are Chrome debugger events, for every Timeline event. Once we've sent this message, we call the webdriverjs callback so that our webdriverjs chain can continue (remember that?).

Now, we perform some Selenium actions for which we want to capture Timeline events—in this case, loading Yahoo! (*http://yhoo.it/XUdP3S*) and then searching for "JavaScript". While all this is happening, Chrome is sending us `Timeline.eventRecor ded` events, which we dutifully capture and keep via the `onmessage` web socket callback.

Finally, after those actions have finished, we shut down Selenium, which closes Chrome, which calls our `onclose` handler, which does some interesting things as well—namely, dumping all our saved events into an HTML file. This HTML file is, conveniently, the same file format used by Speed Tracer, so if you load this HTML file into Chrome with the Speed Tracer extension installed, it will load the Speed Tracer UI with this data—awesome! This allows you to automatically capture Speed Tracer input that you can use to compare against previous versions of your code, or examine at your leisure. Figure 7-15 shows how the HTML code looks when loaded into Chrome, with Speed Tracer installed.

Figure 7-15. HTML code when loaded into Chrome, with Speed Tracer installed

Clicking the Open Monitor! button brings up the Speed Tracer UI with our captured data in it, as shown in Figure 7-16.

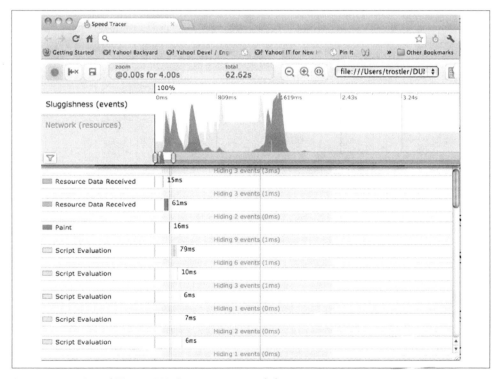

Figure 7-16. Speed Tracer UI showing captured data

Beyond capturing Timeline events from Chrome, you can also completely control the Chrome debugger from a remote location, pausing and resuming scripts, capturing console output, calling and evaluating JavaScript in the context of the page, and doing all the other things you can do using the Chrome debugger directly.

PhantomJS

Similar to Chrome, PhantomJS can be used as a target for remote debugging. But in this case, the remote machine can be headless, or you can run PhantomJS locally without having to fire up another browser instance with its own separate profile.

Unfortunately, you cannot directly interact with the web application running in the PhantomJS browser. Fortunately, you can step through the code and interact programmatically with your running code via a PhantomJS script.

Remote debugging using PhantomJS is most useful for scriptable or programmable debugging. Here is how to set it up using the latest version (1.7.0 as of this writing):

```
% phantomjs -remote-debugger-port=9000 ./loader.js <webapp URL>
```

In the preceding command line, *loader.js* is a PhantomJS script that simply loads your URL and waits:

```
// Open page from the command line in PhantomJS
var page = new WebPage();

page.onError = function (msg, trace) {
    console.log(msg);
    trace.forEach(function(item) {
        console.log('  ', item.file, ':', item.line);
    })
}

page.open(phantom.args[0], function (status) {
    // Check for page load success
    if (status !== "success") {
        console.log("Unable to access network");
    } else {
        setInterval(function() {}, 200000);
    }
});
```

This script will also dump out any syntax errors or uncaught exceptions from your application, which is nice. Once this script is running, open your local WebKit-based browser, type *http://<phantomjs_host>:9000* in the URL bar, and click on the link that is your web application. The familiar debugger will open and you will be live-debugging your application.

PhantomJS provides an `evaluate` method that allows you to manipulate the DOM of the loaded page and execute JavaScript on the page. Note that any JavaScript executed by PhantomJS on the page is sandboxed and cannot interact with the running JavaScript in your application—but that is what the remote debugger is for! One-way interaction from your web application to a PhantomJS script *can* happen via `console.log` messages, and there are interesting ways to leverage that path, as we will see when gathering unit test output and code coverage information and using PhantomJS as a target for automated unit test execution.

Firefox

Firebug also has a remote debugging capability, using the Crossfire extension (*http:// bit.ly/XUeoKQ*). Crossfire is an extension to Firebug that exposes a debugging protocol to the network for programmable debugging. The latest version (0.3a10 as of this writing) is available at their website (*http://bit.ly/XUeoL4*). Once you have installed Crossfire and restarted Firefox, you will see a Crossfire icon in your Add-on bar. Clicking on that icon and then clicking Start Server brings up the dialog box shown in Figure 7-17.

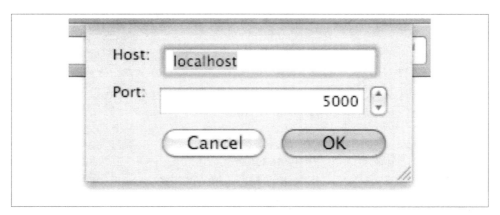

Figure 7-17. Crossfire configuration dialog in Firefox

Click OK to start the Crossfire server on this host, listening on port 5000 (or set the port number to something else).

Alternatively, you can start Firefox with a command-line option to automatically start the Crossfire server on a given port:

```
% firefox -crossfire-server-port 5000
```

Now you can connect to the Crossfire server and start debugging! Similarly to Chrome's tabs, Firebug treats each tab as a separate "context." Unfortunately, the Selenium Firefox driver does not currently support passing arbitrary command-line options to the Firefox executable, and nor does Crossfire support profile-based configuration, so this cannot be automated by Selenium. I hope this changes soon.

Crossfire is not as mature as the debugging server built into Chrome. I expect this to change over time, but currently you are better off using the WebKit/Chrome-based debugger for remote debugging within the browser.

Mobile Debugging

Mobile debugging is just an offshoot of remote debugging. To be clear, we are talking about debugging in mobile browsers. The two main browsers, Chrome in Android and Safari in iOS, are based on WebKit. We've already seen some examples of remote debugging using WebKit-based browsers, and the latest versions of Android (now up to 4.2, Jelly Bean) and iOS (6) allow for remote debugging. If you're sure that all your users will be running these latest versions, then no problem! Let's take a quick look at the native solutions before investigating a more general one.

Android 4

You can install Chrome for Android Beta on Android 4.0 and later from the Google Play store (*http://bit.ly/XUesdB*). This version allows for remote debugging from your desktop using the standard WebKit debugging protocol. Once Chrome for Android Beta is installed, you must go to Settings→Developer Tools to enable remote debugging.

Meanwhile, on your desktop you must install the Android Software Developer Kit (SDK) from the Android website (*http://bit.ly/XUepi1*). We only need one script from this package: the Android Debug Bridge (adb). That executable is available in the stock SDK download and installing it is easy. Once you've downloaded the SDK, run the Android executable, which is the Android SDK Manager. From that tool you have the option to install the Android SDK Platform tools, which contain the adb tool. Simply check the corresponding box and click Install. Figure 7-18 shows what the Android SDK Manager tool looks like on my Mac.

Installing all that stuff will take a long time so if you just want the adb tool, uncheck all the other checkboxes and then click Install. Once the tool is installed, a *platform-tools* directory will exist in the main SDK tree. You must now connect your phone to your desktop using your USB cable. You can run the adb tool like so:

```
% ./adb forward tcp:9222 localabstract:chrome_devtools_remote
```

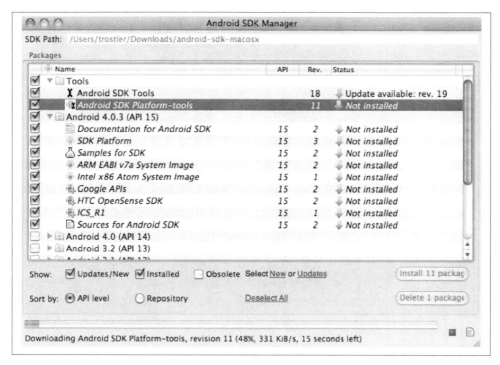

Figure 7-18. Android SDK Manager

On your desktop Chrome, connect to *http://localhost:9222* and you will see a list of the URLs in each tab on the Chrome browser on your phone. Click the tab you would like to debug, and *voilà*, you can use the Developer Tools on your desktop Chrome to debug and control the browser on your phone.

The biggest shortcoming to this approach is that you must be running Android 4.0 or later, you must install Chrome Beta, and your phone must be physically connected to your desktop. This method works only for that exact scenario.

iOS 6

iOS 6 brings a new remote Web Inspector feature to Mobile Safari. Start by selecting Settings→Safari→Advanced to enable the feature on your iDevice (see Figure 7-19).

Now browse to the site you want to debug in Mobile Safari [in this example, Yahoo! (*http://yhoo.it/XUdX3p*)], connect the device to a Mac running desktop Safari 6.0+, and pull down the Develop menu (which must be enabled), as shown in Figure 7-20.

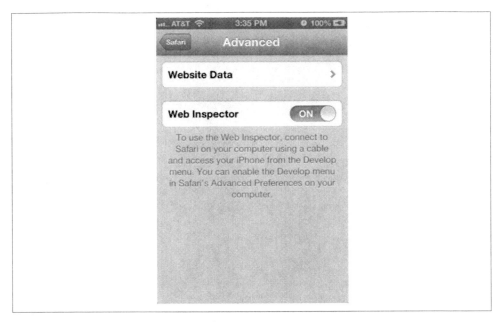

Figure 7-19. Enabling the remote Web Inspector in iOS 6

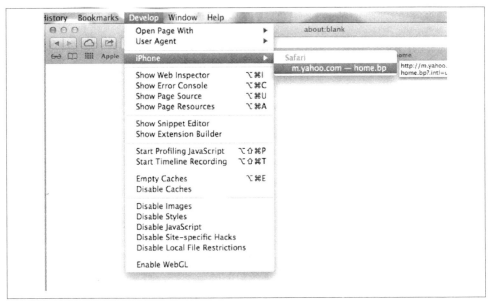

Figure 7-20. Debugging a website on an iPhone from desktop Safari

As you can see here, my iPhone is now available to be Web Inspected remotely. You can choose any open mobile Safari page to attach the debugger to and then debug as usual, setting breakpoints, stepping through JavaScript, and inspecting page elements. Figure 7-21 shows the Safari Web Inspector window for the mobile Yahoo.com page (*http://yhoo.it/XUdX3p*).

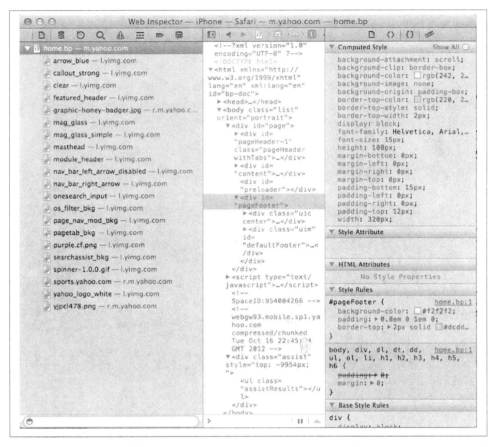

Figure 7-21. Safari Web Inspector window for the mobile Yahoo.com page (http:// yhoo.it/XUdX3p)

Adobe Edge Inspect

Adobe Edge Inspect (originally Adobe Shadow) is a cross-mobile-OS solution that allows remote WebKit mobile debugging on all versions of Android, iOS, and Kindle Fire.

It consists of a desktop Chrome extension, a desktop daemon (similar to adb), and an application on your device. Your device must be on the same local network as your desktop so that they can connect to each other. Adobe Edge Inspect only works on Windows 7 and Mac OS X.

Start at the Adobe Creative Cloud website (*http://adobe.ly/XUeqmc*) and grab the latest version of the Inspect daemon. From that page you can also download the application for iOS, Android, or Kindle Fire and the Inspect Chrome extension.

Start up the Inspect application; to do this you must log into the Creative Cloud website again—Bad Adobe!

In Chrome, install the Adobe Inspect extension from the Chrome Web Store and you will be greeted by the Inspect extension icon on your browser; click it and you'll see something similar to Figure 7-22.

Figure 7-22. Configuring Inspect in Chrome

Make sure the slider is set to "on." Adobe Inspect is now ready to accept connections from a mobile device running the Adobe Inspect application, so grab that from your mobile app store and run it. You will be prompted to add a connection. Although a "discovery" feature is available for this, I have not had success with it. Fortunately, you can manually add a connection by specifying the IP address of your desktop running the Adobe Inspect daemon (see Figure 7-23).

After connecting, you will be presented with a PIN that you must enter into your desktop Chrome browser (see Figure 7-24).

Figure 7-23. Specifying the desktop IP address on an iPhone

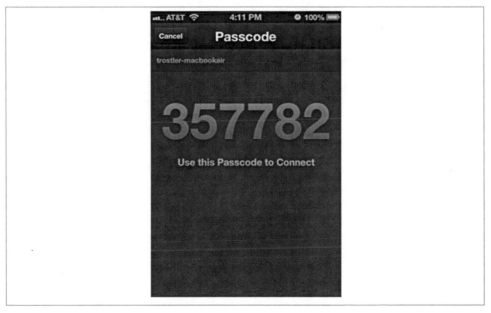

Figure 7-24. Entering the PIN on desktop Chrome

That passcode is entered into your desktop Chrome browser from the extension icon. At this point, the device is ready to be debugged (see Figure 7-25).

Figure 7-25. Debugging a remote device running Inspect from desktop Chrome

Now open a tab in your desktop Chrome browser and navigate to the page you would like to debug; that page will also load on your mobile device. In fact, once you are connected, any URL you visit will be mirrored on that device. Clicking the <> icon from within the Inspect extension will bring up the debugger, and what is being debugged is the version of the URL on the mobile device.

You can now use the debugger as you would on a local page, selecting elements, changing CSS, and debugging JavaScript. It is as though the location being debugged is running in the local browser.

This works on all versions of Android, iOS, and Kindle Fire. The only requirements are that the device (or devices, as multiple devices can be mirrored from a single Chrome desktop simultaneously) must be on the same local network as the desktop, you must use Chrome, and you must be using Windows 7 or Mac OS X.

Things get goofy when a website offers both a "mobile" and "desktop" version of its site, so it's best to set the User Agent of your desktop Chrome browser to match whatever device is being mirrored. You can do this from the Developer Tools menu; click on the Settings wheel in the lower-right corner and select the Overrides tab (see Figure 7-26).

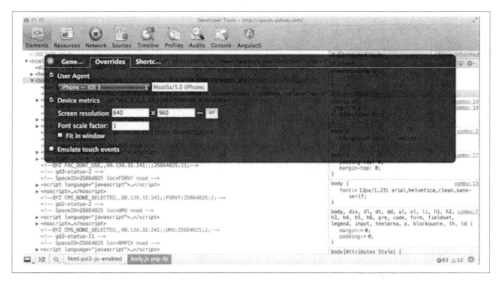

Figure 7-26. Setting the User Agent string in Chrome

Now the site viewable in desktop Chrome will match what is being viewed on your mobile device, making for easier debugging.

While this is a neat tool, with the advent of iOS 6 and good native Android debugging the value of using Adobe Inspect is limited, so stick with the native solutions if possible.

Other Mobile Debugging Options

Other mobile debugging options are also available, such as weinre (pronounced "wine-ry"), which became part of PhoneGap and is now an incubator project at Apache called Apache Cordova (*http://bit.ly/XUetyo*). weinre (*http://bit.ly/XUewtP*)—which stands for WEb INspector REmote—works similarly to Adobe Inspect, but Inspect is more polished. And with the advent of native iOS 6 and Android debugging, its usefulness is minimized.

Jsconsole.com (*http://bit.ly/XUewKk*) is another option: it requires the injection of its JavaScript via a bookmarklet to inject debugging code. The end result is similar, but the method is more clunky and complicated.

Going forward, your best bet for a robust debugging environment is either one of the native options discussed here, or Adobe Inspect. But this space is changing quickly, so keep your eyes and ears open for new solutions!

Production Debugging

The techniques and tools we have discussed thus far are fabulous when debugging in your local development environment. But what about code that is already in production? Minification, combination, and obfuscation make production code extremely hard to debug. We already discussed the fact that WebKit browsers have a "prettify" button to "unwrap" minified code, but what about combined and obfuscated code? Or how about JavaScript code generated from another tool from another language, such as Coffee-Script or even Java (via GWT)?

Minified Code

As previously mentioned, WebKit browsers have a "de-minify" button for the simplest case of only compressed code. Figure 7-27 shows minified code in the Chrome debugger.

Figure 7-27. Minified code in Chrome Developer Tools

As you can see, this is not terribly useful! It is impossible to set a breakpoint, and if the code does stop somewhere it is impossible to tell exactly where. Decompressing the code after clicking the {} button yields what's shown in Figure 7-28.

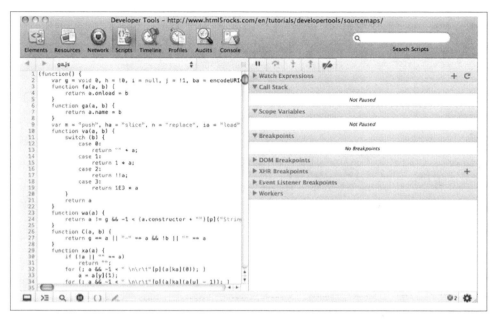

Figure 7-28. Expanded code in Chrome Developer Tools

Great, now this code is readable and breakpoints can be set on each line. But this code was also obfuscated using Google's Closure Compiler (*http://bit.ly/XUeulM*), so we do not have access to the original variable names (similar obfuscation tools will yield similar results).

Source Maps

Source maps come to our rescue here. A source map is a single file containing one large JSON object mapping lines in the compressed, obfuscated, and combined JavaScript code back to the original code. An added bonus is the fact that the "original code" does not even need to be JavaScript! The source map specification is available here (*http://bit.ly/HB8Xtz*) and is currently at Revision 3.

Using source maps, code that has been minified, combined, and obfuscated can be mapped directly back to the original source in the debugger. As of this writing, only Google Chrome supports source maps natively (on the Beta branch), although other browsers are sure to follow. The Google Closure Compiler (*http://bit.ly/XUeulM*)

combines and generates minified and obfuscated code and can also output a source map for that code. Google also supplies the Closure Inspector (*http://bit.ly/XUexhD*), a Firebug extension that lets Firebug understand source maps as well. Hopefully, source map support will soon be supported in all browsers natively.

Let's take a quick look at the process. For this example we will use the `getIterator` function shown earlier. Here it is again, in a file called *iterator.js*:

```
function getIterator(countBy, startAt, upTill) {

    countBy = countBy || 1;
    startAt = startAt || 0;
    upTill = upTill || 100;

    var current = startAt
        , ret = function() {
            current += countBy;
            return (current > upTill) ? NaN : current;
        }
    ;

    ret.displayName = "Inerator from " + startAt + " until "
        + upTill + " by " + countBy;

    return ret;
}
```

As you can see, there's nothing special here—it weighs in at 406 bytes.

Let's grab the latest version of *compiler.jar* from the Google Closure Compiler home page. Now we are ready to run the Closure Compiler on *iterator.js*:

```
% java -jar compiler.jar --js iterator.js --js_output_file it-comp.js
```

Here is our new file, *it-comp.js* (lines broken for readability):

```
function getIterator(a,b,c){var a=a||1,b=b||0,c=c||100,d=b
,e=function(){d+=a;return d>c?NaN:d};
e.displayName="Iterator from "+b+" until "+c+" by "+a;return e};
```

This file weighs in at a svelte 160 bytes! In addition to deleting all the whitespace (and any comments), variable names were renamed: `countBy` was transformed to `a`, `star tAt` to `b`, `upTill` to `c`, and so forth. This cuts down on the size of the file tremendously, and now we are ready to deploy into production!

Or are we? There is still a problem with this code: debugging the code in a browser will be very difficult. Even "unminifying" it using the {} button in a WebKit debugger will not bring our original source code back, due to our renaming of the variables.

Fortunately, the Closure Compiler can make more advanced transformations to our code to make it even smaller. However, these transformations will deviate our code even further from the original.

And here is where this becomes a problem. If we load the code into the debugger as part of our web page and try to debug it, we see that the code is quite ugly (see Figure 7-29).

Figure 7-29. Minified Iterator code

Figure 7-30 shows the unminified version.

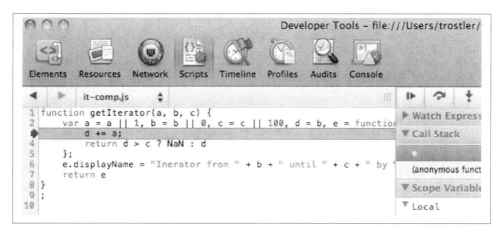

Figure 7-30. Expanded Iterator code

OK, that version is slightly less ugly, *but the variable names are still not correlated to our original source, and the line numbers are different from those in the original file.*

Source maps to the rescue! First we tell the Closure Compiler to generate a source map for us (all on one line):

```
% java -jar compiler.jar --js iterator.js --js_output_file
it-comp.js --create_source_map ./it-min.js.map --source_map_format=V3
```

If we take a look at the generated source map file, *it-min.js.map*, it is indeed a giant JSON object:

```
{
"version":3,
```

```
"file":"it-comp.js",
"lineCount":1,
"mappings":"AAAAA,QAASA,YAAW,CAACC,CAAD,CAAUC,CAAV,CAAmBC,CAAnB,CAA2B,
CAE3C,IAAAF,EAAUA,CAAVA,EAAqB,CAArB,CACAC,EAAUA,CAAVA,EAAqB,CADrB
,CAEAC,EAASA,CAATA,EAAmB,GAFnB,CAIIC,EAAUF,CAJd,CAKMG,EAAMA,QAAQ
,EAAG,CACfD,CAAA,EAAWH,CACX,OAAQG,EAAA,CAAUD,CAAV,CAAoBG,GAApB,CAA0BF
,CAFnB,CAMvBC,EAAAAE,EAAAE,YAAA,CAAkB,gBAAlB,CAAqCL,CAArC,CAA+C,SAA/C,CAA2DC
,CAA3D,CAAoE,MAApE,CAA6EC,CAE7E,OAAOI,EAfoC;",
"sources":["iterator.js"],
"names":["getIterator","countBy","startAt","upTill","current","ret"
,"NaN","displayName"]
}
```

The meat of this object is the `mappings` property, which is a Base64 VLQ-encoded string. You can read plenty of gory details about this encoding, as well as what exactly is encoded, online.

The last bit of magic is to tie the source map to the JavaScript served to the browser, which you can do by adding an extra HTTP header or by adding a magical line to the minified JavaScript telling the debugger where to find the corresponding source map:

```
function getIterator(a,b,c){var a=a||1,b=b||0,c=c||100,d=b
,e=function(){d+=a;return d>c?NaN:d};
e.displayName="Iterator from "+b+" until "+c+" by "+a;return e};
//@ sourceMappingURL=file:////Users/trostler/it-min.js.map
```

Here we added a line to the Closure Compiler output pointing to the source map generated by the compiler.

Now go back to the browser, load it all up, and look in the debugger (see Figure 7-31).

Not only is the code in the debugger window our exact original code, but also the filename in the Scripts pull-down is the original filename. Breakpoints can be set as though this were the exact code running in the browser, but indeed the browser is actually running the minified output from the Closure Compiler.

The biggest issue when using source maps is printing/evaluating expressions, as the original source looks like it is being executed as is, but those original variable names do not actually exist in the browser as it is executing your minified code. You cannot evaluate expressions to determine variable values, nor do you have the mapping to know what the variable was transformed into! Figure 7-32 shows an example.

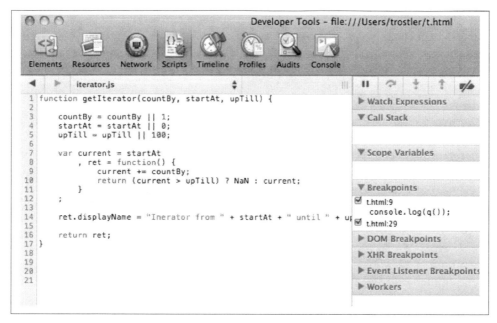

Figure 7-31. Iterator code expanded showing original code

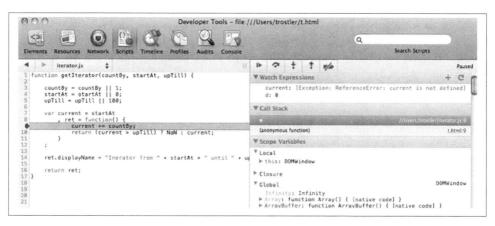

Figure 7-32. Debugging source-mapped code

In the debugger I am looking at code where the variable current should be defined, but my Watch Expressions display reveals that it is not defined! Conversely, some random variable named d is defined with the value 0, but it does not appear to be so defined in the source code listing. This is weird and something to be aware of. Perhaps future versions of the specification will handle this inconsistency.

Google's GWT compiler can also output source maps, and work is being done for the CoffeeScript compiler as well, so as far as you can tell you are debugging your original native code while the browser is actually running the compiled version. As time goes on other tools besides the Closure Compiler will support this format, so get behind (or ahead?) of it!

Recap

There are myriad ways to debug both client- and server-side JavaScript. Debuggers available within (or via an extension to) all the major browsers provide an incredible array of excellent tools for more than just step-by-step debugging, including HTML and CSS live editing, tracing, and profiling. Chrome and headless PhantomJS expose themselves for remote debugging, and Firefox via Crossfire is heading in that direction as well.

Server-side JavaScript is also well served using the built-in command-line debugger, a programmable debugger, or a remote debugger in WebKit-based browsers.

There is also a wide-open field for programmable debuggers. I hope the day will soon come when stepping through code line by line will be mostly a thing of the past. Automated tools to help speed up the debugging process will be a most welcome addition to the current tool chain.

Performance problems can also be quickly tracked down using excellent tools such as Speed Tracer and the Profile or Performance tab provided by most in-browser debuggers, and there is experimental support for profiling Node.js applications as well.

Finally, production and non-JavaScript debugging can be made straightforward with the use of source maps.

So, even though debugging is painful, these modern tools do manage to take away a lot of the tedium. The olden days of "console.log" are (hopefully!) long past.

## CHAPTER 8

Automation

The point of writing testable JavaScript is so that you and your colleagues can easily fix and maintain the code going forward; hence it is a good skill to possess. Writing tests for future versions of the code becomes easy, and this solid foundation makes automation much more effective. Automation ensures that you can write testable JavaScript in a repeatable way as quickly as possible. When considering automation, you must know what to automate, when to automate, and how to automate.

What to Automate

Determining what to automate is easy: automate everything! This includes JSLint and other forms of static analysis, all tests, code coverage reports, application packaging, and application deployment, including rollback, feedback, bug submission, statistics, and bucket or feature testing. Anything you have to do more than once should be automated. Any time you use up front to automate will be more than paid back over the lifetime of your code.

When to Automate

In terms of when to automate, you have three opportunities: while coding, while building, and while deploying. These three points in the software development process all have different requirements, even if some of the tools you use for each process are the same. For instance, the process for deploying your code to test it while under development may be different from the process for deploying the code to production. As much as those two processes should be kept the same, in reality they are different. Deploying code to a test virtual machine is different from deploying it to multiple servers distributed around the world. Similarly, running unit tests and generating code coverage metrics in your local development environment is, unfortunately, slightly different from running all unit tests during the build process.

Of course, you should use the same tool to deploy locally that you use to deploy to production. And the same tool should run unit tests locally, since during the build the particulars will be different. The only way to deal with these differences is to ensure that the process and the tools are automated.

We will not delve deep into the deployment side, as those tools differ the most across organizations due to vast scale differences. For instance, Yahoo! Mail deployments will look radically different from deployments to five servers worldwide, even though the end goals are all the same. Instead, we will focus on development and build automation, which tend to be more similar regardless of application size or reach.

Setting up an automated local environment plays nicely into setting up an automated build environment, which is essentially a superset of the development environment. An automated build environment aggregates tools and tests from the automated development environment and puts a prettier face on them.

How to Automate

Automating your JavaScript environment requires tooling. Whether you roll your own or use something off the shelf, the end result must be a sane continuous integration environment. That means building and testing your code in a simple and repeatable manner.

While your continuous integration system will typically be kicked off automatically (either at timed intervals or as the result of a check-in), developers must also know how to manually kick off a continuous integration run for those one-off situations that always seem to occur. If this process is difficult or arcane to accomplish, it will not get done and chaos will ensue.

Repeatable means the process runs to completion every time without spurious errors in either the build process or the tests. Avoiding too many emails and false-positive test results from the continuous integration environment is paramount, as if too many emails from the build system with bad (either too much or blatantly wrong) information are received, the emails will soon be ignored and your continuous integration environment will be wasted.

Continuous integration automation must be rock-solid.

Automating with Continuous Integration

Perhaps the biggest advantage of a completely automated environment is the ability to do continuous integration. By constantly building and testing (at every commit), you catch errors very quickly, before the code is deployed anywhere.

Developers are responsible for running unit tests before checking in their code, but unit testing is only the beginning. In a continuous integration environment, the code is tested as a whole for any mismatches (and unit tests are executed over the entire codebase in case you accidentally break something else in the process!).

To accomplish this for every commit, you need to run the build and the tests as quickly as possible. You can run unit tests in parallel, followed by a quick deploy to a test environment for some basic integration testing. Not all of your tests need to run while doing continuous integration—typically you just need to run unit tests and several integration tests that test very basic and core application functionality.

You will be able to trace failures directly back to the commit and the developer responsible for the failure. At this point, all builds should be halted until the problem is fixed. (Perhaps the developer's name should go up on a "wall of shame" for breaking the build!) All attention should now be focused on fixing the build so that the rest of the team can continue moving forward.

Upon success, the build can be deployed to a QA environment for more extensive testing, and from there into other environments, and eventually out to production.

A quick, fully automated development build gives rise to a continuous integration environment. Applications with many integration points and pieces are especially prone to errors between all the moving parts. The ability to quickly discern issues in an automated fashion without having to bother developers or QA people speeds development by not wasting time on obviously broken builds.

The Integrate Button website (*http://bit.ly/XUev9i*), maintained by the authors of *Continuous Integration: Improving Software Quality and Reducing Risk* (Addison-Wesley), provides a lot more detail about the process and benefits of continuous integration.

There are very few, if any, reasons why you should not be using continuous integration in your project.

Automating the Development Environment

The software development stage is the most manual, error-prone, time-consuming part of any software project. Until we can teach computers to write code for us, we are stuck typing characters one at a time into an editor. Every modern industry has been completely transformed by automation, with newer, shinier, faster machines doing the repetitive tasks humans once toiled at. Not so with writing software. The "science" and "art" of writing software has not changed in the more than 40 years since the terminal was introduced—the conversion from punch cards to terminals in the early 1970s was the last "breakthrough" in software creation. Instead of writing software on pads of columned paper to be punch-carded, we can now type our programs directly into the computer—woo-hoo.

So, writing software is a very hard, very time-consuming, and very manual process. Any automated tool that can in any way facilitate, speed up, and automate the task is a very good thing. Let's take a tour of some tools that are available for this task and see how we can use them to automate the development environment.

The editor

The most basic and most controversial tool in the developer's arsenal is the editor. The best editor is the one you are most comfortable with. There are fancy IDEs that auto-complete keywords and variable names, but do not have as rich a set of plug-ins as other, more basic editors. There are pros and cons to every editor, so use the one you are most comfortable with. Whatever editor you use, ensure that you familiarize yourself with all its features to make your job as easy as possible. Auto-indenting, auto-complete, brace matching, and other convenience features will improve your life by reducing the amount of time it takes to complete the compile–run cycle. Each editor has its own set of tricks and tips for tons of features you do not know about, so search around and find them! A good starting place is VIM (*http://bit.ly/XUevpO*) ☺.

Unit tests

Having taken the time to write the unit tests, now you should enjoy the fruits of your labor by running them automatically while you develop. Several unit test frameworks provide similar features: the ability to run unit tests from the command line, dynamic code coverage report generation, and multiple browser support. JUTE (*http://bit.ly/XUevGk*) is a handy tool that does all of that, and a bit more. In this section we will focus on integrating JUTE into our development environment to run our unit tests and generate coverage reports as painlessly as possible (in the spirit of full disclosure, I am the author of JUTE).

Available as an npm package, JUTE's biggest requirements are the use of YUI3 Test (*http://bit.ly/XUdGxh*) and your directory structure. From our work with Yahoo! Mail, my colleagues and I determined that the sanest directory structure between application and test code is a mirrored hierarchy. From the root directory there are two main sub-directories, *src* and *test*. The *test* directory tree mirrors the *src* directory tree. All unit tests for each file in the *src* tree live in the corresponding directory in the *test* tree. Of course, your mileage may vary, and you do not have to set up your repository that way—some people like to have their test files in the same directory as the source code, and JUTE can be configured for this scenario. However, my experience suggests that having a mirrored test tree is a superior layout.

Begin by installing JUTE:

```
% npm install jute
```

Use the npm variable to configure it. The most important configuration variable is doc
Root, which is the root of your project. By default, JUTE expects a test directory within
your docRoot:

```
% npm config set jute:docRoot /path/to/project/root
```

Now you must restart JUTE (as you must do after any configuration variable change):

```
% npm restart jute
```

The JUTE UI should be running in your browser at *http://localhost:5883*, where you will
see something similar to Figure 8-1.

Figure 8-1. The JUTE user interface

Starting with the Status panel, you will see all "captured" browsers—in this case there is
only one captured browser, the one I'm using to look at this page. To "capture" a browser,
simply navigate to the root JUTE UI page. Any submitted unit tests will be run through
all captured browsers in parallel.

The middle frame, while not running tests, simply shows all available unit tests. This
list is populated by recursively finding all *.html* files in the *test* subdirectory. To run any
test, click on one of the Run links. You can choose to run either with or without code
coverage. To run multiple tests, check the checkboxes in the corresponding columns
and click the Run Tests button. Remember, these HTML files are the "glue" HTML files
we discussed in Chapter 4.

Finally, the Results panel will display the results and any optionally generated code
coverage reports for all the tests that were run.

You can also run tests from the command line, and they will run within any captured
browser:

```
% jute_submit_test --test path/to/test.html
```

Whatever you set as docRoot will be prepended to the path passed to jute_sub mit_test. Of course, you can run multiple tests from a single command also:

```
% jute_submit_test --test test1.html --test test2.html
```

Finally, you can read in test files from *stdin*:

```
% find . -name '*.html' -print | jute_submit_test -test -
```

This is similar to what the JUTE UI does to display all your tests in the UI.

Running a test with code coverage enabled will automatically generate an LCOV-style coverage report for that test, a link to which will be available in the Results column along with the JUnit XML output from the test itself.

The actual output files are, by default, placed in an *output* directory in the docRoot directory. You can change this using the outputDir configuration variable:

```
% jute config set jute:outputDir results
```

Note that the full path to this directory is docRoot + outputDir, so it must live within your docRoot. All test-result XML files and LCOV data are placed in this directory. The test result filenames are browser User Agent strings, so you can tell how your tests ran in each browser. Figure 8-2 shows the Results panel in the UI after running a test.

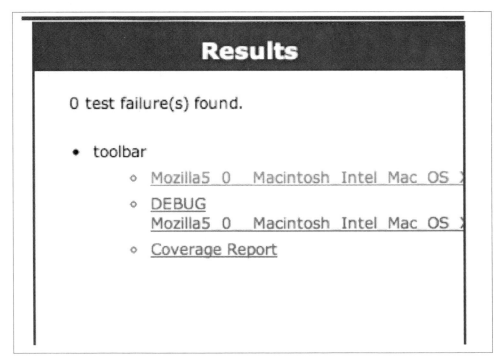

Figure 8-2. The Results panel after running a test in JUTE

The "toolbar" test—the name comes from the Test Suite name—has a JUnit XML results file (which we already saw in Chapter 4), an output file containing debugging information (mainly YUI Test output, anything your code prints to the console, and timing information), and a dynamically generated coverage report. Connecting another browser to JUTE by visiting its page shows both browsers in the Status panel (see Figure 8-3).

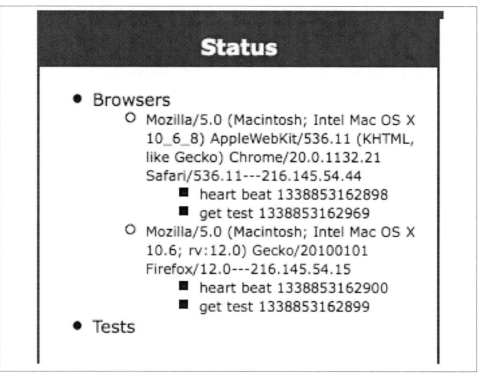

Figure 8-3. JUTE Status panel

Now both Chrome and Firefox are connected to this JUTE instance and are ready to run unit tests.

Running `jute_submit_test` will cause any submitted tests to be run in both browsers in parallel, and there will be results for both Chrome and Firefox in the Results panel. Here is the directory listing after running the "toolbar" test with both browsers connected:

```
% ls output/toolbar/
cover.json
lcov.info
lcov-report/
Mozilla5_0__Macintosh_Intel_Mac_OS_X_10_6_8__AppleWebKit536_11__
KHTML__like_Gecko__Chrome20_0_1132_21_Safari536_11-test.xml
```

```
Mozilla5_0__Macintosh_Intel_Mac_OS_X_10_6_8__AppleWebKit536_11__
KHTML__like_Gecko__Chrome20_0_1132_21_Safari536_11.txt
Mozilla5_0__Macintosh_Intel_Mac_OS_X_10_6_rv_12_0__Gecko20100101_
Firefox12_0-test.xml
Mozilla5_0__Macintosh_Intel_Mac_OS_X_10_6_rv_12_0__Gecko20100101_
Firefox12_0.txt
```

There is only one coverage report, regardless of how many browsers are connected. However, there are now two JUnit XML files and two debugging output files: one set of each for each browser, as named by its User Agent string.

Is your code on a headless server? Want even more automation? Instead of using a "real" browser, JUTE can utilize PhantomJS as a backend! The latest version of PhantomJS (1.6.1 as of this writing) does not require that an X server be running. PhantomJS integration with JUTE is trivial:

```
% jute_submit_test --test path/to/test.xml --phantomjs
```

Now our results will contain another set of JUnit XML results and a debug logfile for the PhantomJS browser. And as a special added bonus, you also get a snapshot of the "browser" right after all the tests finish (see Figure 8-4).

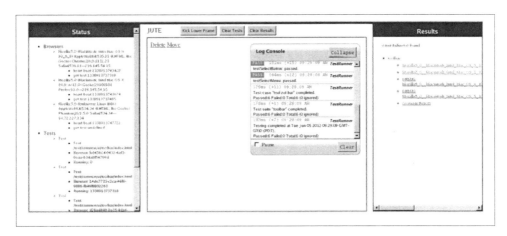

Figure 8-4. JUTE running tests

Figure 8-4 shows what the headless PhantomJS browser looks like on a headless Linux system. You can see the currently running test in the middle panel. You can also see the PhantomJS browser in the Status panel. The yellow highlighted tests in the Status panel are the ones currently running.

A final word on JUTE in your development environment: JUTE requires no changes to your test code (or code under test) to get dynamic code coverage reports and command-line execution, and all the other goodies JUTE provides. You can still manually load your "glue" HTML test files directly into a browser and execute them directly if you wish. When we discuss automating the build environment we will see how JUTE also fits very nicely in that scenario.

With its dynamic code coverage report generation, JUTE allows you to easily track your unit test progress while you are developing code, via either the command line or the UI. That is a big step toward testable JavaScript.

Code reviews

Short of full-blown Fagan code analysis reviews, sharing code with peers to be reviewed before checking it in is crucial to ensuring that both you and your peers are aware of what you are doing. Besides sharing knowledge, code reviews promote style guidelines among the team and help newer members get up to speed more quickly with the code-base.

What should be reviewed? Reviewing a giant chunk of JavaScript makes my eyes glaze over, so going line by line for the bigger chunks is where Fagan analysis really shines. At a minimum, a code walkthrough for large chunks of code with some peers is warranted. However, code reviews for bug fixes are where automation really helps.

Code reviews can be as simple as emailing a diff to some or all team members, but typically a more robust solution is more sustainable. I am very fond of the open source Review Board application (*http://bit.ly/XUeySt*). It is relatively easy to set up (you only have to set it up once!) and has good integration with CVS, Subversion, Git (and other source control systems), and Bugzilla.

Installing the RBTools package gives you the `post-review` command-line script that should be used to create review requests; Review Board also has an HTTP JSON API (*http://bit.ly/XUeySF*) that you can leverage for more complex integrations. I highly recommend using either Review Board or something similar for code reviews. Tying the code reviews into your bug tracking system tightens the loop—to close the loop completely, you need pre- and post-commit hooks into your source code repository.

Commit hooks

Most source control repositories allow pre-commit hooks, meaning you can run arbitrary checks before code is checked in and possibly reject the commit. This is the place to check that code was reviewed, check that this commit is associated with a bug, ensure that unit tests and smoke tests have been run, check code against JSLint, and generally enforce any kind of analysis and checking you want before code gets into the system.

The details of how to set up a pre-commit hook vary for each repository, but typically they are just shell scripts that exit nonzero to abort the commit. Of course, not all developers follow all required processes and practices before checking in, so "trust but verify."

Here is a quick Perl pre-commit Subversion (SVN) hook that will run JSLint on any JavaScript file and fail the commit unless JSLint gives each JavaScript file a clean bill of health:

```perl
#!/usr/bin/perl

# Passed from SVN
my $REPO = shift;
my $TXN  = shift;

# Set up PATH
$ENV{PATH} = "$ENV{PATH}:/usr/bin:/usr/local/bin";

# The log message
my @logmsg = `svnlook log -t "$TXN" "$REPO"`;
#print STDERR @logmsg;

# Get file changeset
my @changes = `svnlook changed --transaction "$TXN" "$REPO"`;
my $failed = 0;
#print STDERR @changes;

# Find JS files
foreach (@changes) {
    my($cmd, $file) = split(/\s+/);
    # Only JSLint *.js files that haven't been deleted!
    if ($file =~ /\.js$/ && $cmd ne 'D') {
        # Text of changed file:
        # my @cat = `svnlook cat "$REPO" --transaction "$TXN" $file`;
        # OR just grab the pre-committed file itself directly
        # This script runs from the directory of the commit itself so
        # these relative paths are the uncommitted versions
            my @jslint = `/usr/local/bin/jslint $file`;
        if ($?) {
            print STDERR '-' x 20, "\n";
            print STDERR "JSLint errors in $file:\n";
            print STDERR '-' x 20;
            print STDERR @jslint;
            $failed++;
        }
    }
}

# STDERR goes back to client if failed
exit $failed;
```

This example grabs the log message but doesn't use it:

```
my @changes = `svnlook changed --transaction "$TXN" "$REPO"`;
```

The code also demonstrates how to get the text of the changed file directly:

```
# my @cat = `svnlook cat "$REPO" --transaction "$TXN" $file`;
```

But it does not use it in favor of the path to the file itself, which is what the `jslint` command-line tool wants.

Grabbing the text of the commit message allows you to enforce a certain format for the message itself, perhaps ensuring that a bug ID is associated with this commit or that a code review was completed by valid usernames (that can then be put into your bug tracking tool, unless a tool such as Review Board already does this for you).

The Git pre-commit hook works similarly—exit nonzero to fail the commit. The difference, of course, is how you grab the log message and potentially committed files.

Let's create a Git pre-commit hook that will reject any commit containing any of these violations: function length greater than 30 lines, more than five arguments, or cyclomatic complexity greater than 9. We'll use the jscheckstyle npm package (*http://bit.ly/XUdsq5*) to get complexity values for each function:

```
% npm install jscheckstyle -g
```

This package has the added benefit of outputting a Jenkins-compatible format, which will come in handy when we automate our build. Here is the pre-commit script (it lives in *.git/hooks/pre-commit*):

```
#!/usr/bin/perl

# Get file list
my @files = `git diff --cached --name-only HEAD`;
my $failed = 0;

foreach (@files) {
    # Check *.js files only
    if (/\.js$/) {
        my @style = `jscheckstyle --violations $_`;
        if ($?) {
            # Send pretty error output to client
            print @style;
            $failed++;
        }
    }
}

exit $failed;
```

This code simply gets the list of files that are to be committed and runs all JavaScript ones through jscheckstyle. If any fail the violation checks, the output is sent back to the client and the commit is aborted.

Here is a sample attempted commit on a complex file from my Injectify npm package:

```
% git commit index.js
The "sys" module is now called "util". It should have a similar
interface.
jscheckstyle results - index.js
```

Line	Function	Length	Args	Complex..
30	Injectify.prototype.parse	197	2	27	
228	Injectify.prototype.statement	42	1	10	

The `parse` function is very complex, and the `statement` function is borderline too complex. You can use Git configuration variables to determine violation thresholds to suit your environment and tolerance for complexity. In this case, the commit failed due to these violations.

Let your imagination run wild with all the interesting bits that can be automated, verified, and checked before spurious code gets into your repository. Any code committed to the repository should be considered production-ready.

Other development tools

Working with JSLint on existing files may drive you batty. You can get a big head start toward fixing basic JSLint errors using fixmyjs (*http://bit.ly/XUeBOo*). It will automatically fix those basic JSLint errors, taking *a lot* of the drudgery out of lots of JSLint errors. Using it is simple:

```
% npm install fixmyjs -g
% fixmyjs myFile.js
```

In the preceding code, *myFile.js* will be updated in place using nondestructive modification; diff the new code against what you had earlier to see the results. If you are afraid, you can do a dry run first to see what it will do:

```
% fixmyjs -r myFile.js
```

Or even output a patch file instead:

```
% fixmyjs -p myFile.js
```

This is a great tool to jump-start your new JSLint-ed life. You will be pleasantly surprised by what it finds (perhaps even some bugs) and what it is able to automatically fix. Once your code is JSLint-friendly it's much easier to keep it that way than it is to rely on a tool to fix it up for you, so get in the habit of keeping it clean.

Of course, if you have to fix a lot of JSLint errors, the first thing to determine is exactly how the code got into that state in the first place. Waiting until later to try to JSLint your code is a recipe for disaster—regardless of whether it's code you've written or code you've just started maintaining, there is no excuse for not keeping it JSLint-compatible.

Automating the Build Environment

The automations made in the build environment are a superset of what is happening in the development environment. You do not want to make large complexity numbers fail the build if they are not also being checked in the development environment. Similarly, do not fail the build due to JSLint errors if you are not also running the code through JSLint in the development environment. We developers hate surprises in the build environment, so don't try to spring any new requirements onto the code in the build environment that are not also present in the development environment.

The build

The steps necessary to actually do a build—any build—are codified using a makefile, an Ant XML file, or some other build system. Like your application, the build should be not a monolithic monster, but a set of smaller pieces. Each piece should do one thing only, and the pieces should then be collected in a specific order to complete the build.

Do not have a single target that minifies and compresses code in one shot—those are two distinct actions. The build itself should also be parameterized, so do not hardcode paths or settings deep within the build; let those be supplied via the command line or some other configurable source. Developers will want to run pieces of the build in their environments, and run a full build to deploy to their local environments while the "real" build runs on a dedicated build machine and deploys out to QA and production, so make sure your build process is flexible enough to handle those varying scenarios. Ideally, developers and build masters can use the same build script to produce similar or identical builds regardless of environment and settings.

Having a build script is great, and being able to execute in isolation the individual pieces that make up a build is great. The next step is to automate it!

Jenkins

Jenkins (*http://bit.ly/XUeClg*), formerly Hudson, is a nice tool for automating the build process. With lots of community-supplied plug-ins plus hooks for even more local customization, Jenkins does a good job of managing and tracking builds, with all the bells and whistles and a nice UI that anyone can use.

Installing Jenkins is relatively straightforward, especially if you have experience deploying WARs (Web application ARchive files), as that is how Jenkins is packaged.

Download either the latest or the Long Term Support version of Jenkins, dump the WAR into the proper container directory, restart your server, and you should be good to go. If you want to get up and running very quickly to play around, simply download the WAR and run:

```
% java -jar jenkins.war
```

Jenkins will start up on port 8080. When it's ready, you will see the Jenkins home administrative page (see Figure 8-5).

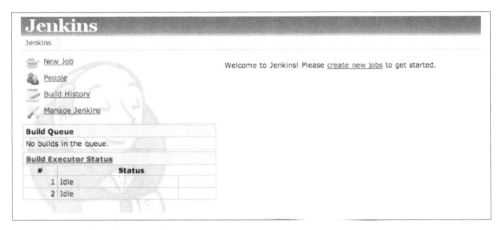

Figure 8-5. Jenkins home administrative page

Before we jump in and create a job, let's take a quick look at some plug-ins that may be of interest. Click Manage Jenkins, and you will see lots of configuration options. For now, click Manage Plugins to be transported to Jenkins's plug-in manager. From here you can update any currently installed plug-ins, install new ones, and see what you already have installed. By default, CVS and Subversion support are enabled; if you need Git support, click the Available tab and find the Git plug-in (see Figure 8-6).

Figure 8-6. Obtaining the Git plug-in

Check the Git Plugin box and install Git, and then let Jenkins restart itself. Be careful about restarting Jenkins on your own! You will have lots of Jenkins jobs, so if you ever need to restart Jenkins, let Jenkins do it. It will wait until there are no currently running jobs and then restart itself (this is done in Manage Jenkins→Prepare for Shutdown).

Now Git will be available as a source code management (SCM) system when you create a new Jenkins job. A lot of plug-ins are available for Jenkins, some of which we will encounter later.

Creating a Jenkins project. Now you can create a project. You basically need to tell Jenkins two things: where to find your source code repository and how to build it. At a minimum, Jenkins will check your code out into a clean area and run your build command. As long as your build command exits with zero, your build has succeeded.

So, go to the top-level Jenkins page and click New Job, and give your job a name. *Do not put spaces in your project name!* Then click "Build a free-style software project." Click OK, and you are ready to configure your new job. Figure 8-7 shows the home page of a Jenkins project.

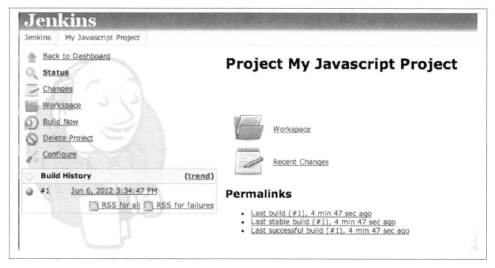

Figure 8-7. Jenkins project home page

Click the Configure link and start filling out the basics. For a Subversion project, the Subversion URL can look like the one shown in Figure 8-8.

Figure 8-8. Configuring an SVN repository in Jenkins

For a local Subversion repository, if you installed the Git plug-in you can put in a Git URL (even something on GitHub).

Under Build Triggers, it's nice to "Poll SCM" repeatedly to pick up any changes. In Figure 8-9 I am polling Subversion every 20 minutes, and if something has changed a build will be kicked off (here is our continuous integration!).

Figure 8-9. Polling Subversion

Finally, you need to tell Jenkins what to do once it checks out your repository to actually do the build.

Here is a quick makefile that will run unit tests on all the code and then compress the code into a *release* directory to be blasted out to production web servers if all is OK:

```
DO_COVERAGE=1
RELEASE=release
UGLIFY=uglifyjs

SRC  := $(shell find src -name '*.js')
OBJS := $(patsubst %.js,%.jc,$(SRC))

%.jc : %.js
    -mkdir -p $(RELEASE)/$(@D)
    $(UGLIFY) -o $(RELEASE)/$(*D)/$(*F).js $<

prod: unit_tests $(OBJS)

setupJUTE:
ifdef WORKSPACE
    npm config set jute:docRoot '$(WORKSPACE)'
    npm restart jute
endif

server_side_unit_tests: setupJUTE
    cd test && find server_side -name '*.js' -exec echo
{}?do_coverage=$(DO_COVERAGE)" \; | jute_submit_test --v8 --test -
```

```
client_side_unit_tests: setupJUTE
    cd test && find client_side -name '*.html' -exec echo
"{}?do_coverage=$(DO_COVERAGE)" \; | jute_submit_test --v8 --test -

unit_tests: server_side_unit_tests client_side_unit_tests

.PHONY: server_side_unit_tests client_side_unit_tests unit_tests
setupJUTE
```

This makefile uses UglifyJS (*http://bit.ly/XUeCSe*) for code compression, but YUI Compressor (*http://bit.ly/XUeAKk*) and Google's Closure Compiler (*http://bit.ly/XUeulM*) work just as well. The makefile lives at the root of our application's repository and has a *src* and *test* directory tree under it containing the application's source and test files, respectively.

Executing the prod (default) target will run all the unit tests and minimize all the code, assuming all the unit tests run successfully. The unit tests are all run through V8, so no browser is required. However, this may not be appropriate for all your client-side Java-Script tests, so use PhantomJS (--phantomjs) or Selenium (--sel_host) to run them through a real browser. You can even use "captured" browsers as long as at least one browser is captured to the JUTE instance running on the machine. Note that in our case we must configure JUTE when running under Jenkins so that JUTE knows where the document root is while Jenkins is doing a build. If you have a dedicated build box you could configure JUTE once to always point to the Jenkins workspace and be done. Regardless, dynamic code coverage information can be toggled on the make command line to turn off code coverage:

```
% make prod DO_COVERAGE=0
```

There is some makefile magic (or insanity, depending on your perspective) with the implicit rule for UglifyJS. Regardless of how you like your makefiles, this will transform all your JavaScript files into compressed versions in a directory tree that mirrors the *src* tree rooted under the *release* directory. When the build is finished, we simply tar up the release directory and drop it on our web servers.

OK, enough fun; let's integrate this makefile into our Jenkins job. (Of course, you could use Ant as your build system and cook up and maintain a bunch of XML files instead; Jenkins merely executes whatever you tell it, so roll your own build system if you like. It can't be any uglier than Ant, can it?)

So, back to Jenkins: simply add make as the build command (this assumes you checked in your makefile in your SVN root directory), as shown in Figure 8-10.

Save it and then execute a build, either by waiting for the SVN check to determine there are new files or by clicking Build Now. If all went well (why wouldn't it?), you will have a successful build.

Figure 8-10. Configuring a build command in Jenkins

Unit testing using Selenium

Let's take a quick detour into Selenium-land. Running unit tests during the build should occur in "real" browsers. You could keep browsers captured to the JUTE instance running on the build box, but there is a faster way, especially since as the number of unit tests increases, the time required to run them and to execute your build will increase as well. Fortunately, when using a Selenium grid, JUTE can parallelize the unit tests against a given number of Selenium nodes connected to a single grid hub. Further, using Selenium you can generate screenshots at the end of each test, which is not possible with "captured" browsers. The screenshots are saved along with the unit test results for easy debugging of unit test failures if the log output is not sufficient.

Setting up a Selenium grid is simple. The idea is that there is a single hub to which all Selenium nodes connect. Any outside process that wants to control Selenium browsers merely connects to this hub, which then passes off the work to a currently idle node. Results flow from the hub back to the Selenium requestor.

Hop on over to SeleniumHQ (*http://bit.ly/XUdI8k*) and grab the latest version of the Selenium server (2.28.0 as of this writing). This single JAR file encapsulates both the hub and node pieces necessary for your grid. Multiple Selenium nodes can run on a single host; in fact, both the hub and the nodes can run on the same box without issue. Virtual machines also make great Selenium hub and node hosts; just do not get too crazy. Depending on the specifications of your host, running a lot of nodes simultaneously can quickly bog down a machine. I have found that Windows running in a smallish-sized virtual machine can handle only two or three Selenium nodes, maximum. Just do not expect to run 10+ Selenium nodes on anything but a large server instance. Also, a hub instance can be connected to from multiple operating systems, so a hub running on Windows can be connected to Selenium nodes running on a Mac, Linux, or Windows machine.

Copy the Selenium server JAR to the hub host and node hosts, and fire it all up. You start the hub like so:

```
% java -jar selenium-server-standalone-2.28.0.jar -role hub
```

The hub listens on port 4444 by default; you can change this using the -`port` option. However, as all nodes and Selenium clients default to using port 4444 to connect to the Selenium master, you will need to change the port values for all of those processes as well.

Now fire up some nodes with the following command (all on one line):

```
% java -jar selenium-server-standalone-2.28.0.jar -role node
-hub http://<HUB HOST>:4444/grid/register
```

The Selenium nodes need to know where the hub is (host and port) so that they can connect to it. Also, the nodes listen on port 5555 by default, so if you run multiple nodes on a single host you must cook up different port values for each node beyond the first one. The port numbers of the nodes do not matter; they just need an open port. So, to start another node instance on the same host as the previous one, use:

```
% java -jar selenium-server-standalone-2.28.0.jar -role node
-hub http://<HUB HOST>:4444/grid/register -port 6666
```

Now you have two nodes running on a single host. These nodes can be on the same machine as the hub or on another box running a different operating system.

Finally, you can configure each node to tell the hub which browsers and which operating system this node can execute. Adding the -`browser` switch to the command line configures all of this information. For example, this tells the hub that this node can run Firefox version 13 on the Linux platform:

```
-browser browserName=firefox,version=13,platform=LINUX
```

Selenium clients requesting specific browsers, versions, and platforms for their Selenium commands use this information. More details about Selenium node configuration are available at the code.google selenium website (*http://bit.ly/XUeEcZ*).

JUTE can now leverage your Selenium grid to run all your unit tests in parallel across the grid. Here is a sample command line (all on one line):

```
% jute_submit_test --sel_host <grid host> --sel_port 4444
--seleniums 5 --test -
```

In the preceding code, `<grid host>` is the hostname of your Selenium hub and -`sel_port` is the port on which the hub is listening—this is only required if the hub is listening on a port other than 4444. The --`seleniums` option tells JUTE how to parallelize your unit tests. This example splits all your tests into five chunks and hits each Selenium node with one-fifth of the total number of tests.

To be clear, using this command line, if you submit 1,000 tests to JUTE each Selenium node will run 200 tests in parallel. Yahoo! Mail has used this setting to good effect, running close to 3,000 unit tests in about 10 minutes across only four Selenium nodes.

JUTE will snapshot the browser after any failed test. If you would like snapshots after every test regardless of result, use the `--snapshot` option.

To specify which browser all these tests should utilize, use the `--sel_browser` option to `jute_submit_test`.

Putting it all together, a nice makefile target to run all your tests in one shot through Selenium would look like this:

```
selenium_tests:
    cd test && find . -name '*.html' -printf '%p?do_coverage=1\n' |
    jute_submit_test --sel_host 10.3.4.45 --seleniums 5 --test -
```

Unit test output

All that remains (besides adding stuff to your build) is to have Jenkins recognize the unit test output (the JUnit XML files that JUTE generates), the coverage data (which JUTE also generates), and any other build data you want Jenkins to consider.

Conveniently, JUTE puts all test output into a (configurable) output directory called *output* by default. This directory exists in *jute:docRoot*, which conveniently is also the Jenkins workspace directory. So, to have Jenkins recognize our unit test results we simply configure our project with a post-build action of "Publish JUnit test result report" and use this file glob to pull in all test results (all JUTE test result output ends in *-test.xml*), as shown in Figure 8-11.

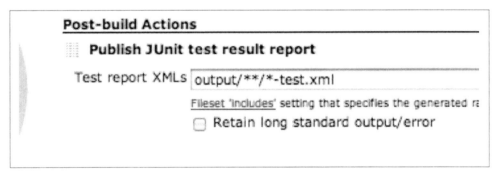

Figure 8-11. Publishing JUnit XML output in Jenkins

Now we'll kick off another build, and when things go right the first time we will see what's shown in Figure 8-12 on our project's dashboard.

Note the link to Latest Test Result and the graph with the number of successful unit tests run—pretty slick!

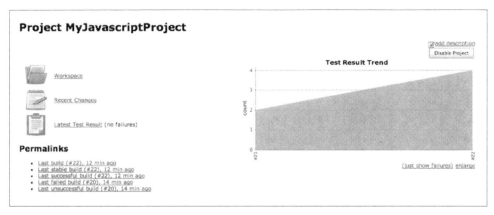

Figure 8-12. Unit test result graph on a Jenkins project home page

Coverage output

Integrating code coverage is unfortunately slightly more complex in the latest version of Jenkins, as support for LCOV-formatted coverage files seems to be missing. So, we must first aggregate all the individual coverage files into one file and then convert that file into another format that Jenkins supports.

Aggregating all the individual coverage files (the *lcov.info* files in each directory) into a single file is easy using the lcov executable. Here is our makefile rule to do just that:

```
OUTPUT_DIR=output
TOTAL_LCOV_FILE=$(OUTPUT_DIR)/lcov.info
make_total_lcov:
    /bin/rm -f /tmp/lcov.info ${TOTAL_LCOV_FILE}
    find $(OUTPUT_DIR) -name lcov.info -exec echo '-a {}' \;
| xargs lcov > /tmp/lcov.info
    cp /tmp/lcov.info ${TOTAL_LCOV_FILE}
```

All this does is collect all the generated *lcov.info* files in the *output* directory and run them through lcov -a ... to aggregate them into a single *lcov.info* file, which will sit in the root of the *output* directory.

Now that we have the aggregated *lcov.info* file, we need to convert it to the Cobertura XML format. We can do this using a handy script provided at this GitHub project (*http://bit.ly/XUeDFY*):

```
cobertura_convert:
    lcov-to-cobertura-xml.py $(TOTAL_LCOV_FILE) -b src
-o $(OUTPUT)/cob.xml
```

Adding those two targets to our original unit_tests target will generate all the information Jenkins needs to display code coverage information.

The next step is to install the Cobertura Jenkins plug-in. Once that is complete the Publish Cobertura Coverage Report option will be available as a post-build action, so add it and tell the plug-in where the Cobertura XML files reside (in the *output/* directory), as shown in Figure 8-13.

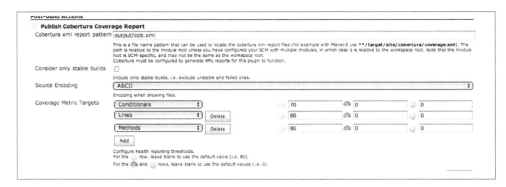

Figure 8-13. Configuring Cobertura output in Jenkins

Rebuild your project, and *voilà*, you have a Coverage Report link and a coverage graph on your dashboard, as shown in Figure 8-14.

Code Coverage	
Classes	100%
Conditionals	100%
Files	100%
Lines	79%
Packages	100%

Figure 8-14. Coverage graph on the dashboard

Clicking on the Coverage Report link will let you drill down to individual files and see which lines were covered by your tests and which weren't. Figure 8-15 shows what a coverage report looks like.

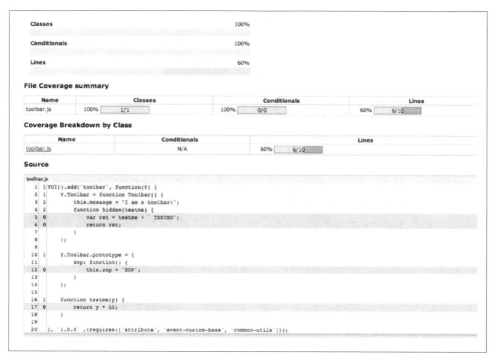

Figure 8-15. Sample coverage report

This output is very similar to the LCOV output format we saw in Chapter 5. Jenkins will now track your code coverage percentages over time, so you can watch the trend go (hopefully) up.

Complexity

We will add one more Jenkins plug-in, and then you are on your own. Earlier we discussed the jscheckstyle npm package, which coincidentally can output its report in Checkstyle format—and wouldn't you know it, there is a Jenkins plug-in for that format! Even though you may be checking complexity numbers pre-commit, it is still a great idea to also generate those numbers as part of your build, for two reasons. One, it is easy to see at a glance the complexity of all the files in your project, and two, you can keep an eye on the complexity trends in your entire application. The dashboard Jenkins provides is also great for nondevelopers to easily see the state of the project. Hopefully that is a good thing.

The flow should be similar: install the Jenkins plug-in, update the makefile to generate the required files, and then configure your project to use the installed plug-in and to point to the generated files. So, let's do it!

First we will install the Checkstyle Jenkins plug-in and then add these targets to the makefile to generate the complexity information via jscheckstyle:

```
CHECKSTYLE=checkstyle
STYLE := $(patsubst %.js,%.xml,$(SRC))
%.xml : %.js
    -mkdir -p $(CHECKSTYLE)/$(@D)
    -jscheckstyle --checkstyle $< > $(CHECKSTYLE)/$(*D)/$(*F).xml
```

This is very similar to the UglifyJS code shown earlier. We are transforming the Java-Script files in the *src* directory into XML files in a Checkstyle mirrored directory. Note the use of the - before the `jscheckstyle` command—jscheckstyle exits with an error if it finds any violations, but that would then stop the build. With a pre-commit hook this is probably overkill; however, failing the build due to violated complexity constraints is not the worst thing in the world.

So, append the `$(STYLE)` prerequisite to the `prod` target:

```
prod: unit_tests $(OBJS) $(STYLE)
```

and all those files will be generated on your next build. Now to tell Jenkins about it: on the Configure screen of your project add the "Publish Checkstyle analysis results" post-build action, and configure it as shown in Figure 8-16.

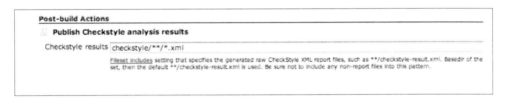

Figure 8-16. Publishing Checkstyle output in a Jenkins project

Here we are just telling the plug-in to look in the *checkstyle* directory of the Work space root and pull out all the XML files to analyze. Click Build and bask in the results (see Figure 8-17).

This graph will now be on your project's dashboard, and clicking on it (or on the Check-style Warnings link that is also now on your dashboard) will show you a history and what all the current warnings are, including any new ones present in this build. You can drill further into the details of each warning and all the way down to the code itself to view the offending code. Great stuff!

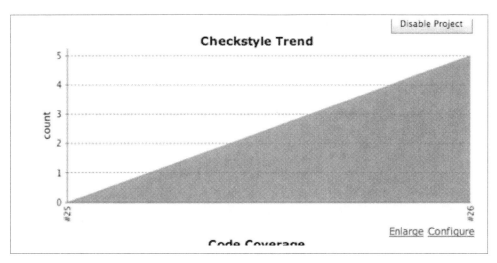

Figure 8-17. Checkstyle output graph on a Jenkins project home page

JSLint

Integrating JSLint with Jenkins is very similar to the previous integrations—for this, you need the Violations Jenkins plug-in. Go ahead and install it, and you will see that it also handles Checkstyle-formatted files. We will look at that later; for now, the Violations plug-in requires JSLint output to be in a certain XML format, which is simple to generate:

```
<jslint>
    <file name="<full_path_to_file>">
        <issue line="<line #>" reason="<reason>" evidence="<evidence" />
        <issue ... >
    </file>
</jslint>
```

If you run the jslint npm package with the `--json` argument, you will see it is a trivial transformation from the JSLint JSON to this XML format. My implementation of the transformation is available at the Testable JS GitHub project (*http://bit.ly/XUeEJT*).

The idea here is to run JSLint on our codebase, output that in XML format, and tell the Violations plug-in where to find the XML. So first we will add the standard stuff to our makefile:

```
JSLINT=jslint
JSL   := $(patsubst %.js,%.jslint,$(SRC))
%.jslint : %.js
    -mkdir -p $(JSLINT)/$(@D)
    ./hudson_jslint.pl $< > $(JSLINT)/$(*D)/$(*F).jslint
```

Then we will add the JSL targets to our prod target:

```
prod: unit_tests $(OBJS) $(STYLE) $(JSL)
```

And we are ready! Of course, to just run JSLint in isolation, simply add this target:

```
jslint: $(JSL)
```

After checking that in, install and configure the Violations plug-in with the location of the *.jslint* XML files (see Figure 8-18).

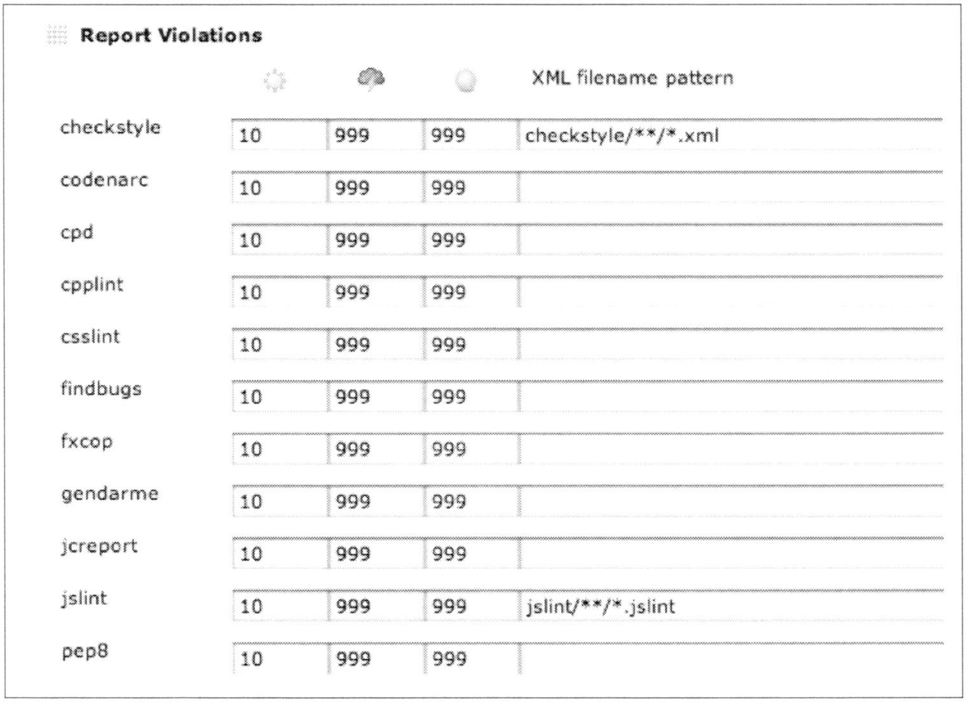

Report Violations	☼	☁	○	XML filename pattern
checkstyle	10	999	999	checkstyle/**/*.xml
codenarc	10	999	999	
cpd	10	999	999	
cpplint	10	999	999	
csslint	10	999	999	
findbugs	10	999	999	
fxcop	10	999	999	
gendarme	10	999	999	
jcreport	10	999	999	
jslint	10	999	999	jslint/**/*.jslint
pep8	10	999	999	

Figure 8-18. Configuring report violations in Jenkins

You'll note that while I was at it I also configured the location of the jscheckstyle output. Now rebuilding your project will embed on your project's dashboard the snazzy Violations graph shown in Figure 8-19.

Clicking on it will give you a breakdown of all the JSLint and Checkstyle errors in your code, and allow you to drill down to each individual file to see exactly what is going on. When viewing the file line by line, hovering your mouse over the violation icon will display detailed error information about that line.

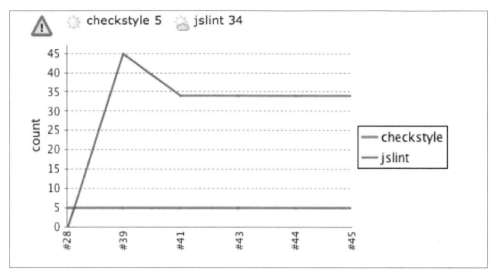

Figure 8-19. Jenkins Violations graph on project home page

Duplicate code

Although doing a build is very helpful in terms of finding all the duplicate code in your project, some duplicate-code-finding tools can be smart about ignoring whitespace and comments and comparing the underlying tokens and syntax tree to really find duplicate or very similar chunks of code.

One such tool is dupfind (*http://bit.ly/XUeGS5*). It parses through all your code looking for duplicated sections. You can tweak the "fuzziness" of the matches and see what pops out. This command-line tool is an excellent addition to your automated build process. It can output a CPD-compatible XML file (*http://bit.ly/XUeH8B*) that—surprise, surprise—a Jenkins plug-in can visualize.

Installing the Duplicate Code Scanner plug-in (*http://bit.ly/XUeHp0*) creates the "Publish duplicate code analysis results" post-commit action, which you can enable in your project (see Figure 8-20).

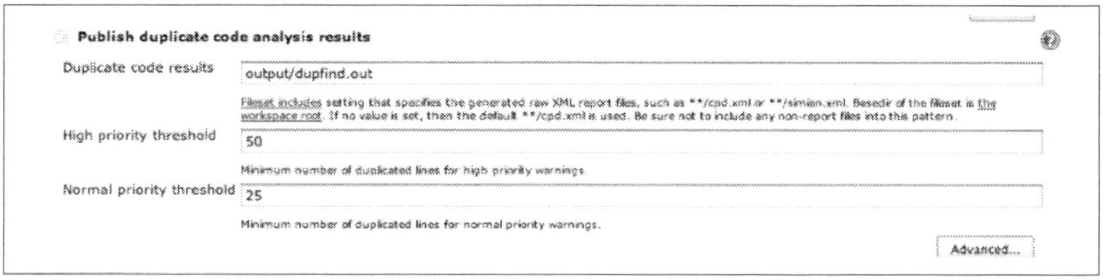

Figure 8-20. Publishing duplicate code analysis in Jenkins

The priority threshold values allow you to configure how many duplicated lines indicate a normal problem or a very big problem. The plug-in will then track and graph all the duplicated sections of code. In the Advanced configuration you can set thresholds for when this plug-in will mark a build as "unstable" or even "failed" (see Figure 8-21).

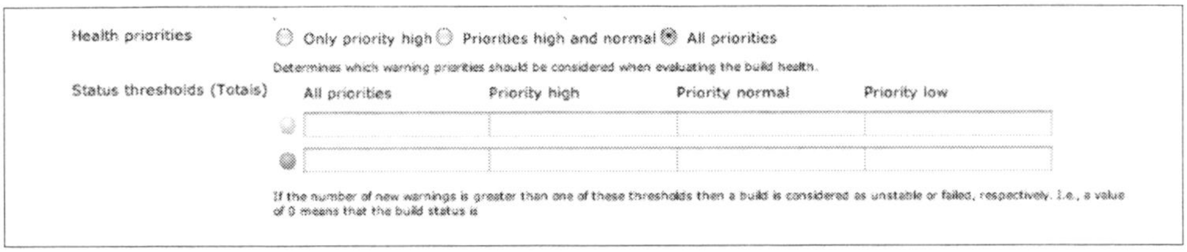

Figure 8-21. Configuring priority threshold values in Jenkins

Installing dupfind is easy; get the *dupfind.jar* file from dupfind's GitHub (*http://bit.ly/XUeGS5*) and add a line similar to this to your makefile:

```
dupfind: $(SRC)
        java -Xmx512m -jar ./dupfind.jar > output/dupfind.out
```

Then add the dupfind target to your prod target, and you are ready to configure dupfind itself. One of the places dupfind looks for its configuration file in the current directory is in a file named *dupfind.cfg*. Here is one now:

```
{
    min:        30,
    max:        500,
    increment:  10,
    fuzzy:      true,
    cpd:        true,

    sources:
    [
        {
            name:   "myProject",
            def:    true,
            root:   ".",
            directories:
            [
                "src"
            ],
            include:
            [
                "*.js"
            ],
            exclude:
            [
                "*/.svn",
                "*-[^/]*.js",
```

```
            ]
         }
      ]
   }
```

This JSON-formatted configuration file tells dupfind specifically what to do. The most interesting bits are the `fuzzy` property that allows dupfind to do fuzzy matches (it will ignore variable names, for instance) and the `sources` array that allows us to fine-tune which directories and files dupfind should investigate and which to skip.

Once you have configured the file, on your dashboard you'll get a snazzy duplicate-code graph, as shown in Figure 8-22.

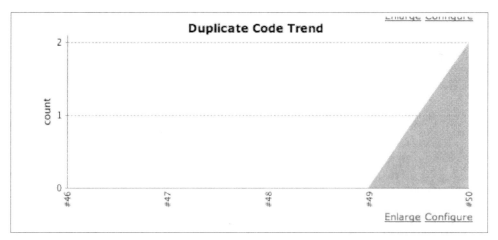

Figure 8-22. A graph showing trends in duplicated code

From this graph you can then drill down into the details, as shown in Figure 8-23.

From here you can drill down to the files themselves and see the detected duplications. In this case, dupfind found a duplicate chunk of code in the same file. Remember, the priority of the duplicated code is set while configuring the plug-in; here the priority is "low" because there are only six lines of duplicated code.

Duplicate Code - Low Priority

Details

| Warnings | **Details** |

t.js:155, Duplicate Code, Priority: Low

6 lines of duplicate code.

Duplicated in:

- src/a/b/c/t.js (162)

t.js:162, Duplicate Code, Priority: Low

6 lines of duplicate code.

Duplicated in:

- src/a/b/c/t.js (155)

Figure 8-23. Details of the duplicated code graph

Other analysis

The latest version of PMD (*http://pmd.sourceforge.net/*)—5.0 as of this writing—has support for some ECMAScript analysis that may be useful to you. Although JSLint does a better/more thorough job, it is relatively easy to add new rule sets to PMD for more custom checking in your environment. PMD output is well supported by various Jenkins plug-ins, which makes it a good choice if you're using Jenkins. Also, as time goes on, hopefully more ECMAScript rule sets will be included with or available for PMD, and ECMAScript will become a supported language with CPD, so keep an eye on PMD!

Finally, I encourage you to browse the long list of Jenkins plug-ins that are available; you can always write your own if you see that something is missing!

Notification

There is no need for Jenkins to operate in a vacuum. Setting up the E-mail Notification" post-build action will email potentially different sets of people when a build changes state. The possible states are "successful," "fail," and "unstable." Jenkins distinguishes between failed builds and unstable builds: a *failed* build occurs when a build command exits with a nonzero exit status, and an *unstable* build is caused by post-build plug-ins noticing that something has gone wrong, such as a unit test failure or code coverage below a certain threshold.

Jenkins can also email only the committers who caused the build to change state from "successful" to "failed" or "unstable," using data from the commit logs. This is an absolutely critical feature to enable!

Dependent builds

You can kick off other Jenkins builds if the current build completes successfully. For instance, you may want to stage the completed build if it completed successfully, or kick off performance or integration testing on the successful build. Breaking these steps into separate Jenkins projects keeps things modular and automated.

The Full Monty

Figure 8-24 shows a snapshot of a Jenkins dashboard with all the aforementioned plug-ins disabled and building—that's a good-looking dashboard!

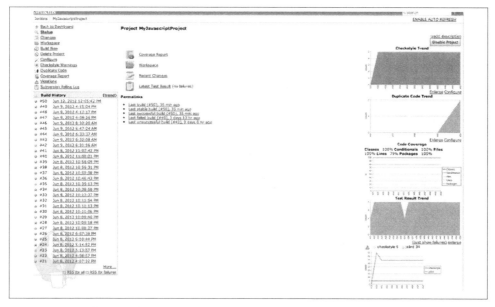

Figure 8-24. A fully configured Jenkins project home page

Non-UI usage

Jenkins can be almost completely controlled via the command line or a remote API. There are two command-line methods of controlling Jenkins: via SSH and via *cli.jar*.

Jenkins starts up its own SSHD server by default on a random port. To determine the port number, make a HEAD request to your base Jenkins URL and find the X-SSH-Endpoint header key; its value is the random port on which Jenkins's SSHD is listening. Alternatively, you can configure Jenkins to listen on a fixed port for SSHD in the Configure System configuration settings area. My random SSH port is 64812, so this command:

```
% ssh -p 64812 localhost build MyJavaScriptProject -s
```

will kick off a build of MyJavaScriptProject and wait for build results.

Visiting *http://<Your Local Jenkins URL>/cli* presents the opportunity to download *cli.jar*, which you can also use to control Jenkins. After downloading the JAR, running this command (all on one line):

```
% java -jar ~/Downloads/jenkins-cli.jar
-s http://localhost:8080 build MyJavaScriptProject -s
```

will kick off a build of the MyJavaScriptProject project and wait for it to complete. Upon completion, you will receive the final status for that build. Jenkins can be almost completely managed via *cli.jar*; visiting *http://<Your Local Jenkins URL>/cli* gives lots more information about what is possible. The commands available via SSH are only a subset of what is available from *cli.jar*.

Deployment

Whether you're deploying to 1 server or 50,000 servers, some things remain the same (and some, of course, are radically different). After verifying that your code is good to go to production, you must shut down the current code cleanly and bring up the new code. The goal is to drop as few connections as possible (if any). Most web servers have a "graceful" restart feature that should be utilized. If you have only one server, connections will be refused while the server is down. If you've got 50,000 servers behind various load balancers, the process will (hopefully) be seamless.

Rollback goes hand in hand with deployment. You should be ready to switch back to the old code as quickly as possible—not that anything will go wrong, of course. Ideally, merely flipping a symlink chooses between the "old" and "new" code—leave the old code on the box while you upgrade.

An upgrade can look like this:

1. Upload new files to the host.
2. Gracefully stop the server.
3. Update the symlink to point to the new code.
4. Start the server.

5. Profit!

For instance, suppose the `DocumentRoot` in your Apache configuration file points to a symlink at */var/www/current* that resolves to */var/www/VERSION_X*. Now you put */var/www/VERSION_Y* on the box, and when Apache is stopped, you change */var/www/current symlink* from *VERSION_X* to *VERSION_Y*.

When a rollback is necessary, simply gracefully stop the server, reposition the symlink, and then start the server. Of course, you will have a script that does all that for you automatically, right?

Recap

Automating your development, build, and deployment processes is crucial for a sane application life cycle. Fortunately, there are a lot of JavaScript tools that (mostly) fit together that can help you with this. Leveraging and melding these tools, from pre-commit hooks to Jenkins plug-ins, allows you to lather, rinse, and repeat as quickly as possible. Like most things, the tools are only as good as their usage. Developers must constantly be vigilant about their code and processes to ensure that everything is running smoothly and that any issues are dealt with as quickly as possible.

Index

We'd like to hear your suggestions for improving our indexes. Send email to index@oreilly.com.

tight coupling, 42–45
toEqual function, 108
top utility, 163
tracking resource usage
    about, 162
    client-side tracking, 163–169
    server-side tracking, 169–172
TWDD (test-while-driven development), 10

U

UglifyJS tool, 225
unicast events, 74, 75, 79
unit tests
    about, xiv, 11
    automating, 212–217
    code coverage for, 115, 118, 126–127, 134
    cyclomatic complexity and, 24–27
    defining functions for, 88–89
    frameworks for, 83
    isolation in, 16, 87
    outputting, 228
    real-world testing, 91–95
    running client-side, 95–107
    running server-side, 107–113
    scope of, 87
    using Selenium, 226–228
    writing, 84–90
user stories
    behavior-driven development and, 6
    defined, 3
users, defined, 3
USR2 signal, 170, 171

V

variables
    declaring in for loops, 21
    global, 31, 57, 119
verify functions, 139
viewing HAR files, 152–154

W

walkthrough process, 54
WAR files, 221
waterfall model
    about, 3

HAR files, 148, 152
web-based applications
    about, 68
    event hubs and, 58
    integration testing, 137
webdriverjs module
    about, 102, 140–142
    HAR files and, 148, 150
    remote debugging and, 187
WebKit Developer Tools
    about, 163
    Heap Snapshot tab, 170
    Profiles tab, 165, 170
webkit-devtools-agent package, 169
weinre debugger, 201
whitespace, 21, 235
window.console object, 175
Working Effectively with Legacy Code (Feathers), ix
writing unit tests
    about, 84–86
    factors of good tests, 86–90

X

XML format
    Cobertura and, 229
    JSLint and, 233
    YSlow and, 154
    YUI and, 127
XMLHttpRequest class, 63

Y

YSlow tool, 154
YUI Compressor, 225
YUI Event Hub module, 62
YUI Library channel, xii
YUI Test framework
    about, 62, 84
    asynchronous testing and, 94, 117
    code coverage tools, 119–121, 126
    Jasmine equivalents, 108
    JUTE tool and, 212
YUIDoc, 48–50

About the Author

Mark Ethan Trostler has been writing and testing code for over 20 years. From humble beginnings as a Computer Science/Philosophy double major at UC San Diego, to working at both startups (IPivot) and large corporations (Qualcomm, Intel, Redback Networks, Juniper Networks, Yahoo!, and currently Google), Mark has always been dedicated to code quality. Previously as a Senior Principal Front End Engineer on the Yahoo! Mail team, he helped spearhead testing and quality for the latest rewrite of Yahoo! Mail.

He is currently employed by Google as a Software Engineer in Test with the Ads team, helping to ensure an excellent customer experience. He has spoken at several internal and external conferences (Yahoo! TechPulse 2010 and 2011, Yahoo!'s Front End Summit, and at YUIConf 2011) about Testable JavaScript and is the author of the Open Source Javascript Unit Test Environment (*https://github.com/zzo/JUTE*). Prior to JavaScript, Mark worked extensively with Perl, Java, and C, but has since drunk the JavaScript kool-aid and is now a full-time convert. With NodeJS and PhantomJS, the future of portable languages is here!

Colophon

The animal on the cover of *Testable JavaScript* is the Doctor fish (*Acanthurus chirurgus*), a tropical fish that can be found in shallow coral reefs throughout the Atlantic Ocean, especially around Massachusetts, the Caribbean, Brazil, and the west coast of Africa. It is the most wide-ranging fish within its genus. All members of the Acanthuridae family are distinctive for the sharp spines on either side of their tail fin—and in fact, Acanthurus is derived from the Greek for "thorn tail." The common name of Doctor fish perhaps arose from these scalpel-like appendages, which the fish can use for defense against predators or other Doctor fish with a rapid side sweep of their tail.

This fish grows to be around 40 cm in length and is typically a blue or brown color. Despite the variations in color, all Doctor fish have 10-12 vertical bars on their body. Its teeth are specially shaped so that the fish can scrape algae and plant matter from rocks; it spends most of the day "grazing" in this manner. At times, Doctor fish will also consume sand, which helps grind food during the digestive process.

Doctor fish spawn within 24 hours after fertilization, and look like floating plankton for a short time. The fish does not typically grow its scalpels until it is around 13 mm in length. It reaches sexual maturity after 9 months.

The cover image is from a loose plate, source unknown. The cover font is Adobe ITC Garamond. The text font is Adobe Minion Pro; the heading font is Adobe Myriad Condensed; and the code font is Dalton Maag's Ubuntu Mono.

Get even more for your money.

Join the O'Reilly Community, and register the O'Reilly books you own. It's free, and you'll get:

- $4.99 ebook upgrade offer
- 40% upgrade offer on O'Reilly print books
- Membership discounts on books and events
- Free lifetime updates to ebooks and videos
- Multiple ebook formats, DRM FREE
- Participation in the O'Reilly community
- Newsletters
- Account management
- 100% Satisfaction Guarantee

Signing up is easy:

1. **Go to: oreilly.com/go/register**
2. **Create an O'Reilly login.**
3. **Provide your address.**
4. **Register your books.**

Note: English-language books only

To order books online:
oreilly.com/store

For questions about products or an order:
orders@oreilly.com

To sign up to get topic-specific email announcements and/or news about upcoming books, conferences, special offers, and new technologies:
elists@oreilly.com

For technical questions about book content:
booktech@oreilly.com

To submit new book proposals to our editors:
proposals@oreilly.com

O'Reilly books are available in multiple DRM-free ebook formats. For more information:
oreilly.com/ebooks

Spreading the knowledge of innovators   oreilly.com

Have it your way.

CPSIA information can be obtained at www.ICGtesting.com
Printed in the USA
BVOW060458180113

310930BV00004B/4/P